The Quakers

by the same author

Manliness and Morality ed. with J. A. Mangan (Manchester University Press)
Slaves and Slavery: The British Colonial Experience (Manchester University Press)
Black Ivory: A History of British Slavery (Fontana)
The People's Game: The History of Football Revisited (Mainstream)
The Life and Times of Henry Clarke of Jamaica, 1828–1907 (Cass)
Questioning Slavery (Routledge)
Fruits of Empire: Exotic Produce and British Taste, 1660–1800 (Macmillan)

The Quakers

Money and Morals

JAMES WALVIN

JOHN MURRAY
Albemarle Street, London

First published in 1997
by John Murray (Publishers) Ltd,
50 Albemarle Street, London W1X 4BD

Paperback edition 1998

A catalogue record for this book is available from the British Library

ISBN 0-7195-5768-2

Typeset in 12/14½ Bembo by Servis Filmsetting Ltd, Manchester

Printed and bound in Great Britain by the University Press, Cambridge

Contents

Illustrations

(between pages 118 and 119)

The author and publisher wish to acknowledge the following for permission to reproduce illustrations: Plates 1, 3, 4 and 5, Library Committee, Religious Society of Friends; 2, Stephen Allott; 6, 9, 11, 12 and 13, Borthwick Institute, University of York; 7, 8 and 10, Cadbury Ltd.; 14, National Portrait Gallery; 15, 16 and 17, C. & J. Clark Ltd.; 18, Wellcome Institute Library; 19, 20 and 21, T. A. B. Corley; 22 and 23, Ironbridge Gorge Museum Trust; 24, City of Aberdeen Art Gallery and Museums Collections

Acknowledgements

It is hard to live in the city of York and not be aware of the remarkable achievements of a local Quaker family: the Rowntrees. This book began in the library of their factory, and I am grateful to Christine Theaker for allowing me access. The J. B. Morrell Library of the University of York provided help, especially its collection of Quaker books inherited from now defunct meeting houses in the North of England. I would also like to thank the staff, particularly Judith Burg, at the Borthwick Institute at the university, where I used the Rowntree papers. In addition, I used the facilities of the library of the Friends Meeting House, Euston Road, London, and the neighbouring library at the Wellcome Institute. Lydia Harris and Sarah Sheils were most helpful in my work on material in the Mount School, York. At Ackworth School I was fortunate to have the guidance of Fred Davies and the friendship of Alan Rothwell. Sandra Holton's scholarly work and conversations were important on a number of occasions. I am indebted to Bill Sheils and Martin Biggs for reading the original manuscript. The University of York Innovation Fund helped me to undertake some of the research required for this book. I thank Grant McIntyre for his initial enthusiasm; Deborah Licorish proved invaluable in her scrupulous editorial improvement of my original text.

Introduction

My interest in Quakers has emerged from separate but converging sources. When working on the British campaigns against slavery in the eighteenth and nineteenth centuries it proved impossible to escape their presence: their importance was critical. Quaker influence has also permeated the city where I have lived for thirty years. When the wind blows in the right direction it is possible to smell the unmistakably sweet scent of chocolate wafting across York, reminding its citizens of the fundamental role that its manufacture has played for a century and more. Today Rowntree is no longer a company of the Quaker founding fathers, but just one among many distant outposts of the Nestlé conglomerate based in Switzerland. Elsewhere in England Fry's and Cadbury have gone a similar route: engulfed by larger corporations, their original Quaker names have been maintained only when closely identified with a particularly successful product.

It was the take-over by Nestlé of the Rowntree company which prompted me to write this book. As the company reorganised its library in the throes of that take-over, the then librarian kindly allowed me access to the company's archive. Following the publication of a company-sponsored history, the full Rowntree papers were deposited in the Borthwick Institute at the University of York. The more I read about the Rowntrees, the more curious I became about the wider influence of the Society of Friends.

By any standards, this one Quaker family, the Rowntrees, have had an extraordinary impact on York. Nor were they alone, for the experience was replicated in other English towns and at other periods, including Reading (Huntley and Palmers), Carlisle (Carr's), Bournville (Cadbury), Bristol (Fry's), Street (Clarks) and Hull (Reckitt and Colman); not to mention the Quaker-founded banks (notably Barclays and Lloyds) which dot most English high streets. And while Quaker economic activities created remarkable industries and businesses from one part of the country to another, a similar tale can be told for Ireland and, of course, North America.

By the last years of the seventeenth century, less than fifty years after the Quakers had emerged from the turmoils of the English Revolution, their contemporaries had become curious about such material success and the commercial culture which accompanied it. Though a relatively small group (never more than 60,000 in Britain), and distinguished from their fellow citizens at large by appearance, mode of address ('thee', 'thou', 'thine') and tone, Quakers had already made their economic presence felt. One of their bitter opponents wrote in 1697 that they had 'Grip'd Mammon as hard as any of their Neighbours; and now call Riches a Gift and a Blessing from God'.[1] A similar picture could be painted for the years immediately before the First World War. By then, however, the power and influence of England's wealthiest Quaker magnates would have staggered their forbears. Both in 1700 and 1914, Quakers were remarkable for and were objects of curiosity because of their business acumen and commercially acquisitive talents. We can gain some sense of that prowess by looking at the number of Quaker-founded companies. By 1826, for example, we know of at least seventy-four banks. Today, the library of the Society of Friends in London has a working list of 216 firms 'with Quaker connections'.[2] However we assess the statistics of Quaker commercial activity, the overall impression remains one of outstanding successes from a limited number of people. This book seeks to describe how that came about.

A great deal has been written about the Quakers, much of it by Quakers themselves, and about the religious culture they inhabited and the rise of modern capitalism. This book, then, follows what are well-trodden literary and historiographical paths, but it is important to state what this book does *not* seek to do. *The Quakers* is not an attempt to argue the thesis, *pro* or *con.*, about religion and the rise of capitalism. It may make a contribution to that broader debate, but this book's aim is altogether more narrowly focused. Nor does it tell the history of the Quakers in England, which has been capably done by many others. Instead it looks at the distinctive role and influence that groups of Quakers came to exercise in particular areas of economic and cultural life in England in the two and half centuries between the emergence of the Society of Friends and the onset of the First World War.

The Quakers does this by examining the careers of certain Friends and their commercial interests, in the hope that such accounts will illuminate more general cultural forces, but the story is offered within a broader narrative and chronological framework. Throughout, I have explained the story of these people within the defining context of the history of the Society of Friends. Stated crudely, I do not think it possible to understand the rise and success of Quaker businesses unless we grasp the basic nature and culture of the Society itself. The crucial link is not that between Quaker business and a particular theology, so much as Quaker membership of a powerful organisation and the culture it created.

In their beginning, the Quakers seemed just one of many small religious sectarian groups spawned by the convulsions of the English Revolution. Yet the seeds of later success were there, and can be detected in the words and actions of the founding fathers, most notably George Fox. I therefore consider their seventeenth-century origins (Part I) in order to trace the intellectual and organisational foundations on which subsequent Quaker life and success were built. What followed – the rise of Quaker prosperity in the eighteenth and nineteenth centuries (Part II) – took varied and unusual forms and ranged from engineering to banking. It was, however, a prosperity which followed a pattern of mutual self-help, meticulous bookkeeping and financial scrutiny, and all under the watchful eye of the local Quaker community. The worldly wealth unleashed by these various successes forms Part III of this book. The consequences reached far beyond the boundaries of the Quaker community in the years up to the First World War, and left a permanent mark on modern British society.

What follows, then, is the history of what I have called *The Quakers: Money and Morals*. It is an attempt to say something new about Quaker history and English social history. More crucially, perhaps, it seeks to bring the two together: to describe the role that successful Friends played in the broad process of English cultural change over a period of two hundred and fifty years. It is a large canvas and I am painting with my favourite broad brush, but to understand the story that follows, we first need to go back to the founding days of Quakerism itself; to those years of revolutionary turmoil of the mid-seventeenth century. Let us begin with the peculiar story of the young George Fox.

PART I

Origins

1

George Fox and Friends

George Fox, founder of the Quaker movement, was a tormented man. Convinced of his own inner strength and rectitude, in his public utterances at least, he was privately assailed by doubts and worries. From first to last he is an enigma. In the early 1640s he was a troubled youth, racked by theological and social doubts. In his last years he was domestically contented and had seen his following develop into a nationwide movement despite vicious persecution. But throughout he poses serious problems for the modern reader. Fox was a man who wrote his own history, most notably in his *Journal*, but he also generated a vast and continuing literature by other people – friends and enemies. Yet the more we learn about him, the more remote he seems and the more mysterious a figure he remains. This problem has increased with the passage of time in that he does not fit easily into the lexicon of character-types available to the contemporary biographer and easily understood by all. Resolving such a difficulty is the historian's basic job: to conjure forth images of a remote, disconnected past in terms which make sense to the contemporary reader. But despite all we know about George Fox, he remains elusive.

We are not even sure what he looked like. The few portraits that exist are less lifelike than many of the descriptions of him which accumulated over the years. He was a 'bulky person', with long hair 'like rats' tails'. He needed little sleep and was capable of enduring extreme hardship and physical privation, at first in his early years when forced to sleep rough, and later when repeatedly exposed to the misery of prison cells. More unusual than his looks or physical strength, however, were his inner qualities. Even as a child he stood out from others – or at least he said he did: 'I had a gravity and stayedness of mind and spirit, not usual in children'.

Fox was born in 1624, the son of a devout Puritan who was a reasonably prosperous weaver and an equally 'upright woman' in Leicestershire. He was destined in childhood for the Anglican ministry, but instead he became an apprentice shoemaker to a Nottingham man who also dealt in sheep and wool. In his youth, Fox was conspicuous for his piety and aloofness. ('When rude people and boys would laugh at me, I let them alone.') Famous for his honesty, he proclaimed that 'The Lord taught me to be faithful in all things . . . and to keep to Yea and Nay in all things.' Then at the age of 19 he underwent a crisis that changed his life. It was prompted by a simple but symptomatic incident.

In the summer of 1643, Fox sat with a cousin and other Puritans at a fair. The young men tried to goad him into joining their drinking round: the proposing of health and the custom that the man who refused to drink should pay for the round. George Fox was shocked. He paid for his own drink, and left. That night he could not sleep, paced his room and called to the Lord for guidance. Divine intercession advised him to abandon his friends and family, and to seek truth and spiritual guidance elsewhere. Over the next four years Fox wandered throughout England, often living rough (though he clearly left home with cash in his hand), badgering clerics and divines, and seeking guidance in prayer and isolation. His sole attachment was to his bible and to the occasional companionship found among the proliferation of sects and divines that had been spawned by the turmoil of the English Revolution. For Fox it was a period of mysticism and personal doubt, but he found no satisfaction – no truth – in the protestations of priests and 'professors' of any description. Just when he despaired most, in 1647, 'When all my hopes in them and in all men, were gone . . . I heard a voice . . . '[1] The Lord spoke directly to Fox. Henceforth his path was clear, though rarely straight or untroubled.

George Fox, now in his mid-twenties, embarked on his lifetime's mission. His aim was not to create a sect but to persuade his fellow men and women to worship honestly, not through the intermediary of the priesthood or any religious organisation but from within themselves, directly to the Almighty. He set out to persuade people to be true to themselves and to others, and to be frank in their private dealings with the Lord. Yet we will never fully understand Fox simply by scrutinising his own words. For all his uniqueness he was also a man of his time. Fox and the Quaker movement established in his wake were, first and foremost, creatures of the English Revolution.[2]

Fox was not alone in suffering turmoil in the 1640s. The entire nation was racked by personal and social agitations that had been whipped up by a bloody and vengeful civil war. That decade, and the Interregnum years of the 1650s, formed what Christopher Hill has described as 'the greatest upheaval in English history'.[3] Old assumptions and beliefs – old certainties – were shattered by the convulsion of religious and political freedoms which had scarred most people in some way or other. The traditional acceptance that all English people belonged to the national Church and must worship as a matter of obligation was destroyed for ever. As the world turned upside-down, religious and political groupings of the most varied (and sometimes most bizarre) kind sprang up across the nation. Unleashed by the collapse of draconian censorship laws, books and tracts flew off the presses in unprecedented numbers, speaking for each and every sect and radical splinter group. The printed word was eagerly devoured by a curious readership that had been previously kept in check.

As the old restraints melted in a new climate of freedom, there was a parallel blossoming of political and religious activity. Men and women found a voice previously denied them. They could be heard everywhere: in homes and alehouses, at crossroads and army camps, on the street corner and inside parish churches. The old order of church and formal worship collapsed before a nationwide spiritual agitation. Authority of all kinds, whether monarchical or priestly, was swept away by an upsurge of secular and theological individualism. Levellers and Diggers, Ranters and Muggletonians, Fifth Monarchists and Millenarians: these and many others flourished in proportion to the discomfort of the old order. King, lords and bishops were mocked and humbled, levelled by those of no previous consequence.

The political tumult after 1642 was unprecedented: civil war, the eventual victory of Parliament, the abolition of lords and bishops, and the trial and execution of the King all followed in quick and disturbing succession. In this confusion of change, anything seemed possible. Even those who proclaimed the imminence of the Second Coming did not appear unduly unrealistic. The 1640s were, in effect, a political and religious free-for-all that heralded a democratic tradition of the most fundamental and varied kind, and which would be bequeathed to later generations. The personal anguish experienced by George Fox in 1643 did not, then, seem out of the ordinary.

Men who later became Quakers played their part in the fighting of the Civil War with no hint of their subsequent squeamishness about bloodshed. Indeed, the Quaker vernacular that emerged from those upheavals was suffused with military imagery, itself forged in the battle for freedom against the royalists in the 1640s. But the years of the Interregnum, between the execution of Charles I in 1649 and the restoration of Charles II in 1660, witnessed a progressive disillusionment with Oliver Cromwell's rule. During the 1650s, when the victories of the preceding decade turned into the dust of Cromwellian compromise and failure, George Fox placed himself at the head of those whose formative memories had been the libertarian experiences and expectations of the 1640s, and who now formed the first shock troops of the Quaker movement.

By 1647 Fox had found his voice, and he began to preach, at first only a 'few, but powerful and piercing words'.[4] His reputation soon spread, but his words were not always welcome as he was an uncompromising preacher, hurling disputation and contradiction at the heads of his opponents. In 1649 he experienced his first imprisonment for rising in a crowded church in Nottingham to dispute the resident cleric's biblical views. Not surprisingly, 'the officers came and took me away, and put me into prison, a pitiful stinking place'.[5] It was to become the first of many similar experiences. The years of sleeping rough in the mid-1640s now seemed like an apprenticeship for the even starker rigours of detention in various English jails. A year later Fox was back in prison, this time in Derby, committed for six months for blasphemy. The man who convicted him, Justice Bennet, was the first to call Fox's followers Quakers, 'because we bid them tremble at the word of God'.[6]

As Fox trekked across the North of England he encountered crowds of people keen to hear his words and anxious to share his thoughts. Many were striving for a new way to express their beliefs in the wake of the fragmentation of religious experience and ideals, much of it related to the splintering of other political groupings. Bands of worshippers had turned their back on other sects, most notably Puritanism, and were therefore ripe for the appropriate message and leadership. For example, Fox found a sympathetic audience among agricultural workers, who by instinct had spurned their betters and clashed with landlords about rents or tithes.

The recruitment to Quakerism was rapid. In the course of the 1650s, numbers swelled to 40,000, perhaps even 60,000, equalling the Catholics and overtaking the older, more famous sects.[7] The movement effectively began and thrived in the poor, backward and remote North-West of England. One contemporary Quaker propagandist compared the North to Bethlehem, in that it was the focus of Quaker strength. It was here, among people who felt ignored or rejected by Church, State and powerful landowners, that Quakerism first took root. And it was from the North-West that the first Quaker ministers, men and women, fanned out to take the message to other regions and towns. These missionaries, sixty-six in total (almost all from Lancashire, Yorkshire and Westmorland, and almost all recruited from older, highly individualistic Seeker communities) travelled southwards in 1654–5 to London and Bristol, later to Scotland, Ireland, Europe and on to America. It seemed as if London had been invaded by 'plain North Country ploughmen'.[8]

In the North of England Quakerism quickly assumed a shape which was to survive successive waves of persecution in later years. Quaker organisation, financial structure and headquarters were established in the region. Money for the cause was raised from local sympathisers, administered from Kendal, and spent on sending missionaries to other parts of the country and on providing relief for Quakers in prison. The Monthly Meeting was introduced 'to look after the poor and to see that all walked according to the Truth'. Elders from those meetings met other county representatives at the Yearly or General Meeting. It proved an ideal structure for an expansive movement. The location of the headquarters came about more fortuitously, however. In 1652 Fox visited Swarthmore Hall near Ulverston, where he converted Margaret Fell and three of her children.[9] Her husband, Judge Fell, was a powerful local figure whose support ensured protection for the Quaker activity that became centred upon his wife and home. Swarthmore in effect became the headquarters of the movement, and Margaret, the 'Quaker matriarch', managed the finances for the missionary activities that spread the cause through the South of England.[10] (In 1669, Fox was to marry the then-widowed Margaret Fell, thereby establishing the first Quaker dynasty.)

In the 1650s, the movement began to establish itself in other parts of the country, with strongholds in London and Bristol, but the richest Quaker seam remained rural. Many of those attracted to Quakerism tended to be traders and artisans, yeomen and husbandmen. They were also likely to be literate. Few were very poor and few came from the ranks of the gentry. As had happened in the North, many turned to Quakerism after rural agitation, mainly against the tithe; others had seen their radical instincts finely honed in the military conflicts and the associated political wrangling of the war years. There was also a sizeable number of women who turned to the cause, where they found a freedom of expression and activity denied them in other spheres.[11]

What Quakers actually believed during their explosive growth of the Interregnum years is less easily described. There was at first no clear outline of principles or tenets. Instead they tended to define their views by rejecting the ideas of others. They proclaimed the prospects of salvation for all, and announced a sense of unity with God. Most important of all, indeed central to Quaker thought, followers were urged to turn to the light of Christ within themselves: they were 'spiritual millenarians'.[12] They relegated the importance of the Scriptures in favour of the pre-eminence of this inner spirit, and so rejected the necessity for an educated clergy to lead and interpret. Even the Bible was demoted, to become, in the words of Christopher Hill, 'a book like any other'.[13] What mattered was not so much biblical stories about Christ and the past, but one's own feelings of the present. Heaven was *within* the Quaker believer. Nathaniel Smith turned to Quakerism for this very reason, that 'the Kingdom of Heaven was in Man'.[14]

This led certain Quakers to claim miraculous powers. Fox himself claimed to have effected no fewer than 150 cures by the laying on of hands. Naturally they had their failures, the most spectacular of which concerned the Worcester Quaker who dug up a corpse, commanding him 'in the name of the living God, to arise and walk'.[15] Quakers formed an ecstatic movement, hence their name, and in their early years were renowned for the frenzy of their responses. That first generation of preachers often provoked shrieks and communal tremblings from the congregation. When Fox spoke at Ulverston in 1652, 'the steeplehouse shook'. A year later, when preaching in Carlisle, the effect was even more remarkable: 'A dreadful power of the Lord there was amongst them in the steeplehouse, that the people trembled and shook, and they thought the steeplehouse shook and thought it would have fallen down.'[16] Fox seemed able to sway even the doubters. From Tickhill in 1652, he reported that the priest who 'scoffed at us, and called us Quakers' was swept along by the power of the spirit and 'fell a-trembling himself, so that one said unto him "Look how the priest trembles and shakes, he is turned Quaker also".'[17]

From the first, the Quakers inherited the anti-clericalism of the English Revolution. Fox's *Journal* records his repeated conflicts with 'priests', yet he was only the most prominent of a host who regularly clashed with the authorities. It was perhaps natural that they should dispute with other theologians (a favourite tactic was to bellow objections at a priest in his own 'steeplehouse'), but it was equally inevitable that such frictions would spill over. Congregations, parishioners, local townsfolk, government officers and the military all joined in the arguments. What began as a polemical dispute often ended in a brawl, with the Quaker assaulted by a baying mob inside and outside the church, before being expelled from the district or flung into the local jail. And the trouble did not end there. Fox, for example, sought to win over his jailers (sometimes successfully), but most tended to be as cruel and vindictive as the outside rabble. Thus, in those early years, Quakers became familiar with the prisons of England as they found themselves persecuted not only for their actions but also because they refused to bow to demands made of them by the political and ecclesiastical authorities. What made the Quakers so dangerous and troublesome was their resolute refusal to accept authority.

So the Quakers were heirs to an older radical tradition of dissent and vocal opposition that had been forged in the Civil War, and their evolving beliefs engaged in political matters, as much as questions of faith and theology. They were destined, from the first, to clash with authority of all kinds as there was to be no compromise. They had the inner light and were not to be diverted by injunctions to obey, or to accord to the demands of Church and State. The Quakers' first and most obvious enemy was the church and its officers, the priests who were maintained in luxury by the labour of the poor, thanks to the iniquitous tithe.[18] Quakers sought an end to the university-educated clergy, allowing instead the rise of 'a ministry of simple men and women'; people who 'spoke plaine words, and reached to the consciences of men of the meanest capacity'.[19] But since the church was a pillar of the state, and the tithe was the tax which financed that church at parish level, the Quaker challenges therefore involved matters of fundamental political importance.

Quakers may have lacked a clear philosophy in the early years, but there was an unmistakable emergent Quaker sensibility with a levelling, democratic tone, articulated by a growing band of preachers. They attacked privilege and rank on all hands. Aristocracy and gentry, lawyers and priests, the wealthy and the privileged all found themselves denounced by these preachers and pamphleteers. The rich man, argued Fox, is 'the greatest thief' because he acquired his wealth 'by cozening and cheating, by lying and defrauding'.[20] At times, Quaker views had uncomfortable echoes of the old Levellers. One Quaker wrote in 1653 that 'the earth is the Lords . . . he hath given it to the sons of men in general, and not to a few lofty ones which Lord it over their brethren'.[21] They were unequivocal in their support for the winning side in the Civil War, but they also believed that the revolution had not gone far enough. In the course of the 1650s they became progressively disenchanted with Cromwell's regime, disliking the compromises with the old order and hating what had become a rapacious army that seemed interested solely in its own well-being and future.

Quaker demands, backed by the growing strength of their numbers, began to spread alarm among men in authority. 'These vipers', said one MP, 'are crept into the bowels of your Commonwealth, and the government too . . . They grow numerous, and swarm all the nation over; every county, every parish.'[22] Fox submitted to Parliament a series of fundamentally egalitarian reforms involving a massive programme of expropriation. These ideas reminded men of substance everywhere of the wilder fringe groups of the previous decade. There was reason to fear that this increasingly numerous and vocal body of people, who espoused 'such principles as will level the foundation of all government into a bog of confusion', would usher in a 'social anarchy'.[23] The Quaker refusal to recognise rank seemed corrosive of the very fabric of social life itself. They refused to bow, to remove their hats to superiors, to acknowledge titles, and they spoke to their betters with the common, plain 'thee' and 'thou'. It was a style, a tone, a vernacular of equality which could be interpreted as showing disrespect and disdain; it was a message which could prove utterly seductive to the common people.

Quakers were successful in garrison towns, for example, where their egalitarianism posed a military threat. Their principles, thought Henry Cromwell, 'are not verry consistent with civil government, much less with the discipline of an army'. Not surprisingly some regiments were purged of their Quaker soldiers.[24] Quaker successes, however, often depended on local patronage. Where they secured the sympathy or the conversion of a local powerful figure (notably Judge Fell), they could weather the storm of local hostility and persecution which they endured throughout the 1650s; but more common was the banding together of local (especially urban) interests to deny them a platform or even entry to the town. Time and again, their preachers were cruelly dispatched from the area and any sympathisers persecuted. Officials dragged Quakers before the courts on a range of charges, conjuring forth whatever Act or by-law seemed most likely to secure a conviction.

By the late 1650s Cromwell's government felt obliged to heed the voices of provincial alarm and authorised local magistrates to use old vagrancy laws against travelling Quakers. A new Act allowed prosecution for the interruption of Sunday services (a favourite Quaker tactic) and reinstated the obligation to attend these services. Magistrates took full advantage of these measures, continuing to imprison and persecute wherever they could, but even that failed to staunch the rising popularity of Quakerism. By

1659, many felt that only a swift restoration of the monarchy would stop the encroaching tide of egalitarianism and the drift of people to the Quakers and other sects. It was ironic but obvious that the rise of Quakerism emboldened the reactionary forces intent on restoring the King.

The Quakers were set against the restoration of the monarchy in that, whatever its altered form, it would usher in many of the men, ideas and relationships against which they had struggled. The greatest risk to the return of Charles II was the hostility within the Army and the fear that it would go over to the Quakers *en masse*. Here surely was a remarkable phenomenon: a group which had scarcely existed a mere decade earlier was now feared for its potential influence within the most powerful body in England. But just when Quakers seemed poised for even greater influence, they were subjected to acute persecution by the vengeful forces unleashed by the return of Charles II.

The men who came back to England with the King in 1660 knew very little about the Quakers, who had scarcely existed when the royalists had fled the country in defeat. It was therefore difficult for them to distinguish the Quakers from the other, more overtly revolutionary sects of the previous two decades who had been anxious to turn the nation back to the basics of democracy. The Restoration, notably the Clarendon Code, sought to reimpose loyalty to Church and State. This inevitably spelled persecution for those who refused to obey. Following an uprising of Fifth Monarchists, a wide-ranging clampdown was launched against all those sects thought to be subversive and dangerous. Despite protestations of loyalty, the Quakers were plunged into a spiral of oppression, the scale and depth of which surpassed all previous agonies. By the end of January 1660, jails across the country were filled with them.

From one town to another the story was the same: of Quakers detained in stinking prisons and mouldering detention rooms in appalling, sometimes fatal conditions. More than 4,000 men were incarcerated - including 500 in London, 400 in Yorkshire and almost 300 in Lancashire – and women and children were not exempt from these miseries. In Aylesbury, John Whitehead and Isaac Penington joined sixty or seventy others in an old malt-house 'so decayed that it was scarce fit for a dog-house'. Quakers in Norwich were housed in a recess in the castle wall; one in Dover was thrown into a hole, 'a place very filthy . . . overrun with maggots and other insects'.[25] Yet in York, where local Quakers were of 'the better sort', unwilling to antagonise their local business associates and neighbours, their community did not suffer as such.[26]

During these years the 'Society of Friends' was 'the most vilified of all the sects', denounced and physically attacked by both the propertied and the poor, in town and country alike.* Stories from across the country told of frenzied assaults which in retrospect are hard to comprehend. When James Parnell preached in Colchester he was viciously attacked 'by a blind zealot who struck him a violent Blow with a great Staff, saying There, take that for Christ's Sake.' The first Quaker preachers to arrive in Cambridge were women who were publicly whipped in the market place 'so that their Flesh was miserably cut and torn'. Such acts of parochial violence were often prompted by a dislike of outsiders trying to interfere in local matters. It is easier to understand such feelings in the context of Quakers disrupting church services, burials and the like. Sometimes the offending Quaker seemed to be merely crazy. Solomon Eccles walked through Smithfield in 1663 'with his Body naked, and a Pan of Fire and Brimstone burning on his Head'. He was promptly dispatched to Bridewell.[27]

The growing hatred for Quakers flared up even when they were going about their normal business. When the Huntingdon shopkeeper Robert Raby and others traded on Christmas Day, they had 'Dirtt and Mire cast upon them'. Quakers were also attacked as they worshipped. In Sawbridgeworth, a local 'rabble' threw

*Note that the name 'Society of Friends' was not used in the seventeenth century. Indeed, it gained acceptance only in the early nineteenth century.

'Showers of stones, Dirt, rotten Eggs, human Dung and Urine' into the meeting house. Their hats were filled with dirt and placed back on their heads. After the widow Ann Cock disrupted a service in Cambridge, an angry local tailor threw a 'piss-pot of Urine' at her.

The animosity against Quakers clearly ran deep, for they were described and considered as less than human – as cannibals, satanists and the like – a process which allowed their tormentors to punish them in the most violent and bloody fashion.[28] Men were herded through the streets like cattle, crammed into stinking confinement, beaten, starved and roundly abused. For that first generation of Quakers, these humiliations on a ghastly scale and from all quarters was a regular occurrence.

The severity of these post-1660 persecutions which lasted for more than a decade shaped the course of Quaker history. It was from the violations of these years that their 'peace principle' gradually evolved. Fox declared that 'The spirit of Christ will never move us to fight a war against any man with carnal weapons.' Thereafter Quakers eventually became wedded to this new concept and practice of non-violence.[29] Indeed, many of the features we today associate with Quakerism emerged from this difficult time. For example, it was necessary to devise and maintain a form of discipline primarily to withstand attacks from others. It was also imperative to present their case to the outside world, and important to exclude those who failed to abide by the movement's basic tenets. Thus, in the climate of persecution, Quaker organisation gradually assumed the recognisable shape of quarterly and national meetings, with an accountable financial system.[30] Those sects who failed to reorganise – who tried to exist as they had before the Restoration – simply disappeared. A small number of Quakers, it is true, periodically rose up in opposition over the next generation; others took strident issue with the imposition of tight discipline upon a movement which was highly individualistic in origin and spirit. But these were exceptions. Most quickly accepted the new order of the Society of Friends, thereby ensuring its survival.

This discipline born of necessity attests to the political alertness of the movement's leadership. As the 1660s advanced, the Quakers were clearly led by George Fox. His obvious competitors died out (often from the rigours of imprisonment) or resigned. Fox's leadership was strengthened by his marriage in 1669 to the widowed Margaret Fell and he began the process of rewriting Quaker history. Henceforth all Quaker commentaries and histories had to pass his scrutiny and approval. Not surprisingly in such publications his role in the formative years came to the fore, and the work of other men was relegated or removed entirely. It was through this revised – purged, even – historiography that subsequent generations have come to view the original Quakers of the 1640s and 1650s, but the Quakers of the last years of the seventeenth century were very different. This peacable, industrious, plain-speaking, plain-acting second generation stood in sharp contrast to the motley collection of political and religious revolutionaries and anarchists, of whom Quakers were one group, at the heart of the English Revolution. These origins discomforted older Quakers. Who wanted to recall the image of James Nayler in 1656 riding into Bristol on a donkey as a sign of the Second Coming, or the adoration by those followers who believed him to be the true Messiah?[31]

Consequently, the Quakers' response to persecutions after 1660 was stoical, sometimes apocalyptical. They would unnerve their tormentors even in the midst of their sufferings by seeking to convert them. More than that, those on the outside remained undaunted by the imprisonment of fellow Quakers, continuing in their 'insolence' to meet in worship. The pattern repeated itself everywhere: no sooner was a prominent member arrested (Fox at Swarthmore in January 1664; Margaret Fell a month later) than even bigger congregations came together. The persecutions were clearly counter-productive.[32] And predictably, whenever a leading Quaker was brought to trial, he or she was effectively given the floor to preach and convert. The despairing judge at Fox's Lancaster trial in 1664 sighed, 'I would the laws were otherways.'[33]

They endured long months of the harshest of prison regimes, often made worse by the victimisation and cruelty of prison officers and governors. Francis Howgill, for example, festered in misery (but never relented in his faith) at Appleby until his death in 1669, 'stuffed up for want of air, and at the mercy of a tyrannous gaoler'.[34]

Quakers were an easy target. Whenever a plot, real or imaginary, was discovered, it was assumed that they (or Catholics) were involved. The prominent Puritan William Prynne was convinced that the Great Fire of London had been started by Catholics, and that Quakers were merely Catholics in disguise.[35] Moreover, the law allowed relatively easy arrest and trial, though proving a case was more difficult. Quakers could be prosecuted for attending their own services, and imprisoned when they refused to take the oath in court. For that simple offence they could also be transported to the West Indies or North America, or heavily fined. Their meeting houses were knocked down in London, so they gathered in the rubble. Even when acquitted, they bounced back for more, inviting authorities to do their worst. Often they did.

Even though national political stability suggested the need for greater toleration, the forces of revenge were spurred on by sharp and durable memories of the troubles of the past twenty years, and endured in Parliament and Church. The immediate impetus to end the persecutions was the changed international and diplomatic climate in the 1670s, and the threat of war with the Dutch. Conflict abroad demanded greater domestic harmony, and from that need emerged the Declaration of Indulgence in 1672. Relief was immediate and Quakers turned their efforts to securing the release of 'Friends' languishing in jail. Though Parliament sought to renew the attacks on Quakers in 1673, the high tide of persecution seemed to have receded, but many of the old hateful memories lived on.

From 1670, the Friends, always swift to record the catalogue of attacks they suffered, now began to record incidents of toleration and sympathy. Non-Quaker neighbours would stand up for them when their goods and possessions were impounded by local officialdom. Sometimes even the officials themselves refused to implement what they knew to be unjust orders against Quakers. Gradually they were accepted into the local way of running things: made executors of wills, for example, or given a role in helping the poor. Non-Quakers even began to attend Quaker funerals.[36] Mutual trust developed and Quakers came to be accepted where once they had been reviled and attacked.[37]

The best remembered political disputes of those years were concerned with more elevated issues: the power of Parliament versus the King, and the right of the King to choose his own faith. In the struggle against the Catholic James II, Parliament found itself locked into a more fundamental battle than it had experienced with Quakers, but in some regions the authorities continued to feel the need to persecute Quakers and others as a means of enforcing and maintaining political power. Meeting houses were pillaged and destroyed (Bristol and London were especially badly hit); Quaker children were not spared. Often the authorities had to dig out old legislation to sanction their actions, so that even in relatively benign times there were hundreds of imprisoned Quakers. When James II ascended the throne in 1685, there were 1,383 in jail (200 of them women) and more than 100 had died in custody over the past eight years. It was owing to these circumstances that the 'Meetings for Sufferings' were convened and continued thereafter to record details of Quaker affairs.[38]

Much of this persecution was inspired by high politics in London, but the details, the specific pains and penalties heaped upon Quaker heads, had more to do with local enmities and jealousies. Informers or worried clerics, uncertain landowners or hesitant officials all felt the need to exact social and political reprisals as a means of securing their own position, and perhaps grasping some bounty afforded by the Quakers. The balance sheet of 'suffering' – death, personal endurance, fines, confiscated property, ruined businesses and expropriation – was long. The Restoration period had witnessed perhaps more than 15,000 such instances.[39] Yet this miserable litany of pain and distress elicited a remarkable display of fortitude and durability from the Quakers. Far from being destroyed, bankrupted or downhearted, they thrived. It was becoming clear that intimidatory Acts of Parliament, punative magistrates and judges, and hateful neighbours were not having the desired effect but quite the contrary. In the late seventeenth century Quakers were flourishing: one Cumberland Friend remarked that 'they flock to our meetings like doves to the windows'.[40]

Suspicions on a more national scale continued to come the way of the Quakers whenever a plot or rebellion was uncovered (most spectacularly, Monmouth's rebellion in 1685), but dissenters found themselves largely tolerated and sometimes encouraged. Friends were even invited to take local office. The lesson that a greater degree of toleration was the only way to secure national political stability, whatever the theological bent of the incumbent monarch, was quickly learned by William III when he landed at Torbay on 5 November 1688 to remove James II and protect the Protestant Establishment against the threat of Catholic control.

The new monarch believed that the nation would be best served by harnessing the abilities and talents of its dissenters, men and women of enterprise, initiative and strength; still less could it afford costly and counter-productive persecutions for reasons which seemed increasingly anachronistic. Within months of the accession of William and Mary, the Toleration Act of 1689 had moved quickly through Parliament. It was designed, as the preamble stated, to be 'an effectual means to unite Their Majesties' Protestant subjects in interest and affection'; in practice, toleration was to be more liberal than the Act specified.[41] Major discrimination continued, of course (and was not to be legislated against until the early nineteenth century), but the year marked a major turning-point in the history of the Quaker community.

Two years later George Fox died having endured a life of persistent persecution, as had his followers. Yet Fox had lived long enough to see his efforts (allied to others) rewarded by a large, thriving and committed following. From the upheavals of the Civil War, through the factional disputes of the Interregnum and the oppression of the Restoration, they had survived. It was appropriate and typical that when the pall-bearers gathered to carry Fox to his grave in London's Bunhill Fields, 'for a considerable time there was nothing but deep sighs, groans and tears and roaring to admiration, and, after that all had vented and eased themselves, and grew quiet in their minds'. One man present thought that the occasion 'resembled that day when the apostles were met together and the mighty power of God fell upon them'.[42] At the end of Fox's life it was hard to recall that troubled youth wandering the lanes of the Midlands and the North in search of spiritual satisfaction. Though his leadership was often disputed, by the time of his death the movement he had come to personify had grown to an estimated 50,000 Quakers (quite apart from those thriving in Pennsylvania).[43]

By the last years of the seventeenth century, the Quakers were led and managed from London. Membership had taken root in many other regions and the North was no longer the main centre of activity, though it could still claim to be their spiritual birthplace. But Quakers everywhere were *different*; different from other religious groups in almost every respect. They had evolved a style of conduct both at worship and in their private lives which stood in sharp contrast to the world at large. The first Quaker organisations emerged, naturally enough, to cater for their parochial needs. Regional meetings had begun to spread in the North in the 1650s, then, prompted by Fox, annual meetings were called in London. In the counties, Quakerism organised itself through the Particular, Monthly and Quarterly Meeting (the last charged with monitoring the overall conduct and well-being of local life). There was an inevitable overlap in the concerns of these various meetings, but they formed a structure of management which allowed the London headquarters to keep in touch with events and developments in the smallest of communities.

Between 1699 and 1798 the Northern Yearly Meeting reflected the origins of the movement, but the Yearly Meeting in London served to co-ordinate business at national and regional level, while the Monthly and Quarterly Meeting channelled business upwards from local meetings. Yet Quaker feeling continued to be characterised by strong individualism; by an element of 'religious anarchism'.[44] Reactions against Fox's centralised form of organisation periodically surfaced, especially in the North, where in the 1670s John Story and John Wilkinson threatened separation. Such tensions were partly theological, but they also challenged Fox's authoritarian leadership. Many bridled against his tone and his conviction, which came out repeatedly in the London meetings, that he alone had a monopoly on truth.[45]

However, the Quakers needed more than an efficient organisation; they also required principled rules and specified conventions which could provide the basic tenets of Quaker conduct and belief: the bedrock of Quaker life and behaviour. Beginning in 1682, the Yearly Meeting asked three simple questions of the various representatives about numbers, imprisonments, and the state of local Quakerism. They were designed to provide the factual information that they required to function properly. By the early eighteenth century, the number of such questions had greatly increased, replies were recorded and the whole exercise had subtly changed 'to ensure consistency of conduct among Friends and to obtain information as to the state of the society'. As problems were revealed (a fall in Quaker membership, for example) new strategies were devised, and a more coherent structure of control and discipline evolved.[46] There thus emerged the *Queries* and *Advices* which, though changing from time to time, became their guiding rules. In the words of Quaker Elders in Yorkshire in 1652, 'these may be fulfilled in the Spirit – not from the letter, for the letter killeth, but the Spirit giveth life'.[47] If we are looking for a written code or constitution for Quakerism, it can be found here in the varied *Advices* published over the years. These *Advices* provided the precepts which shaped their personal and communal lives; not only the theological outlook but also the conduct of daily life, including outside businesses.

The London Yearly Meeting dispatched *Queries* to the Quarterly Meeting, seeking answers and advice. By the end of the eighteenth century such missives going back and forth had become the broad outline of contemporary Quaker philosophy; an accumulating corpus of judgement and suggestions which, though never sanctified as philosophy, in fact acted precisely in that way. They formed, in effect, the ideology and principles of the movement which was paralleled by an ever-tighter control exercised over Quaker life and worship. An ad hoc London committee read and monitored all their publications, excluding unwanted ideas and rejecting those manuscripts which diverged too sharply from Fox's ideas of harmony and organisation. From about 1675 onwards, the key decision-maker had been the 'Meeting for Sufferings'. It regulated ministers and meetings, negotiated with the authorities, helped Quakers in distress and acted as a pressure group on behalf of their broader interests.[48] Throughout, the conduct of Quaker business was undertaken in the spirit of worship; none the less it was businesslike, thorough and meticulously minuted from first to last.

As Quaker philosophy evolved, it was inevitable that disciplinary action would be taken against those who transgressed. A much tighter control developed than the early Quakers could ever have imagined, and those who 'walked disorderly' could expect at least a reprimand, even exclusion. Individualism was gradually brought to heel and subordinated to what was deemed the broader general good. This evolution took place during years of persecution to defend Quaker interests and individuals, and to deflect external enemies and threats. This self-regulating, self-supporting community thus devised a form of organisation that survived till modern times, the foundations of which were laid as a means of self-preservation and mutual protection in the years from 1650 to 1700.[49]

At the same time there emerged the distinctive physical face of Quakerism. They needed a place of worship and to meet, so local groups consolidated and pooled resources, and they acquired, constructed or converted buildings for their own unique use. In the early years, Quaker preachers had spoken wherever was necessary, preaching in open spaces to large crowds, converting, praying and working from within private homes. Subsequent meeting houses sometimes betrayed their domestic origins: 'Sarah Sawyers', 'Widow Webbs', and 'The Bull and Mouth' revealed their varied sources. Often built by the co-operative help of members, meeting houses developed standard features: the simple benches, the gallery, an upper room (initially used by women). Like Quakers themselves, these houses were simple, unpretentious and functional; early ones were often remote, in part a reflection of Quaker farming roots. A number were pulled down and destroyed in the persecutions; others have decayed and been lost in the intervening years. But a clutch of those early original buildings survive to this day – some in private hands, some still in use as meeting houses – where we can catch some sense of their appealing tranquillity.[50]

This tranquillity stood in contrast to the early history of the movement. Conceived in the upheavals of revolution and civil war, by the time of Fox's death in 1691 it had been refined into a national organisation with headquarters in London, committed to active missionary work across the country and alert to the need for self-preservation. The instinct to be mutually helpful was to become of prime importance as Quakerism moved into a new phase. With the age of persecution passed, Quakers were able to flourish in a more tolerant climate. Henceforth they directed their energies to assisting each other, no longer as a defence but for personal and communal self-advancement. The tactics, organisation and ideology which had been fashioned to stave off hostility provided the very basis for a great deal of Quaker success to come in a more benign religious and political world.

2

The Shaping of Quaker Culture

By the late seventeenth century, Quakers had become well known as a prospering people. A critic wrote in 1697, 'For tho' the Quakers, at first, left their Houses and Families to shift for themselves, to run about and Preach And cryed down Riches, when they have none', now they were wont to 'Call Riches a Gift and a Blessing from God'.[1] It was a trait noted by friends and enemies alike that, from their early days, many Quakers had seemed to thrive and that even when they fell on hard times, others were on hand to help them out. This had been the saving grace of Quakerism throughout its years of greatest persecution: the banding together to help fellow Friends in times of suffering. But it does not explain the emergent prosperity in Quaker ranks which contemporaries jealously noted. Few seemed abjectly poor. Many, it is true, were not 'in affluence', to use a contemporary Quaker phrase, but neither was poverty a striking characteristic. From the seventeenth century onwards, contemporaries – to say nothing of recent scholars – simply *assumed* that Quaker life was conducive to material improvement. It is true that they were, by law and by their own theological choice, excluded from wide areas of everyday life, but were they propelled towards economic success by the same process? And were they also *encouraged* to acquire this money?

Again, we need to begin with George Fox. When he embarked upon his tortured travels in the 1640s he had cash in his pocket. He had quit a modest but comfortable family home and wandered the country with no apparent financial worries. As his following grew he acquired more substantial funds, some of which was bequeathed to him. Not surprisingly, enemies raised the issue of his personal wealth as an implied criticism, though Fox dismissed such accusations with the claim that his money had merely been a 'birthright'. Later in life he was able to make investments and at his death his will revealed a respectable inheritance.[2] Fox was, in short, more prosperous than all but a handful of his contemporaries. But what of his followers?

In recent years, historians probing the origins of provincial Quakers have produced a composite picture of regional similarities: far from being the hard-pressed group portrayed by earlier commentators, Quakers seem to have been drawn 'mainly from the middle ranks of society'. Historians, as we might expect, continue to disagree about the finer details – local studies show Quaker fortunes varying from one place to another – but it is generally agreed that members prospered with the passage of time (though so, too, did many others).[3] In York, the provincial capital of the North of England, Quakers belonged to the 'comfortably off', and were to be found among the ranks of shopkeepers and craftsmen. Some even took their place alongside more affluent citizens. None, however, belonged to York's mercantile élite, though some of the town's early Quakers were described as 'Gentlemen'. The group was, therefore, 'comfortably bourgeois in character' and lacked any significant number of the 'poorer sorts'.[4]

The formal conduct of York's Quaker business was from the first dominated by the more prosperous, as poorer Friends lacked the time, opportunity or necessary social skills to involve themselves in such time-consuming and demanding activities. Try as they might, well-to-do Quakers failed to persuade humbler Friends to play a major role in their local affairs.[5] Despite that, Quakers remained rootedly egalitarian.

On the surface at least, rich and poor shared common ground in their appearance. They could be recognised at a glance in that they dressed as plainly as possible, choosing to deny themselves the 'wearing of needless things and following the world's fashions in . . . clothing and attire'.[6] The London Yearly Meeting in 1691 decreed that 'Friends take care to keep to truth and plainness, in language, habit, deportment, and behaviour . . . and to avoid pride and immodesty in apparel'.[7] In 1669, William Penn had denounced 'personal pride', wishing that people 'could spare but half the time to think of God, that they spend in washing, perfuming, painting and dressing their bodies'. Such finery, he felt, was an insult to the poor.[8] Quakers therefore wore simple shades of black, white and grey, but such plainness could have its problems. In the 1680s, when the 10-year-old Thomas Chalkey walked the two miles to school he was often assailed by other children, 'by beatings and stonings along the streets, being distinguished to the people (by the badge of plainness which my parents put upon me) of what profession I was'.[9]

Simplicity became the Quakers' watchword. They constructed their homes and meeting places, designed their furnishings, gardens and ceremonials with this in mind. At worship, at home and at work, they were urged to 'choose what is simple and beautiful'.[10] The vogue for 'great ruffling periwigs' was denounced; so too was the company of 'guzzling drinkers and company-keeping smokers'.[11] 'Plainness' was a feature of a number of sects and communities that had arisen from seventeenth-century Puritanism on both sides of the Atlantic, but in the case of the Quakers theirs was an appearance which did more than speak to a sense of public or personal decorum. It was part and parcel of a much wider commitment to straightforwardness in all things, rather than just sartorial style. To be simple and above reproach in the eyes of all was the Quaker way, and this was especially true in matters of commerce and business.

The large numbers of early Quakers who were in trade and business, though often at a lowly level, were guided by the evolving ethical code of the Society of Friends. The tone had been set by George Fox in the first days of his preaching, when in 1653 he hectored Carlisle market traders with the assertions that 'the day of the Lord was coming upon their deceitful ways and doings, and deceitful merchandise; and that they should put away all cozening and cheating, and to keep to yea and nay, and speak the truth to one another'.[12] The *Advices* issued to Quakers throughout the country paid increased attention to this subject. As early as 1688 members were told that none should 'launch into trading and worldly business beyond what they can manage honourably and with reputation; so that they may keep their words with all men'.[13] From the outset the dangers of debt was a stern refrain in Quaker missives ('the payment of just debts be not delayed').[14] But those keen to embark on business had more than society's codes to concern them.

In many towns, Friends faced serious difficulties in terms of local politics. Their refusal to swear oaths prevented them from becoming freemen, but commercial activity was often confined to the local fraternity. The Affirmation Act of 1722 allowed Quakers to affirm (rather than swear) an oath, but even before that date many had managed to circumvent the rules. Local officials and other freemen came to realise the value of energy and initiative in business, and could ill afford to exclude Quakers from economic life owing to the formalities of oath-taking, but their refusal to do so could be used against Quakers by ill-disposed officials or by those merely wishing to settle old scores.[15]

Once established in local business, Quakers faced other difficulties. Honesty and plain-dealing often ran counter to the way others conducted their affairs. William Tout of Lancaster admitted that he 'always detested that which is common, to ask more for goods than the market price, or what they may be afforded for; but usually set the price at one word, which seemed offensive to many'. Yet it seemed to bring its own rewards, for, as Tout observed, 'such plain dealing obliged worthy customers and made business go forward with few words'. Naturally enough, some Quaker businesses did fail despite close scrutiny by other Friends, but such upsets were normally explained in terms of the victim not adhering to Quaker principles. Lancaster Friends blamed 'freedom in company and in some houses of no good character and his dealings in merchandise with loose partners' for one Quaker's insolvency. Another failure was put down to extravagant spending 'in purchasing buildings and other superfluities'.[16] Personal weaknesses, bad company and straying from life's basic necessities were all proof of the need not to wander too far from the Quaker way.

Quakers in business were expected to conform to the principles issued from the Yearly Meeting in London and laid down in the *Advices*, but they also had to answer to their town peers. In commerce, as in private life, their behaviour was subject to the critical scrutiny of local meetings or the nominated officers. The implementation of Quaker policies was in their hands. Thus a complex but efficient bureaucracy was put to work to ensure that even the humblest of Friends accorded with Quaker standards.

Quakers could therefore find their business activities criticised for what today might seem the most innocent of transactions. Having determined to live and dress as plainly as possible, they were sometimes uneasy about satisfying the more exotic tastes and habits of their non-Quaker customers. This was a particular problem for those involved with the 'luxury trades', not least because the consumer revolution of the late-seventeenth and eighteenth centuries was driven forward by the proliferation of such goods, ranging from imported foodstuffs (tea, sugar and coffee) to domestic furnishings and fashions.[17] Enterprising Quakers could scarcely ignore the commercial opportunities of an evolving market, but at the same time to trade in these luxuries might attract critical attention. Lancaster Friends were urged to avoid the 'making or selling of striped or figured stuffs or other cloth for apparel' (presumably owing to its excessive gaudiness).[18] Quaker shopkeepers in Malton burned their silks and ribbons. But as contemporary fashion changed in the course of the eighteenth century, many of the fripperies of consumer taste became ever more pronounced and increased the dilemma. York's wealthiest Quaker, milliner John Todd, determined 'to give over his trade and cleare the Truth as it may be with him concerning those unnecessary things sould by him'.[19]

This hostility towards luxury goods posed many problems for Quaker traders. What seemed to outsiders to be a simple matter of trade and business could plunge them into an agitated moral debate in the local meeting house. Should they make 'draught, figured or striped work, or to sell such or make them up into cloth'? Some tailors were stymied: commercial potential was enormous, but they felt that they could not 'answer the world's fashion'.[20]

However, the ethics of commerce cannot be easily divorced from the much broader world of Quaker values, for the Friends' behaviour was expected to be consistent in all matters. Honesty and plain-dealing were fundamental to life itself. Friends were instructed in 1732 'to have a watchful eye over all their members', and those heading for commercial trouble should be warned and, if required, helped in their difficulties.[21] Time and again throughout the eighteenth century, as increasing numbers of Quakers involved themselves in commercial ventures, the *Advices* returned to the question of reconciling their business practices with their faith. Though it was too much to expect that all would inevitably follow the true path, those who fell by the wayside could expect to be called to account by their neighbours. The end result was that Quaker businesses were carefully scrutinised during a time when the commercial world was generally free from outside control.

As Quaker unease with worldly gain had dated from the era of Fox himself, their enemies were likely to use any such success as a snide insult. Some critics alleged that Quakers used their growing economic prosperity as recruiting bait; others liked to deal with Quakers as they were always direct in their dealings and paid their dues on time.[22] But the world of commerce brought its own dangers. In the wake of the disasters following the collapse of the South Sea Bubble in 1720, in which some Lancaster Quakers lost money,[23] they were all warned to 'be very careful to avoid all inordinate pursuit after the things of this world, by such ways and means as depend too much on the uncertain probabilities of hazardous enterprises'. Instead they should 'labour to content themselves with such a plain way and manner of living as is most agreeable to the self-denying principle of Truth'.[24]

Yet worldly success was not so easily avoided, not least because it had begun to diffuse itself throughout British society in general as the fruits of overseas trade and dominion yielded ever more prosperity. A simple case will suffice. By the early eighteenth century the British had become a nation of tea-drinkers. The tea came from the merchants of Canton and was mixed with cane sugar grown by African slaves in the West Indies. At first, tea seemed a luxury beyond the reach of most, involving elaborate ceremonial with lavish displays of porcelain tableware (itself imported from vast distances) and all with its own complex etiquette of sociability. In its more ostentatious forms it attracted disapproval. In 1714, Quakers were urged to 'refrain from having fine tea-tables set with fine china, being it is more for sight than service . . . It's advised that Friends should not have so much china or earthenware on their mantlepieces or on their chests of drawers, but rather set them in their closets until they have occasion to use them'.[25] Such objections might have deterred Quakers at home, but it did little to hold back the rapid expansion of tea consumption. In town after town, Quakers set themselves up as shopkeepers and traders to buy, retail and repack tea in its various forms. Dozens of former pupils from the Quaker school at Ackworth, for example, made their careers in the tea trade.[26]

Quakers disliked a range of customary pleasures and worldly pursuits. Long-established popular traditions were rejected if they failed the simplicity test. Feastings at weddings and christenings, or the exchange of gifts at certain seasons and ceremonies were dismissed for their popish or pagan past. Quakers struggled against behaviour which was Catholic in origin; they denounced such amusements which were likely to spill over into drunken or sexual abandon. Popular culture, with its turbulence, irreverence, drunken excess and licence, was a favourite and recurring target of this Puritan-inspired hostility on both sides of the Atlantic. Quakers were anxious to ensure that members resisted the earthly temptations of high days and holidays, remembering instead to keep them holy.

Before the massive industrial and urban changes of the nineteenth century, Britain had a well-defined ceremonial regime associated with the Christian calendar, the agricultural year and local festivals. Their origins had been lost in time, but what concerned Quakers was not their antiquity, or even their deep-seated popularity, but their appeal to basic sensual feelings. Quakers disowned all traces of such rituals and histories: they refused to use the names for days of the week because of their pagan origins, preferring for example 'First Day' for Sunday; the gift of cheese or biscuits at burials incurred their disapproval; hunting, and at times fishing, drew Quaker fire. More violent popular pastimes – animal-baiting, cock-fighting and the like – were predictably denounced.[27] In 1739, young Quakers were urged to 'avoid all such conversation as may tend to draw out their minds into the foolish and wicked pastimes with which this age aboundeth; . . . those nurseries of debauchery and wickedness'.[28] Friends were instructed to 'Avoid sports, plays and all such diversions; as tending to alienate the mind from God, and to deprive the soul of the comfortable enjoyment of his presence and power'.[29]

During the course of the eighteenth century, popular and highbrow culture was enhanced, like social life in general, by the diffusion of new material artefacts. The proliferation of books, commercial theatres and music, of spa towns, assembly rooms, racecourses and other new commercial delights all provoked fresh Quaker instructions.[30] Friends were urged to stick to 'useful and commendable employments' and to avoid spending their time 'amusing themselves with the pernicious works of stage-authors, and romances; which strongly tend to excite irregular passions, and to introduce them into the giddy pursuits and pollutions of a degenerate age'.[31] Music-making was also frowned upon in part because many contemporary songs addressed some of those issues of love, drinking or fighting which offended Quaker ideals. Mastering a musical instrument was considered to be too time-consuming, likely to place the instrumentalist in spiritual danger. Quakers were even 'disowned' (expelled) from their meeting for giving children music lessons. The stage, in demanding false expressions of the actors (they were not in fact angry or sad, for instance) inevitably called for insincerity. It was false and therefore dangerous. Visual arts were similarly disliked because they too elevated the 'worthless and the base'.[32]

Quakers were not alone in many of these objections. By the late eighteenth century there was a growing sense of propertied disgust towards the most cruel and violent of contemporary amusements, but Quakers were once more ahead of the pack in their objections, and it took many years for a broader sensibility to emerge and follow their lead. Quakers were not seeking to convert the world to their view, but rather to ensure that their own members resisted the temptations to stray from the path.

Yet there was no certainty that their culture would survive such challenges. Indeed, many seventeenth-century sects had simply faded away. From the outset it had been appreciated that a way to ensure the survival of Quaker culture was through appropriate childcare and education. As in matters of daily life and commerce, this determination to raise children in the Quaker way was perpetuated by a combination of instructions from the London Yearly Meeting and the intrusive scrutiny of local Friends.

Quakers had been obliged to educate themselves in the era of persecution and state-sponsored exclusion, in that they were denied access to, among other things, the old grammar schools and the two universities. Like other dissenters, they therefore devised their own tuition system for their children. George Fox, who had written about the nature of schooling as early as 1656, was among the first to establish Quaker schools: one for boys at Waltham Abbey in Essex in 1668 and another at Shacklewell 'to instruct young lasses and maidens in whatsoever things were civil and useful in the creation'.[33] Friends across the country followed his lead. The Westmorland farmer and botanist Thomas Lawson opened a small school at Strickland in the 1650s, his early pupils travelling long distances (as with other pioneering Friends schools, though normally from within the region) to study with him. It was a sign of Lawson's growing fame as a schoolmaster that more and more people entrusted him with their children. This included non-Quakers, a number of whom subsequently graduated from Oxford and Cambridge. But Lawson, like other Quaker teachers and preachers, was seen as a threat by some non-Quakers and was subject to bouts of prosecution and fines for his schoolmastering.[34] Yet he and others persevered, and by 1671 there were fifteen Quaker schools, quite apart from a host of smaller institutions, sometimes open to all comers.[35]

With the relative thaw in persecution following the Toleration Act of 1689, and as part of the establishment of a tighter discipline among Quakers, Friends tried to put schooling on an organised footing. The Yearly Meeting of 1690 urged that they 'provide schoolmasters and mistresses who are faithful Friends, to teach and instruct their children. And not to send them to such schools where they are taught the corrupt ways, manners, fashions, and languages of the world, and of the heathen in their authors.' Under Quaker instruction, the young were expected to be trained 'in that plainness and language which becomes truth'.[36] Educational philosophy hinged on this necessity of hiring devout Friends as teachers, but they were often hard to find. Friends at Lancaster had trouble appointing a suitable teacher throughout the 1690s even though there were successes elsewhere, notably at Penketh School near Warrington, where teachers were trained for service throughout Lancashire. Such difficulties in providing suitable education continued well into the eighteenth century, and even when suitable candidates were found finances were often troublesome. The most common way to raise money for the lowly paid teacher was via subscriptions, benefactions and fees from non-Quaker pupils.[37] In

York there was rarely enough money for teachers and, in any case, they were in short supply – not surprisingly, perhaps, because they faced prosecution for teaching without a licence. But the most pressing educational need concerned the children of poorer Quakers. The more prosperous could make private provision for their offspring; they worried about providing free or cheap education for the others.[38] Quakers in London had sought to educate the children of their poor as early as 1674, and it was easier to find teachers in the capital than in provincial and certainly rural England.[39]

The Quakers wanted education for both sexes. Women had been prominent in their ranks from the founding days – indeed, their enemies were quick to point out how numerous and vocal Quaker female preachers were. Statistics confirm this presence. Wherever historians have analysed the data, women formed a substantial part of the active community. They shared the miseries of persecution, bore a comparable burden of social disgrace and worked vigorously in local meetings. One-third of those accused of disrupting church meetings between 1654 and 1659, almost half of those migrating to America between 1656 and 1663, and large numbers of members in local meetings were women. Of all those sects and groups thrown up by the English Revolution and the Civil War, and which lent support to spiritual equality, it was 'among the Quakers that the spiritual rights of women attained their apogee'.[40] Of course, they shared all the disadvantages of contemporary women at large, and at worship women were separated from their menfolk inside the early meeting houses. In some cases they even had their own side room.[41] But Quaker leaders had always been keen to assert the 'equality of men and women in spiritual privilege and responsibility', choosing to refute biblical or philosophical claims to the contrary. In the words of Fox, 'The Lamb of God, the Son of God, is but one in all His males and females, sons and daughters, and they are all one in Christ, and Christ one in them all.'[42] The Society of Friends did not offer women genuine equality, but it certainly granted more autonomy than could be found elsewhere: they 'preached, proselytised, wrote and printed tracts, participated in church government (though in separate meetings and mainly in the area of welfare), and assumed a militant role in the sect's various campaigns.'[43]

It was, then, natural enough that the Friends should be concerned about girls' education, but inevitably Quaker schoolmistresses were harder to find, though the wives of schoolmasters played a part at a number of schools. In 1697 Esther Storrs was hired in Derbyshire to teach children to 'read, knit and sew'. Margaret Ker, appointed in Aberdeen in 1682, was subsequently encouraged by visiting female Quakers 'to accomplish herself in arithmetic and writing for the education of the children'. Quaker women made financial donations to their school, one being for 'a schoolmistress to teach three girls in the art of reading their mother tongue and sewing and making plain work'. Other girls' schools were founded across the country, at Warrington, Ramsey, Huntingdon and Brighton, in addition to more transient establishments, the existences of which are barely registered in the normally copious Quaker records.[44]

Teachers were expected to do more than simply instruct the three Rs; they also sought to encourage the spirit of the Quaker movement. However, parents often had their own ideas about what that involved, sometimes taking issue with theological questions raised at school. In 1677 Elizabeth Couldam, schoolmistress in Norwich, saw children removed from her care by parents who disagreed with her about discipline. Teachers and parents alike faced a peculiar mix of problems: they wanted a useful education which would fit their children for life (and work), and consolidate their attachment to Quaker culture. Aside from various local idiosyncrasies (clashes of personalities, disputes about theology, ill-educated teachers and the perennial shortage of money), they had to bridge the gap between their commitment to education and practical realities. The founding fathers, most notably Fox and William Penn, had paid great and detailed attention to the question and nature of schooling, but these high ideals, and the ambitious promptings from various London meetings, had to be set alongside the everyday problems of money and manpower faced by provincial Quakers. They were, in effect, being urged to make educational bricks without financial straw.

The education offered sought to remain faithful to Fox's basic principles: he was opposed to music and dancing in schools, and believed that classical learning should be replaced by more practical, useful subjects. William Penn suggested that boys should be taught the rudiments of construction and agriculture, and girls taught to 'spin, sew, knit, weave, garden, preserve'.[45] Thomas Lawson was keen to pass on his own love and knowledge of botany, encouraging children to work in the garden for practical results. He wanted 'a Garden School-house' where pupils would combine classroom learning with horticultural skills.[46] In 1695, John Bellers proposed the creation of 'A Colledge of Industry' to provide a practical education which would consequently generate prosperity for poor and rich alike.[47] This emphasis on functional schooling persisted in the various faltering efforts throughout the eighteenth century, but the real blossoming of Quaker education – the establishment of their 'Public Schools' – had to wait until the last years of the eighteenth century, by which time funding had become available, derived from the efforts of commercially successful Friends.

Of all the heirs of the Puritan Revolution who survived into the eighteenth century, the Quakers were perhaps the most conspicuous. They had emerged strong, relatively united and very well organised, and their distinctive way of life was not merely an adjunct to Quaker faith; it was a living embodiment of that faith itself. The Friends recognised that in order to secure their future they needed to bequeath their common culture to future generations by the careful education and rearing of their own children. Education itself was clearly important, but the crucial force in laying the foundations of Quaker culture was the family and community, and the formal management and government of the Quaker movement as a whole. By the end of the seventeenth century, to ensure that all Friends remained faithful to the Quaker way, an intrusive system of bureaucracy and management had evolved around a structure of local, regional and national meetings which seemed to many to rest uncomfortably with the freedoms which had been won by that first generation of Quakers. Ideally suited to the maintenance of discipline and uniformity, this system of government effectively supervised the evolution of Quaker culture. But as the eighteenth century advanced, this culture was itself in conflict with the rapid changes transforming British society, most notably the gradual diffusion of nationwide material betterment. And among those who benefited from and who helped make possible this improvement was a growing number of Quakers.

Exclusion from many areas of contemporary social and economic life had indeed obliged Quakers to look to their own efforts for careers and economic well-being, and to the support and assistance of other Friends. In this they were greatly helped by the organisation and essence of Quaker life itself, which was ideally suited to the rigours of commerce. The financial rewards of industry, sharp-eyed commercial opportunism and the accumulation of considerable family wealth (with all its public manifestations) came the way of an increasingly powerful group of Friends. Yet it all seemed out of kilter with their plainness and other-worldliness. It was to prove hard to adhere to Quaker culture while enjoying the rewards of economic success.

PART II

The Rise to Prosperity

3

Plainness and Plenty

Few groups kept records like the Quakers: family records; genealogies; birth, marriage and death statistics; private letters and diaries; minutes of local, regional and national meetings. These all add up to a detailed documentary and statistical archive of evidence, which was initiated in an era when such data was relatively scarce and continues through to the present. Quakers devised and perfected a process of tabulating information about themselves, centred on London, which predated by more than a century the census system established by the British state. For this reason alone, their records have proved invaluable for demographic historians keen to reconstruct the nature and changing patterns of the Quaker population over the past three centuries.

This obsession with minutiae originated, like much else, in the early days of the Quakers. They needed to record their own affairs because they had opted out of other formal institutions. For example, marriage ceremonies required the permission of Quaker parents (and hence documentary proof of this); family and business life demanded inheritance data; and since Friends tried to look after their own poor (rather than leaving them to rely on the parish), that too required confirmation that the applicant for assistance was a Quaker. In time, such record-keeping at each and every level, by individuals and by the Society of Friends, became an integral part of Quaker life.

These records are not infallible, of course. Some were kept more conscientiously than others, and names were removed if those Quakers were deemed not faithful to the cause, if they dabbled with other faiths, or for a string of other social or religious transgressions. In addition, much of this data has simply not survived the passage of time, yet all these inevitable blips scarcely dint its overall value.[1]

Here, then, was a group of people who believed in the necessity of keeping accounts about themselves, but many also recognised the need for an educated following who would be able to make their way in the world. We have seen how Quakers valued teaching. They also encouraged carefully monitored apprenticeships, letter-writing and all forms of record-keeping. In short, they cherished and came to depend upon the written word, both as an authentic account of their own personal and communal struggles, and as a means of regulating and monitoring their private and their working lives. It was, from the first, a highly literate culture.

Quaker meetings produced volumes of writings as minutes, news, decisions and queries passed back and forth from the local Particular Meeting, to the regional Monthly Meeting, thence to the county Quarterly Meeting and finally to the national Yearly Meeting. Instructions and suggestions from London (the *Advices* and *Epistles*) gave Quakers the practical and moral guidelines for every aspect of their lives. A fine web of literate contact was spun, linking Friends across the country and keeping British Quakers in contact with those overseas, more especially in Ireland, North America and the West Indies. Quakers sought to educate themselves and to persuade their opponents, through tracts and booklets, reprinted sermons, journals and letters. It was a drive both to refute in print the calumnies flung at their own heads, and to rally and strengthen the faithful. And the print that flew off the Quaker presses is testimony to the literacy of the movement itself.

More than 2,500 pieces of writing were published in the first forty years of Quaker history – an average of one per week despite serious obstacles. Books were censored and controlled between 1662 and 1678, and 1685 and 1693; even in other years, local officials were likely to impound and destroy Quaker publications, and to harry and persecute the authors or distributors. Yet the flow of publications continued, mainly because of the number of sympathetic printers. Theirs was a precarious business, however, for they faced the destruction of their presses, seizure and burning of any books, and a prison sentence. But private presses, some run by women, survived when all else seemed lost. From 1673 the Quakers appointed official printers, and a group of senior Friends vetted and authorised manuscripts submitted for publication. This editorial group also served a broader function, for they scrutinised published criticisms of their faith, issued rebuttals and saw to it that any official denial was on its way to the printer within the week. This system also curbed alternative dissenting views within the movement. Writers, preachers and polemicists whose opinions had previously found their way into formal print were now excluded. Old favourites, most notably Fox's *Journal*, were edited and re-edited, and those parts thought unsuitable or dubious were excised. Quaker history was thereby rewritten as theologically contentious factions found themselves effectively dispatched from Quaker memory.

The Quakers' nationwide network formed a ready-made readership and purchasing public for all their books. It ensured that these publications had a guaranteed sale and a relatively swift means of distribution throughout the country, and were thus relatively free from commercial risk. Neither did they need to use professional booksellers, for books were simply passed on, via meeting houses and personal connections. In time, even the smallest of local meetings built up their own circulating library of texts, and Quakers became regular book borrowers.* Books which would

*The books from a number of these northern Quaker libraries can now be consulted in the J. B. Morrell Library of the University of York.

have been costly for the individual to buy thus became more widely accessible by general subscription. The development of these libraries also served to unify the movement, to give it an intellectual and theological coherence (monitored by the London Yearly Meeting), but it also helped to whet the Quaker appetite for literature and create a reputation for studiousness among them all.[2]

Quakers became avid readers, and parents ensured that their children were nurtured on a love for the printed word. Such a literacy had its own clearly defined limits, but is notoriously corrosive and not easily contained or directed only to chosen texts. Indeed, Quakers recognised this fact by the internal censorship they had set in place for the vetting and editing of approved texts. But it was to have a much wider significance than engagement with religious writings: it was an invaluable tool in the successful conduct of business.

The Quaker attachment to this culture of literacy may have been rooted in their broader, distinctive style of education and child-rearing, yet they were insistent that their children's instruction should remain firmly in their own hands. This posed no real problem for the more prosperous, but how best to educate poorer children proved more troublesome. The prevailing system of the parish placing them in apprenticeships seemed designed to lure Quaker children away from their faith, so from the 1650s meetings supervised the training of boy apprentices. They were also expected to pay for that training, with some money coming from Quaker bequests. Naturally enough, meetings took great care in choosing the trades and masters, carefully monitoring progress throughout the seven years of their traineeship. The supervision of apprentices sometimes fell to the women's meeting as part of their role in welfare matters.[3]

Apprenticeships were more widely used throughout most trades and professions than we might imagine. They were not restricted to humbler or artisanal skills, as became the case in industrial Britain, but spanned a wide range of occupations and activities, from shopkeeping to medicine. Even prosperous and professional

Quakers dispatched their young to an apprenticeship, and many of the most successful learned their basic skills through such a route. Dr John Fothergill, the founder of Ackworth School, was of North Yorkshire yeoman stock, and had been educated at day and grammar schools before serving a seven-year apprenticeship to Benjamin Bartlett in Bradford, where he trained in 'the art, trade, mystery or occupation of an apothecary'. At the age of 20 he moved on to study medicine at Edinburgh, and ultimately to a successful medical career.[4]

As a young apprentice became more accomplished or experienced in his chosen trade, he was granted more responsibility. William Tout, apprenticed for some years to a Quaker grocer and ironmonger in Lancaster, found himself put in charge of a branch shop. Later he made business trips to the Isle of Man, though for most of his apprenticeship 'I had scarsly been ten miles from home'.[5] With his training completed, Tout raised loans from his family, faithfully documenting their repayment, to set up his own shop. He borrowed a horse and money, and rode to London with a group of local associates to buy goods from 'such tradesmen as I was recommended to'. A week after his return to Lancaster, most of his goods arrived by sea and his shop was ready for business. Through industry and application, Tout's shop prospered; he took little time off, save for a mile walk each morning and evening. When business was slack, he 'passed [his] time reading religious books, or history, geography, surveying or other mathematical sciences'. In his turn, Tout took in apprentices from among poor Quakers, rearing them *in loco parentis* and seeking to ensure that they remained faithful Friends.[6]

Apprenticeships in shopkeeping and commerce allowed boys from rural yeoman backgrounds to settle into urban mercantile trades and professions. They also inculcated the value of persistent industry and application in a variety of skills, which also served to insulate these youngsters against the outside world. They worked long hours with little free time and were obliged to swear that they would forgo the pursuits characteristic of other youths. When

Fothergill signed his indenture he agreed, among other things, that 'his master well and faithfully shall serve; his secrets shall keep; taverns he shall not haunt; at dice, cards, tables, bowls or any other unlawful games he shall not play'.[7] But such demands were not peculiar to Quakers. English apprentices (and servants) were notoriously exploited in the eighteenth century. They had a virtually non-existent private life, sometimes their names were changed, and they received little recompense for their long and arduous labours. Towards the end of the century, Robert Owen often worked until two in the morning as a haberdasher's apprentice.[8] As the century advanced, it seemed to many that the institution had become outdated: it was dubious in declining industries and 'positively irrelevant' in the new trades.[9] Yet its usefulness to the Quakers lay in socialising the young in the disciplines of their faith. It was part of their determination to build a cordon sanitaire between their children and the world at large. Mary Ann Galton, reared in a Quaker household in the 1780s, recalled that her mother 'took the greatest pains that we might receive no contamination from ignoble minds, no vulgarism or habits or ideas'.[10]

The Quaker story in the eighteenth century poses a curious paradox, however. On the one hand they sought to distance themselves from the world and reject its temptations, its transient and material pleasures, yet they also set out to prepare themselves and their offspring to make the most of its economic potential. What were the qualities of industry and application designed to produce if not worldly success? Moreover, it was a process greatly helped by the structure of Quaker faith. They worshipped and lived within a highly efficient organisation which reached from the remotest of communities into the heart of London. As Quakers travelled from one meeting to another, there evolved an impressive network of personal contacts, friendships and family ties. These networks had cemented a literate (and literary) culture which was also ideally suited to commercial activity. And yet through all these developments there ran a Quaker uneasiness – a distaste, even – about material success.

As the eighteenth century progressed, the idea of useful industry was transformed, in the eyes of Quaker opponents, into a love of money-getting. When Thomas Clarkson wrote a sympathetic history of the movement in 1806, he devoted a whole chapter to this problem. Here was a characteristic 'belonging so generally to the individuals of this Society, that it is held by the world to be almost inseparable from Quakerism'. Clarkson readily accepted that they were a people who seemed to have 'discarded the amusements of the world, to be more in their shops and counting-houses than others'. And despite Quaker contribution to philanthropy, they were better known for material prosperity. They were a 'sedate, thoughtful, sober, diligent, and honest people', whose habits were likely to bring their own rewards.[11] But it was a lifestyle which necessarily rejected many of the pursuits and pleasures so widely enjoyed by their contemporaries, and strict Quakers were on hand to ensure that temptation was kept at bay. Friends who 'follow pleasure, drunkenness, and gaming' were visited and brought to heel. The Society's disciplinary system (wielding the ultimate penalty of exclusion) dealt with those who 'slipped into the spirit and friendship of the evil world in keeping ill-hours, ill-company, sitting idly and excessively drinking and tippling and haunting ale-houses and taverns, gaming and neglecting of their own affairs'.[12] Yet the fact that this issue was frequently raised throughout the eighteenth century suggests that back-sliding was far from unknown.

Young Quakers were especially warned against the dangers of gambling which, along with other temptations, came their way as they grew older and were likely, say, to mix with more worldly colleagues. Christopher Story, later to become an important Quaker preacher, confessed that 'as I grew in years, I was drawn forth after the vain pastimes which are in the world; as, vain shooting with guns, and bows, and following them that played at cards; and I was successful in playing . . . for this the Lord gave me a sore rebuke'.[13] Yet where was the dividing line between, for example, gambling and speculative financial investments? In 1788, the Yearly Meeting declared itself 'deeply affected' by the actions of Friends who 'through an evil covetness, have engaged in illegal dealings in the public stocks, or government securities; which is a species of gaming, and altogether inconsistent with our religious principles'.[14] Gambling and the related impulse to acquire ever more wealth was the stuff of covetousness and was frequently denounced, but injunctions issued from various Yearly Meetings implies that the problem did not go away. As early as 1676, it was urged 'Let none covet to be rich in this world, in these changeable things that will pass away.' The same message was issued forty-four years later in 1720, and again in 1740: 'We beseech you to stand upon your guard against the allurements and temptations of this evil world'.[15] Such enjoyments multiplied and proliferated in the course of the eighteenth century, dangling temptations of every conceivable kind especially before the young. The 1739 Yearly Meeting complained of 'particularly balls, gaming-places, horse-races, and playhouses'.[16]

The issue of personal clothing also created difficulties for Quakers, and Yearly Meetings repeatedly returned to the need to avoid elaborate garments, and especially that parents warn their children (or servants) when they 'lusteth after the vain customs and fashions of the world, either in dressings, habits, or outward adornings'.[17] None the less, increasing numbers of Quakers, known as the 'gay Friends', broke away from the more rigorous application of the clothing convention. All were urged to stick 'to truth and plainness, in language, habit, deportment and behaviour',[18] children were reminded that 'immodest apparel, or foolish garbs, or other extravagances' incurred 'God's displeasure and judgment'.[19] Impressing such ideas upon Quaker children was of the utmost importance, in that 'they, being thus instructed in the way of the Lord when they are young, they may not forget it when old'.[20]

Quakers were not alone in denouncing the rise of luxury, however. Jonathan Swift railed against 'all Excesses in Cloathing, Furniture and the Like', but it was a losing battle. By the time Adam Smith published *The Wealth of Nations* in 1776, he assumed that luxurious material consumption was built into the very fabric of British society.[21] Excess was all around: in elaborate clothing, the profusion of new furnishings for the home, and that proliferation of shops across the face of urban England which so tempted the passer-by with their window displays of each and every fad and fashion. Dr Johnson invited Goldsmith to 'take a walk from Charing Cross to Whitechapel through I suppose the greatest series of shops in the world'.[22] Oxford Street's 153 shops of the late eighteenth century displayed all 'the whim-whams and fribble-frabble of fashion'. Behind their bowed and lighted windows there lay 'absolutely everything one can think of'. It was, according to a Russian visitor, 'a continuous fair'.[23] Outside London provincial shops also multiplied, and their owners were keen to tell local customers that the goods on offer were the latest 'fashionable assortment', fresh from the capital.[24] Even in the remotest of places – highland villages or hamlets in rural mid-Wales – the smallest of shops (sometimes no more than a counter in the front room of a cottage) could be relied on to sell goods which, only two generations previously, had been too costly and exotic, and available only to the prosperous.[25] The chorus of criticism became increasingly shrill as the century advanced, but this tide of consumption seemed irreversible.

Quakers therefore needed to be vigilant in defence of their plainness, not least because their style appeared ever starker against a society devoted to the philosophy of conspicuous consumption. In this and in other matters Friends were increasingly at odds with the times. Quaker homes were expected to provide life's domestic essentials in simple and functional terms. We know about Quaker furnishings because much of it survives today – notably in meeting houses which were soundly constructed, the craftsmanship always of the highest order and hence so durable. In stone, wood and glass, Quaker craftsmen produced artefacts which reflected their ideals.[26] It was a style at once useful and part of an aesthetic of plainness where starkness could acquire an attractiveness of its own, and owed much to the founding years of Quakerism. There was a tone about Friends' buildings of the late seventeenth century (their homes and places of worship) which stood steadfast against the changing styles of eighteenth-century interior design. There were few colours, few items of furniture and simplicity in each item. Quaker tables carried only the essential eating and cooking implements, at a time when the potteries, china and metalworks of Europe and Asia were producing domestic items in remarkable volume. The people of eighteenth-century Britain welcomed enthusiastically and absorbed an increased flow of 'blankets, linens, pillows, rugs, curtains and cloths', in addition to the 'pewter, glass and china; and brass, copper and ironware'.[27] Even large sections of the labouring population acquired a number of items which their ancestors could have only dreamed about. Bishop Berkeley approved of the fact that they were now able to acquire goods which previously only the more affluent could afford.[28] Sometimes the poor came into the possession of such artefacts as they passed down the chain of ownership. Goods which had been soiled, damaged, chipped, or had become out-dated trickled down the social scale as society's élite discarded them, often via servants. The Quakers must have provided lean pickings for anyone hoping to acquire such second-hand goods.

As the western world at large turned with ever greater zest to the consumption of ever more fancy possessions, Quakers were repeatedly warned to be on their guard. They were cautioned against 'fine and fashionable furniture and apparel equivalent, with dainty and voluptuous provision, with rich matches in marriage'. As early as 1703, the Yearly Meeting complained that 'some under our profession' had turned to 'the excess of apparel and furniture'. The same point had to be made fifty years later: 'And, dear friends, abide in humility, let neither the apparel of your persons, nor the furniture of your houses, carry with them any appearance of contradiction to the plainness of your profession'.[29]

Not all Friends heeded the call, however, for in 1755 it was alleged that some had 'run into the corrupt customs and vain fashions of the world, in speech, habit, behaviour, or furniture'.[30] As society became more materialistic, it was understandable that some Quakers would succumb. Yearly Meetings continued to reiterate the need to guard against 'the deceitfulness of riches; the nature of which is to choke the good seed, and to render men unfruitful. An eager pursuit after the grandeur of this world is a certain token of earthly mindedness'.

As increasing numbers of Quakers established themselves in business, such riches and prosperity were not the only problems to worry them. Friends had a dread of business failure and especially of indebtedness. Monthly Meetings were asked 'to be properly watchful one over another, and early to caution all against running beyond their depth, and entangling themselves in a greater multiplicity of trade and business than they can extricate themselves from with honour and reputation'.[31] The bureaucratic machinery was galvanised to monitor the business affairs of Quakers in the localities. Thus their policy was not only to issue repeated statements in defence of their ideals, but rather to ensure that Friends actively observed and upheld their principles. Quaker organisation, created to defend themselves against their enemies, had become by the early eighteenth century a powerful instrument for the implementation of Quaker policy. Its ultimate power was in disciplining and expelling back-sliders, but it also operated in a more constructive, less draconian fashion by serving to question, scrutinise and *help* Friends in trouble. This was particularly important in matters of finance, more so as regards the question of debt.

Indebtedness remained a persistent theme in Quaker pronouncements from one generation to another, a reminder of their continuing concern about the monetary dealings of Friends, and further evidence of their involvement in commerce and trade. They were especially anxious to insist on the prompt payment of debts, and not to be seen to be benefiting from the indebtedness of others. Complaints were levelled against those who failed to pay debts on time 'to the great scandal and reproach of our holy profession.'[32] Friends were warned to give 'timely caution to any such, as either break their promises, or delay payment of such debts, or otherwise render themselves suspected'. The aim was 'to prevent the great scandal and reproach which any professing truth' might bring to the Society.[33] It was noticed that some Quakers, while claiming that they could not pay their debts in full, still managed to live in some style. Not surprisingly, this was frowned upon, 'it being exceedingly dishonourable for any to live in ostentation and greatness at the expense of others'.[34]

Quakers feared the public shame that commercial failure would bring to the Society, so they made provision for experienced Friends to intervene with advice for their financially troubled members. They advised 'that all Friends that are entering into trade, or that are in trade, and have not stocks sufficient of their own to answer the trade they aim at, be very cautious of running themselves into debt, without advising with some of their ancient and experienced Friends among whom they live'.[35] It was *assumed* that Quakers would turn to each other for business advice; that more experienced heads would help the less so. Co-operation, not rivalry, was their commercial watchword.

Any form of activity which might rebound on the Society was frowned upon. Whatever their capacity, Quakers viewed themselves as representatives of their Society; ambassadors not only of a particular faith but also of a way of life. Their faith was not put on hold the moment they left the meeting house, but entailed a consistent style of personal and social behaviour. And where failings or shortcomings became apparent, the local meeting was on hand to step in, advise and correct. Or to exclude.

The subject of indebtedness endured throughout many Quaker annual meetings in London, but warnings were ignored when individuals were tempted by the prospect of greater gains for greater risks. Some Friends, for example, had been badly hit by speculative investments in the disastrous South Sea Bubble of 1720.[36] The annual missives were in response to information provided from the localities, and it is clear that Friends across the country were periodically alerting London to the financial danger they saw close to hand.[37] Quakers everywhere were expected to exercise some restraint on the more impetuous, more speculative instincts of others in their community.

While Quakers fought to distance themselves from the taint of commercial failure or wrong-doing, they were also not entirely happy with the rewards of success. The tension between such success and Quaker other-worldliness had been widely acknowledged by the close of the seventeenth century. It was alleged, for example, that London's Gracechurch Street Quaker Meeting consisted of 'the richest trading-men in London'. Such men, claimed another, 'seem to be of late years as much busied in thoughts how to increase in wealth and riches as any'.[38] Eight days before his death in 1691, Fox had confronted the question of Quaker material success among those 'who embrace the present world and encumber themselves with their own businesses and neglect the Lord's and so are good for nothing'.[39] In 1680 Stephen Crisp of Colchester had complained of the 'too eager and greedy pursuit after the things of this world. Diligence in their outward callings had been turned into slavery to them'.[40]

One possible antidote to 'the riches and possessions of this world' was philanthropy.[41] The early Quakers had been anxious to promote concern for the poor as a traditional virtue. This had arisen from the care of those who had been fined, imprisoned or were otherwise impoverished. A great deal of early effort and organisation had been directed towards such 'sufferings', but they became committed to a much wider philanthropy. In 1696, 'liberality to the poor' was thought a virtue, especially for those 'friends as are endowed with plenty of substance'.[42] Two generations later, in 1768, Quakers were reminded of the same point: 'let us impress it especially upon Friends in affluent circumstances, to submit to a becoming frugality in their manner of living, in order to relieve the wants of the needy of all denominations with a liberal hand'.[43]

Whatever the cause, Quakers were generous with their time and money towards their favourite charities. In York, for example, they were active in no fewer than thirty-four charities (and seven schools) between the years 1740 and 1860.[44] But such charitable deeds were not enough to calm the unease about the emergence of more affluent members. By the early years of the eighteenth century, prosperity was proving a troublesome force in Quaker affairs, and the resulting debate about wealth and 'worldliness' was but one aspect of a much more fundamental struggle at the heart of the Society of Friends. The debate was, in essence, about the very soul of Quakerism itself.

There is no doubt that Quaker life had changed in many respects. Fewer (perhaps only a small minority) believed that they could bring about an utter transformation of the world around them. Quakers had also changed politically. Among other things, the Affirmation Act had allowed them to become more at ease with the machinery of the British state (allowing them to affirm rather than swear oaths), not least because they were left to their own devices rather than persecuted on all sides. As a result, the path to the corridors of local civic power had become smoother, for example. However, there were differences between each region, most strikingly the divide between more 'worldly' London Quakers and their provincial contemporaries.

On the other hand the Quakers had become a clearly defined sect. They looked, sounded, behaved, dressed and lived differently, and over the course of the first seventy years of their history, from 1650 to 1720, a 'group discipline' had developed, designed primarily to keep individual Friends 'in the community of the godly'.[45] Quaker culture had proved itself an increasingly powerful socialising force over these years: the grass roots of Quaker life were more tightly controlled from the centre than early Friends could have imagined possible. Conventions and rules were issued from the London Yearly Meeting, but were implemented by the local meeting, so that very little escaped the watchful eye of Quaker officialdom. Personal foibles and unsuitable associates caught the attention of other Friends; public behaviour was inevitably subject to greater scrutiny, particularly in their relatively close-knit communities. At home, rest and work, Quakers were under the permanent gaze of their critical peers (and outsiders).

The rapid economic and social transformation of Britain consequently created particular difficulties for Quakers in the eighteenth century, and no one could have predicted the material bounty that the economy would yield. Large sectors were directed towards providing a range of possessions and pastimes previously unknown to earlier generations: sweet cups of tea or coffee served in decorative chinaware; rolls and pipes of tobacco. Yet all of these items and their related social habits became integral to social life among all manner of people. This transformation of Britain into a consuming society, serviced by Adam Smith's 'nation of shopkeepers', created myriad commercial opportunities for those with the right skills, training and networks, and few were better placed to make the most of such openings than certain Quakers. Yet it was to be a commercial world replete with the obvious dangers inherent in the tension between 'plainness' and 'plenty'. This set the theme for those successful Friends who strove to reconcile the conflict between money and morals as their businesses thrived.

4

Money Matters

When the Lancaster Quaker William Tout decided to establish and equip a new shop in 1687 he turned initially to various relatives for the money. He raised cash by selling land bequeathed by his father, and persuaded his mother and brother to advance money from the same will. The final piece in his financial jigsaw fell into place when 'I borrowed of my sister £10 which I kept many years'. He fitted out his shop and headed for London, at the age of 22, with £120 cash in his pocket. There, helped by recommended business contacts, he bought the goods he needed for his shelves, paying for half with cash and getting the rest on credit. Tout started his journey home with £20, 'which I laid out . . . in Sheffield and Birmingham manufactories'.[1] This was a model example of money-raising and commercial dealing among small Quaker businessmen in the late seventeenth century. Their rise was inextricably linked to their access to finance, but before we can understand how that system evolved, we need to look in broader terms at the development of money (coins and bills of exchange) and banking in these years.

Banking had played an important role in earlier epochs of European history: Florence in 1300, or Genoa in the late sixteenth century, for example, had seen a rapid expansion in banking and credit (although this ultimately ended in collapse).[2] Many of the major enterprises of the Renaissance period had been backed by the great European bankers. British financiers had also acted in a similar role, lending their own and other people's money, dealing in bills of exchange and handling deposits. Merchants, jewellers and lawyers, for example, had followed their lead. Even though money was being physically moved around the country all the time, it was much safer to use the services of brokers and their bills of exchange. Those who saved money (generally depositing it with a local merchant or businessman) could pay for goods and services with written notes: 'a cheque in all but name'. These promissory notes to pay fixed amounts at specific dates were issued, exchanged and circulated, and effectively became paper currency, yet Britain still lagged behind its main European trading and commercial rivals, most notably the Dutch. By the mid-seventeenth century the need for a more organised banking system had become clear.

This need was intensified by the upheavals of the Civil War, with its major repercussions on land-holding and finance, and the social and political changes that followed. At the same time the Treasury was exercising growing control over state financial affairs, at a time when the House of Commons was empowered to scrutinise public and royal expenditure. Finally the late-seventeenth-century rise in prosperity, fuelled partly by overseas trade and dominion, made the need for more sophisticated financial services an imperative.[3] It is worth noting that Samuel Pepys, himself involved in the debate about creating a formal system, was so distrustful of bankers that he kept his own money variously in an iron-bound chest and buried in a country garden.[4] None the less, the growing public confidence in bankers was reflected in an increase in deposits, with a substantial part of the funds invested in London banks coming from provincial investors. In its turn, this money was passed on primarily as loans to the government and the monarchy.

In Parliament, opposition to establishing a national bank came in the form of the 'landed' members who distrusted any form of usury, but a series of proposals in the 1670s and 1680s finally culminated in the Act that established the Bank of England in 1694. The Bank's paper money issued to its depositors began to circulate in the economy, but in its early days the Bank's main function was to provide financial services for the state. It is hard to imagine today that it was an outsiders' bank, heavily influenced by and related to the economically powerful, though numerically small, dissenting groups in the City, many of whom were immigrant in origin. Not surprisingly, it attracted more than its share of criticism.

In return for loans to the Crown at fixed rates of interest, the Bank of England was able to negotiate a monopoly on joint-stock banking (other banks were limited to a maximum of six partners), a role which survived from 1710 to 1826. Henceforth it became the government's banker, dealing in gold, silver and cash, issuing stocks, receiving loans and 'handling the government's overseas business in finance'. The Bank also issued paper credit, or bank notes, which passed into circulation and were redeemable with the bold assertion, still there for all to see, 'I promise to pay'. Until 1793 the lowest denomination of note was £10 (far too high ever to be in widespread circulation) and remained redeemable until 1797.[5]

The new Bank also served London's main trading houses and merchants, for whom they discounted bills of exchange and offered loans (the sum of which was often greater than the Bank's total bullion holdings). In fact, the whole operation was metropolitan: the Bank of England was, in the words of its historian Sir John Clapham, the Bank of London.[6] Other private banks had also begun to appear in the capital in the late seventeenth century, challenging the financial dominance of the older goldsmiths' houses. During the course of the eighteenth century these banks multiplied and by 1800 there were almost seventy in the City specialising in dealings with provincial banks, stockbrokers and other commercial activities.

At the same time, a new financial market dealing in stocks and shares began to emerge in London as young companies sought capital for a range of speculative enterprises, especially overseas. Many such ventures proved disastrous, some were successful, but there was mounting unease, expressed in print and Parliament, about the tactics of the stock 'jobbers' and their trading culture. It inspired greed and was, according to Defoe, 'founded in Fraud, born of Deceit, and nourished by Trick, Cheat, Wheedle, Forgeries, falsehood'; its practitioners he thought 'mere original Thieves and Pick-Pockets'. Many like Defoe hated this world 'of easy money and easier virtue'.[7] A number of financial scandals, sometimes suffused with the rivalries of party politics, confirmed a growing hostility towards money men and their institutions. By the early eighteenth century there was a nationwide unease about these financial masters. Above all else, those who wanted to borrow money, to invest it or to entrust their financial livelihood to others wanted security and honesty.

The fraternity of London banking was divided between the West End and the City. The former, including Hoares and Coutts, fought shy of the sort of commercial activity which was booming elsewhere, preferring instead to maintain its traditional business links with the aristocracy, the gentry and the legal profession.[8] These banks also handled the London accounts for the nation's rich, buying property on their behalf and investing in government stock. But most of London's banks were in the City, physically distant and socially distinct from their West End peers. Their numbers increased dramatically in the eighteenth century, from fewer than 30 in 1750, to 50 in 1770, and 70 by the very end of the century. They discounted bills for merchants and industrialists, lent money to stockbrokers and provided loans 'on call' (they had to be repaid as and when the bank needed the money).[9] It was a form of banking that required substantial cash assets, or the ability to drum up cash at short notice, which meant that the City banks were best suited to financing trade rather than long-term projects (investments in building or land, for example), which yielded profits more slowly.

London's banks were conducting increasing amounts of business for the 'country banks', which proliferated throughout the eighteenth century. This flow of bullion from the provinces to the capital, the movement of bills of exchange and Bank of England notes, was both expansive and profitable. As Britain's economy was transformed, new financial institutions began to appear throughout the country. Bristol, heart of a remarkable overseas trade and the centre of inland business stretching from Birmingham to the West Country, became in 1716 the first city after London to have its own bank. In mid-century there were an estimated 12 such banks throughout the country. In 1784 this had increased to about 120, 270 in 1797 and 370 by 1800. Ten years later there were 650.[10]

Country banks therefore emerged along the shifting contours of regional economic activity and growth, and flourished on the crest of a commercial wave, following whatever was the dominant form of local trade. Successful businessmen evolved into country bankers as a by-product of another main line of work. The bank has been described as 'just a separate counter in his office'. In Cambridge, the Fosters were millers and corn merchants (the main trade of the region) before founding a bank in 1804 which later became part of Lloyds. The Mortlake family were prosperous drapers who moved into banking in the 1750s. Liverpool's banks emerged from the merchant houses involved in overseas trade, Birmingham's from the iron trade, and Nottingham's from the hosiery industry. The mining trade in Cornwall provided its bankers; brewers in various parts of the country seemed especially likely to convert. These men would assume the role as a means of utilising the cash and local expertise acquired through their other business ventures.[11] In this way, Quakers began to appear among the ranks of eighteenth-century country bankers because they had also begun to emerge as a local economic force.

One such Quaker was Edward Pease in Darlington, the principal market town which served the agricultural district of Teesdale, at the junction of the Great North Road and the border between North Yorkshire and County Durham. As well as agriculture, this community of 3,300 people thrived on the woollen and worsted trades, tanning and linens. Edward had entered his uncle's wool-combing business in the 1740s, and from 1752 began to modernise operations by gradually relocating each production process into one single factory complex (as opposed to 'putting out' the various stages of manufacture). When he died in 1785, he was able to bequeath substantial property, business holdings and personal effects (silver plate, delft and Chinaware, and other valuable household items) to his five sons and two daughters. But in addition to the woollen business, Edward bequeathed a banking concern.[12]

The Pease Partners Bank held 109 accounts in the years 1765 to 1799, most of them scattered throughout the local district. It was a natural step for a manufacturer to provide credit for his suppliers when cash was in short supply and there were in-built delays between each stage of production. The Pease business empire thrived under Edward's son, Joseph, a Quaker who was better known for his links to industry and business. A rival Darlington bank was J. J. Backhouse. The family were originally Quaker flax dressers and linen manufacturers who made a similar transition to banking after 1800, their financial services being greatly strengthened by their role as agents for the Royal Exchange Assurance Company.[13] The two families and businesses came together in 1774 in the marriage between Jonathan Backhouse and Anne Pease (Joseph's younger sister). The strength of the Pease dynasty may have become regional – it had forged trading links into central Scotland and as far away as the West of England – but its banking interests remained local.

The Pease fortune burgeoned under the stewardship of Edward Pease, son of Joseph, who was born in 1767 and educated at a Quaker school in Leeds. He entered the family worsted business at a lowly level, travelling the region on horseback. He was a 'plain Friend', orthodox in dress and speech, turning his back on life's frivolities (including the reading of 'pernicious books or novels'), and was supported in his style by his devout wife Rachel Whitwell, a Kendal Quaker and preacher. Edward was convinced that 'the accumulation of wealth in every family known to me in our Society carries away from the purity of our principles, adds toil and care to life and greatly endangers the possessions of heaven'.[14]

Yet here was a man whose commercial acumen, and his ability to capitalise on his business and Quaker contacts, was to generate wealth on a grand scale. The opportunity came from an unexpected direction.

There had long been a thriving regional coal industry, the development of which had been severely limited by transport problems. The need for a better communication network was recognised as early as the mid-eighteenth century, and the Pease family were involved in early discussions about canal construction. The matter took a different tack in 1818 when a subscription was raised for the development of a railway line between Stockton and Darlington. The Pease and Backhouse families were heavy investors, but so too were Friends from outside the region (notably the Gurneys of Norwich). Indeed, the whole venture was spearheaded by those who drummed up investments in London, mainly among business associates and relatives of the North-East Quaker families. At this time the concept of a railway was both novel and highly speculative, and the fact that outsiders had invested substantially in such a distant project was testimony to the reliance they placed on the judgement and advice of those Friends local to the project. When the railway was finally opened in September 1825 it became known as 'the Quaker line', and much of its subsequent success was down to Edward Pease. In the 1830s, when railway construction began in earnest with the opening of the Manchester–Liverpool line and the success of Stephenson's Rocket, one of the new ironworks which fed the massive rail-track expansion received substantial investment from Pease.

Despite inevitable commercial problems and financial setbacks, by the time Pease stepped down from business life in 1827 he was a very rich man, retiring to a fundamentally plain Quaker lifestyle but worried by the apparent conflict between his religious ideals and his accumulation of wealth. Throughout, Pease had maintained a relatively humble existence. He lived in the same modest house from 1798, happily cultivating fruit in his greenhouse; an excellent table and wines his only luxury. He was a regular attender at the London Yearly Meeting, was indefatigable in the anti-slavery cause, and a regular traveller among Quaker Friends and groups. He had risen from local textile manufacturing to preside over investments in banking, railways, ironworks and a host of related concerns, yet he chose to end his life as he began it – as a simple Quaker.[15]

In 1902, J. and L. W. Pease bank was taken over by Barclays, which was itself forged from an amalgamation with Backhouse and Gurney banks, all three of which had been Quaker in foundation and development, and each illustrating that typical transmutation from a particular local economic activity into banking.[16]

One of the best-known examples is the Gurneys of Norwich. In the early seventeenth century Francis Gurney had acted as London banker for a local family, but the family came to the fore through the efforts of John Gurney. He was a Norwich wool merchant who had been a Quaker since 1683 (his business was managed by his wife during the periods he served in jail during anti-Quaker persecutions). His sons, John II and Joseph, successfully continued the family concern. One generation later, Henry, the eldest son of John II, founded a local bank, the origins of which, like those in the North-East, lay in the organisation and management of the local textile industry. The Gurney family received yarn from the worsted spinners and provided cash in return to pay for the associated labour. They flourished as middlemen between producers and consumers, but in the process generated enough money, and developed systems of loans and repayments, so that they were effectively acting as a bank even before formally establishing the Gurney Bank in 1775. Soon, they had opened branches across East Anglia and absorbed various regional rivals.

All over the country, Quakers created similar textile or shop-based loan schemes: the Birkbeck family in Settle, Yorkshire, for example, who later established banks in other parts of northern England (the Birkbecks also developed business and later family links with the Gurneys). Shopkeepers were set on the road to banking as it became common, for example, for their customers to deposit any spare cash for security. In providing advice, and through partnerships forged with established Quaker bankers, they were able to evolve into a more sophisticated banking service.[17]

Family links were often crucial to this evolution, in that carefully selected Quaker partners for sons and daughters produced new generations who could be trained in the business. When the young Samuel Gurney (son of John) finished his formal schooling, he was dispatched to an apprenticeship in the London home of his brother-in-law, the banker Joseph Fry, who also had 'an extensive business in the tea trade'. In the words of Mrs Thomas Geldart, his early-Victorian biographer, it was 'very important that the young men of the family should be educated in an intimate acquaintance with monetary and commercial transactions'. Samuel was drilled by his brother-in-law in the systems and procedures of contemporary financial life, all the while supervised by his sister, 'by which means the temptations and dangers of a London life were guarded against'.[18]

These inter-family connections, as well as forming an extended web of professional and educational links, also provided a forum for discussion. When senior Quakers travelled on business (especially to the London Yearly Meeting) or personal matters (often at one and the same time), they took the opportunity to talk over mutual commercial interests with other Friends and relatives. More than that, they were eager to point out to each other, in their journals and to those who might care to read their publications, that their faith gave them a resolve and grasp which stood them in good stead in financial or commercial crises (which sometimes came thick and fast). They were able to take comfort in God's blessings in times of adversity, but they also thanked Him when they enjoyed good times.[19]

The male world of eighteenth-century business meant that Quakers concentrated on schooling their sons in such matters, and great trouble was taken to secure appropriate positions for them. The Gillett family of Oxfordshire was a case in point. William

Gillett, a farmer and woolcomber, like so many others branched into financial services in the 1820s, extending credit, and handling cash for customers and suppliers alike. Joseph, one of his eight children, was sent to the then new Quaker school at Ackworth and thence to an apprenticeship with a Leicester Quaker woolcomber. Before returning to join his father and brothers in the family business he was also employed as an agent by Cobbs, the Banbury banker. This thorough training for his career was rounded off by marriage in 1821 to Martha Gibbins, daughter of Joseph Gibbins, the Birmingham and Swansea banker. With a considerable wedding settlement of £5,000 he was able to buy a partnership in Whiteheads Bank, which rapidly led to the purchase of the Banbury Bank in 1822, renamed Gilletts Bank in 1823.[20] The bank survived until 1919 when it was also taken over by Barclays, by then one of the nation's leading concerns.[21]

Barclays Bank underwent a bewildering variety of name changes throughout the eighteenth and early nineteenth centuries: revisions were made as the associated Quaker commercial and family alliances waxed and waned. Barclays' origins lay in the activities of London goldsmith John Freame, whose business interests included the mining of precious metals and the grocery trade. In 1736 his son Joseph took James Barclay as a partner in a firm which was becoming increasingly devoted to banking. Thereafter the Barclay name remained, and ultimately became dominant, through the ebb and flow of changing allegiances. Over the years, partners in Barclays Bank developed a range of other business interests (including funding the establishment of Ackworth School in 1777).[22] David Barclay traded extensively with America, where he was active in Pennsylvania politics; another partner, Silvanus Bevan III, brought connections in the older brewing industry; the Tritton family had ties to London's goldsmith banking traditions. Slowly, however, the main concern of Barclays shifted and by the mid-eighteenth century it had distanced itself from its old trading associations.[23]

By the late eighteenth century, this changing pattern of Quaker trading had become commonplace. Wherever money was saved, borrowed or loaned in the conduct of local business, the commercially active would seize the opportunity to diversify their interests. (Of course, this proliferation of banks in London and across the country went beyond the Quaker community, with entrepreneurially minded groups capitalising on the transformation of Britain's economy.) The history of Lloyds Bank begins with a Welsh Quaker family who, after thriving in the local iron industry, moved to Birmingham in the late seventeenth century to avoid the worst persecutions. The Lloyd family maintained their interest in iron production, but consolidated it by various marriages into other Black Country ironmaster families, which produced a dynasty of truly royal complexity.[24] The Lloyds began to lend money to the smaller manufacturers who provided them with their basic iron. There followed a succession of changes of name and partners before their business finally emerged as Lloyds Bank. Initially, most of their dealings were local, and were closely involved with iron manufacture and other tradesmen. Soon, however, the bank was yielding greater profits (£10,000 in six years) than the family's original iron interests. As the financial side flourished, links with London became vital and, in 1770, Lloyds opened up an office in the capital, forging partnerships with established concerns there. They also began an association with (and take-overs of) smaller banks in the Black Country until the twentieth century, when it became one of the country's five major joint-stock banks, along with Barclays, Midland, District and Martins.[25]

Most of these names survive today, but a similar process unfolded, with less memorable results, in other Quaker communities. The West Country textile industry had long provided a natural economic niche for local Quakers. The Were family, serge manufacturers who dispatched their textiles throughout Europe, were linked by marriage to other Quaker business dynasties in the West, and in 1787 they moved into banking. The Fox family of Falmouth was perhaps the most famous in shipping, who, like others of the 'Quaker cousinage', had links through marriage to a number of important Quaker families in other parts of the country. In 1754, in order to formalise his existing credit arrangements, George Croker Fox established the G. Fox and Company bank.[26]

The short-term success of such new ventures could persuade a Quaker family to relinquish its previous business interests in favour of finance. Joseph Gillett's father-in-law, Joseph Gibbins, who was initially in the metal trade in Swansea and then Birmingham, joined up with his associates and opened banks in both towns. His son gradually disassociated himself from the metal industry (but retained his shares), concentrating instead on banking. This switch perfectly suited his many brothers when they required loans for their own business ventures.[27]

To describe the dynastic lines of prosperous Quakers in detail runs the risk of sliding into antiquarian family history, but a general pattern does become evident when looking at the most famous banking interests. From emerging as banks, there followed a process of consolidation, often via family ties. Then these banks made their financial services available to other Quaker commercial interests. Of course, banks were supposed to help a variety of investors in all manner of ventures, yet it was no disadvantage for Quaker businesses to be able to turn to other Friends for financial help. In the early nineteenth century, a group of prosperous Quakers established a special fund to help their 'young men of small property but high virtue . . . small farmers and mechanics [but] not mere Labourers'. They were able to borrow up to £100 for six years at a mere 2 per cent interest. By 1820, twenty-four had used the facility.[28]

The Society of Friends provided institutional help in that it served as a regulator of such activity, and it is important to relate these money matters to the rituals and organisation of the Society itself. As we have seen, businessmen were under the permanent scrutiny of their immediate meeting. Whenever a member was in financial trouble, when doubts or complaints surfaced about business practice, bad debts, poor judgement or, worst of all, insolvency, a deputation from the meeting would examine the matter and question the people involved. In Norwich, for example, sixty insolvencies were reported between 1701 and 1773; in twenty-six of those cases, a Gurney family member was involved in the subsequent investigation. In August 1770, John Gurney and Robert Seaman examined the insolvency of Thomas Neale, 'which he acknowledges to be in Part owing to his Indiscretion; for which he expresseth himself deeply concerned'. The problem, however, was how to distance the Society from such shortcomings: 'to clear our Society from the reproach brought thereon by his Misconduct, We can do no other than testify our Disunity with him, until he shall make such Satisfaction as becomes this meeting to receive'.[29] Such measures were to prove increasingly difficult as the world of finance and banking became ever more complex and subject to government regulation during the course of the nineteenth century, but in these formative years, when Quaker economic power began to grow beyond its relatively compact, localised and generally small-scale origins, the power of such scrutiny and control over Friends' business affairs was formidable.

Honest conduct was not merely a result of external assessment. Quaker culture inculcated the duties of plain business-dealings in the home, the school, the meeting house and the workplace. Theirs was a form of Puritanism which, far from rejecting the unregenerate world and withdrawing from it like other sects, was driven forward by the view of 'the material world of daily toil and daily bread as God's world in which men were called to do his Will'. William Penn denounced monasteries where monks practised '*a lazy, rusty, unprofitable Self-Denial*, burthensome to others to feed their Idleness'. The true 'Christian Convent and Monastery', he argued, was within each person, 'And this Religious House the true Followers of Christ carry about with them, who exempt not themselves from Conversations of the World, though they keep themselves from the Evil of the World in their Conversation'. True godliness, he argued, 'enables them to live better in it, and excites their Endeavours to men it'.[30]

This was a refrain which was repeated in *Advices* and *Epistles*; in minutes of meeting houses across the country (and in North America); in diaries, memoirs and letters. When Israel Pemberton set out from Philadelphia on a business trip to England in 1748, his father reminded him 'let not the Cares, Profitts or Pleasures of this Transitory life divert thee from the pursuit of a holy self-denying life'. When a year later Pemberton lost a ship, and a small fortune, he told his father that such incidents 'tend to wean the Mind from delighting in transitories and if rightly improv'd – dispose us to look after Enjoyments more certain and permanent'.[31]

Quakers believed that hard work would be divinely rewarded. Thomas Chalkey, a merchant and sea-captain, recorded that he 'followed [his] Business with Diligence and Industry, and throve in the Things of the World, the Lord adding a Blessing to [his] Labour'.[32] Their duty was to be busy and active, wherever they found themselves. Fox had discovered a group of Quakers in prison who when not at prayer were active in whatever trades they could manage: 'The jail by that means became a meeting-house and a work-house, for they would not be idle anywhere.' The Truth also demanded that Quakers be frugal, though there were, as we have seen, more practical reasons involved. Dress, homes and furnishings were all expected to be consistent with a way of life ruled by prudence, industry and sincerity.[33] Quaker books about discipline were regularly reprinted and revised, and provided guidelines for business and personal life which were strictly adhered to by many. One Quaker trader insisted on paying a ransom extracted by a privateer as he felt morally bound by his own promise (even though it had been made under duress);[34] another abandoned the Birmingham button trade in the 1790s when he was expected to pass on shoddy goods to customers.[35] York's meeting told its members 'that none stretch beyond their compass, and that they use few words in dealing and keep their word in all things, lest they bring through their forwardness dishonour to the precious Truth of God'.[36]

Friends were directed to inspect their financial affairs annually and to seek the help of other Quakers if in trouble, but the meeting sometimes felt obliged to take matters into its own hands. The York meeting regularly discussed the general problem of Friends' debts, but the examination of particular cases was delegated to suitably experienced members. In 1707 one Quaker from the town was ordered to sell his house to make repayments. In 1740 Benjamin Holme, York's most widely travelled minister in the eighteenth century, confessed to debts acquired through business dealings for which he had no skills. He was given help with the repayments, but the meeting demanded to know why he had not revealed the problem earlier. Others were less fortunate: Mrs Armitage was told to make savings in her housekeeping to help settle her husband's account; Mary Lee was disowned when it was discovered that she had hidden some silver to avoid using it to repay her husband's debts.

Indebtedness was so important an issue that it could reach beyond the grave: the trustees of George Pearson's will settled his debt to Elizabeth Cross. Illness, too, was regarded as no obstacle to repayment. When a husband and wife were 'incapacitated through paralytic complaints', the York meeting sought to secure settlement of their debts, even by pursuing money they had given to their son. Not all incidents were as a result of personal failing. Stephen Proctor, who often repaired York's meeting house, slid into debt because of 'frequent want of employment when he had two apprentices'. A local farmer was similarly affected by the 'fluctuating value of agricultural property'. When Friends raised such problems with local Quakers, they generally received help and consideration; where their difficulties stemmed from personal weakness, from greed or foolishness, the meeting tended to take a firmer line.

The fear of bankruptcy hovered over business affairs, 'the nightmare of the eighteenth-century bourgeoisie', with its unlimited personal liability, threat of imprisonment and public shame.[37] Quakers understandably struggled to avoid its dangers and ramifications, but inevitably the business affairs of a struggling Friend would become a matter of dispute inside the local community, with decisions bounced back and forth, overturned or reinstated, through the various tiers of Quaker hierarchy. Many of these issues could not be readily reduced to the stark alternatives of black and white, right and wrong, which were fundamental to Quaker commercial ethics. When John Linney, York's main Quaker publisher, made losses and could not repay his debts, he simply refused to allow others to examine his accounts.[38] This, too, offended basic Quaker sensibilities, yet in itself was not an unreasonable line to take. Why should an independent concern open up sensitive financial details to public scrutiny? The assumption, however, was that such an examination, undertaken by carefully selected Friends, would be unimpeachable and honest, with no risk of violation of commercial privilege or betrayal of trust.

Consequently Quaker finances and business were regulated like no other, which had major consequences for Friends in their potentially troublesome relationship with the British state. Quakers had every reason to feel at the very least distrustful of a state which had been the instrument and cause of their greatest persecutions, and had ultimately sought their demise. Moreover, the most intrusive and deeply resented relationship between it and the world of commerce involved taxation and excise duties.

Throughout the eighteenth century, one of extensive global warfare, the British state was in permanent need of income. Its fiscal officers were forever looking for ways of enhancing the power and range of taxation, and were alert to the fact that many were determined to thwart their efforts. Taxation of all kinds was deeply unpopular and the nation's commercial communities felt their progress was being retarded by what they took to be a rapacious government keen to separate them from their hard-earned money, despite the fact that much of this revenue was being swallowed up by naval and imperial protection for the trade routes which underpinned national prosperity.[39]

Many showed little reluctance to circumvent the fiscal and excise exactions of the state – avoidance, fraud, smuggling and deception became a way of life – but such tactics were not for the Quakers.

Their reference points were biblical and spiritual, and their conduct had to comply with the strictest of instructions emanating from local meetings and from London; moreover, they had to be *seen* to be leading their lives accordingly. Needless to say, certain Friends succumbed to the full range of human failures, including drunkenness, cohabitation and sexual transgression, and not all erring Quakers took their punishments unflinchingly. Among resistant York Quakers, Elizabeth Nellist refused to be browbeaten by the local meeting, telling them that she had no intention of marrying the man with whom she lived. It proved easier to disown father and daughter Joseph and Dorothy Reader in York in 1772 as they were sharing the same bed (and that under the very roof of the local meeting house).[40]

Such frailties, however, were seen as mere unfortunate incidents compared to the threat of financial irregularity. From their early days Quakers had been objects of suspicion, and felt their reputations to be most at risk in trade and financial dealings with their local communities, the wider region and the nation at large. They were particularly sensitive about such dealings with the state, which had to be strictly honest 'so that no reproach may be brought upon our holy profession'.[41] Any Quaker found defrauding the government 'by endeavouring to diminish any of the customs, excise, or any other public dues' was to be dealt with by the local meeting, 'that our holy profession may not be blemished thereby'.[42] They were urged dutifully 'to render unto the king what is his due, in taxes and customs payable to him according to the law'.[43]

From the first, Friends had been urged to be law-abiding citizens, and 'not to defraud the king in any branch of his revenues, nor to deal in goods clandestinely imported . . . and that friends keep clear of purchasing such goods, either for sale or private use; from motives of gratitude to the government, and justice to our fellow-subjects . . . be punctual in the payment of every tribute . . . ' In 1719 they were directed not to cheat the King out of 'any of his customs, duties or excise'; in 1786 they were specifically instructed not to become involved in smuggling or buying goods from smugglers.[44] By the mid-eighteenth century, smuggling had grown into a major industry. Merchants, traders, shippers and shopkeepers all sought to avoid their obligations to pay the onerous duties on the imported staples of ever-growing popularity (especially tea) which had effectively doubled the price to the British consumer.[45] There were extraordinary escapades and episodes of violence as entire communities connived to defeat the best efforts of the excise men. Not until 1784 did the government take the obvious step and slash the duty on tea from 120 to 12.5 per cent.[46]

Smuggling so reduced the cost of certain items that those traders who abided by the letter of the excise law were at a commercial disadvantage. The 1733 Yearly Meeting felt confident that Quakers in general were keeping 'themselves clear of defrauding the king'.[47] There must have been few other groups quite so confident in their claims to civic honesty, but this was not mere self-satisfaction, for it reflected what Friends reported from the localities. We know that local meetings recorded their blemishes and weaknesses as well as their strengths. Reliable members were instructed to keep a watchful eye over those thought likely to cut corners in their tax affairs.[48] Those who failed to comply were 'disowned', but to reject them was a simple way of ensuring that those left behind remained relatively untarnished. They therefore took great trouble when examining commercial transgressions in their midst. When in 1779 George Peacock, a York tallowmaker, was fined by local magistrates for defrauding the excise, local Friends were bemused by the trade's technicalities. They therefore recruited three Quaker candlemakers to make an assessment, after which they still 'could not believe him clear of the design of a fraud' and he was partially disowned (not allowed to subscribe to Quaker funds or to take up any appointment within the Society).[49]

The pressures on Quakers to conform to these rigorous (and, in some cases, self-denying) demands were enormous. Businessmen had to satisfy not only their partners, customers and suppliers, but also their fellow Friends – they were expected to open their ledgers, show their receipts, reveal their bills and correspondence to satisfy their co-religionists. But that outsiders were aware of these internal pressures upon Quakers served to strengthen their reputation. Which other commercial interest could make such claims of probity? The money lent to or borrowed from a Quaker seemed to be in the safest of hands. In eighteenth-century Britain – a society where the huckster, the rogue and the fraudster personified the world of commerce and trade – the Quaker stood out as the consumer's reliable, upright and trustworthy servant. Just as money mattered to them, money matters were safe in their keeping.

The Friends were attached to shared religious beliefs and practices which came to exercise a powerful control over their business conduct. They formed networks of like-minded associates, held together by ties of family, faith and mutual trust, which were to prove vital in the subsequent emergence of Quaker commercial successes.

5

Networks

Quakers kept in regular contact with each other, not only at the local meeting house. The Society of Friends was structured around the travels of Quakers back and forth from the local meetings to the national annual gatherings in London, but they also wrote to each other, exchanged and discussed publications, and used each other's homes as staging posts on their various social and commercial wanderings across the country. Any travel, by horse or carriage, was arduous; accommodation was sparse and to Quakers uncongenial. But Friends felt safer than most, for they knew that they could rely on a national network of others in distant parts to welcome them and provide hospitality.

When in 1808 the aged John Thorp was making his way back to Manchester, he progressed via the homes of a string of Friends *en route*: 'I staid nearly four days at Worcester, and was at most of the Friends' houses; and from thence I went to Coalbrook Dale, where I stopped about fifteen days. I was at most of their houses, and at the New Dale, and from thence, by the monthly meeting at Shrewsbury, through Chester home.'[1] Jabez Maud Fisher, a Philadelphia Quaker, relied on his English Friends for accommodation and transport during his business travels of the

1770s.[2] Such networks had been vital since the pioneering days, when, like George Fox, itinerant preachers had wandered the country, and had been dependent on Friends and sympathisers for shelter and comfort. It remained fundamental to the way Quakers conducted their religious lives, as they made their regular excursions to meetings, but it also became a key element in the conduct of their trade and business. Quaker homes could be a forum for discussing mutual commercial interests, where business advice was proferred and accepted, where deals were struck and opportunities pursued.

Annual London meetings provided the opportunity to visit the country's financial and commercial capital, and to combine Quaker with secular business. This national gathering was itself a perfect venue as it brought provincial Friends into contact with the major metropolitan families and dynasties, and offered commercial possibilities both at home and abroad.[3] William Tout, the acknowledged leader of Lancaster's Quakers in the early eighteenth century, travelled extensively to meetings. He would use the chance to clinch his own business deals in London, pay bills, order new goods and arrange their transport back to Lancaster.[4] Wherever he went, Tout promoted the Quaker way with painstaking vigour, but he also made the most of the help of fellow Quakers, trusting their judgement on quality, good and bad. Friends listened closely to each other about unreliable traders and manufacturers, and who to avoid.[5] This sort of information proved invaluable to the Quaker businessman who sought to operate on the nationwide network.

Such a system created an organisation which served to shape Quaker identity and ensure the conformity of its members (and because the numbers of Quakers remained relatively limited, it was ideally suited to that task).[6] But at the same time Friends were able to use the system to their advantage. Their networks extended beyond Britain to reach the far points of colonial settlement in the Americas, and proved crucial in the rise of eighteenth-century Quaker prosperity. Few personify this better than the apothecary and merchant Thomas Corbyn.

Corbyn was among the plainest of plain Quakers. He dressed in liver-coloured clothes; his demeanour and lifestyle were sober and strict. No one doubted his probity, his charitable instincts, his love for those closest to him and his compassion for the unfortunate. Yet even other Quakers found him excessively rigid and 'a little too severe in his notions'. Always quick to chide his fellow Friends, acquiring the unQuakerlike nickname 'Pope Corbyn' in the process, he was a legend among his peers. He was also a remarkably successful businessman.

Thomas Corbyn emerged as London's leading apothecary in the mid-eighteenth century, manufacturing and selling drugs throughout Britain, Europe and the Americas, at a time when men of his profession were able to make the leap from shopkeeper to magnate and in a trade which seemed especially attractive to Quakers.[7] Writing in *The English Tradesman* in 1747, Robert Campbell remarked that the apothecary was in 'a very profitable trade . . . His profits are inconceivable'. Few, however, could rival Corbyn's pharmaceutical success, much of which flowed directly from the fact that he was quick to capitalise commercially on a network of Friends on both sides of the Atlantic. Page after page of his voluminous business correspondence illustrates the way he used his connections to advance his interests.[8]

Born in 1711 in Worcester, Corbyn served his apprenticeship in London to Joseph Clutter, whose company he subsequently took over. With money borrowed from other Friends, Corbyn embarked upon a programme of major investment, acquiring a warehouse and laboratories, and building up a string of domestic and overseas customers.[9] Like so many others, he offered Quakers favourable credit and trading arrangements. In 1750, for example, he wrote to Cadwaller Evans, an associate in Jamaica, 'if Thou send over any Merchandise [we] will dispose of it for thee to the best Advantage and not charge any Commission, only Brokerage'.[10]

The Quaker network proved vital in the initial development of Corbyn's trade with provincial doctors and apothecaries. When he travelled throughout Britain on Society business, he took the opportunity to find out about local markets, and to seek appropriate outlets and contacts. (American Quakers visiting England did precisely the same.)[11] But Corbyn's most spectacular successes were built on overseas trade, where, again, the network was central. From Nova Scotia to Barbados, he dispatched pharmaceutical goods to Friends for sampling and distribution, knowing that they would transact his business fairly and honestly. And he tapped into their intimate knowledge of America and the West Indies to follow up the payment of bills and generally to acquire information which would help his commercial activities.

A single reliable contact could create entirely new commercial openings. Corbyn thanked Cadwaller Evans in 1750: 'Thy Intention to recommend me to the Doctors and Planters I take very kind as also the Candid Informative [?] Situation of Affairs . . .' Two years later, he approached Evans again: 'I shall take it very kind if thou wilt please to recommend us to any safe Apothecaries on the island . . .'[12] In Antigua, Corbyn used the good offices of Alexander Shuttleworth, who had been recommended by other Quakers on the island, to promote his business, sending him boxes of drugs 'that they may serve the Doctors and Considerable Planters'. Corbyn also filled an order from a customer in Barbados via a Quaker contact, Dr Gamble, with the warning, 'if Thou knows him to be a Respectable Person please deliver the Chest and Inclosed Letter unopened, but if doubtfull not without paying sufficient to purchase a Good Bill of Exchange for 16.10.7 shillings'.[13]

Such men would also forward to London a range of local produce requested by Corbyn for his pharmaceutical preparations. In effect, they acted as his agents; in return, they secured preferential treatment in their dealings with London. International trade was notorious for its risks – including unreliable contacts, bad debts and faulty distribution – but thanks to the Quaker network, business across the Atlantic could be conducted much more efficiently. Trust between supplier and agent, in so volatile and uncertain a world as international trade in the seventeenth and eighteenth centuries, was an invaluable commercial advantage, and therein lay Corbyn's rewards.[14]

Corbyn took every opportunity to mix profitable trade with the promotion of his strict Quaker views. Writing again to Cadwaller Evans in 1749, he noted, 'Strict Honesty to do as we would be done by, is not so Easy a Matter as some boast it to be. Please advise me whether Men's shoes and Pumps, Women's Stuff and Silk Damasks are good Articles, Specify the Sorts particularly and what they will sell for Dozn.'[15] He assumed throughout his dealings with Friends that there was no dividing line between faith and practice. Denouncing the immorality of Jamaica (a byword for vice in all its forms in the mid-eighteenth century), Corbyn thought it a place where 'Pride, Idleness, Dishonesty, Using and putting out to Interest other men's Money' was rife. It offered a perfect lesson that 'nothing but a Close Attention to the Divine Principles and Witness is able to preserve and keep Men from running with the Multitude to do evil'.[16] Ironically, here was a theological view of the world which yielded remarkable material benefits. Unbending and severe in his Quaker style, Corbyn applied precisely the same rigid rules to his everyday business affairs. Though always concessionary to his Quaker associates, provided they paid on time, he was relentless towards his debtors and was undoubtedly besotted with money, as he almost admitted: 'though I don't love money, yet it affects me very much.'[17]

Corbyn died a very rich man, one of many Quakers whose fortunes secured for them a niche among London's great and good (there were at least fourteen families with fortunes of about £100,000 in the eighteenth century). In every case, these wealthy dynasties utilised the Quaker networks to secure their personal and business interests by carefully arranged marriages of sons and daughters into other appropriate families. Quakerism itself did not, of course, guarantee success, but among those who did prosper, their commercial well-being was invariably cemented by access to such a network.

The Barclays were one such family. Of Scottish descent, with an impeccable Quaker pedigree (Robert Barclay, the 'Apologist', was the promoter of a settlement in East New Jersey), their origins lay in the linen trade. By the 1720s the direction of their business had shifted overseas, particularly to Pennsylvania and trusted Friends in Philadelphia, from where the Barclay trade blossomed throughout British America and the West Indies. Their success was secured by marriage to another Quaker family, Freames the bankers. From 1776 onwards, when North America broke free from British control, the Barclay sons turned their commercial acumen towards banking rather than the family trading business. They were active in the negotiations to prevent the outbreak of war between England and America, and seem to have turned ever more surely towards their new venture because of the transatlantic disruption caused by the conflict. In 1776 the family bank was renamed Barclays.

As we have seen, this concentration on banking did not prevent the Barclays from pursuing other commercial opportunities whenever they arose. Their most spectacular investment was the purchase of Henry Thrale's Anchor brewery, a business which offered, in the words of Dr Johnson, 'the potentiality of growing rich, beyond the dreams of avarice'.[18] The wealth which flowed from this lucrative mix of banking and brewing into the Barclay coffers placed enormous strains on the family's Quaker loyalties. The material and social trappings which such wealth inevitably brought lured some members away from the older, stricter dictates of the Society of Friends.

The Barclay fortunes were augmented by marriages and business associations with other families, notably the Trittons and the Bevans. The latter had achieved their early successes in copper refining in South Wales, but had risen to prominence, like Thomas Corbyn, through pharmaceuticals, especially in trade to the Americas. Apothecaries were infamous for their adulterated and shoddy products, but the founding father, Silvanus Bevan, had offered reliable reasonably priced goods. His shop in Plough Court was ideally located at the hub of London's commercial life, close to the banks, not too far from inns and coaching houses, hard by a number of coffee houses and accessible for the docks. For a Quaker, Silvanus lived very stylishly in a splendid Hackney house, able to afford the latest and best in furnishings and foods. In 1765 the business was taken over by his brother, but his sons moved on, via marriage and other prospects, into Barclays Bank and the Anchor brewery.[19] In 1775 the pharmacy business was bequeathed to Joseph Gurney Bevan (related to the more famous Norwich Quakers), whose colourful and sprightly early years gave way to an older man of uncompromising principles. Bevan expected prompt payment, though he would never pursue debts through the courts, nor accept money earned from the slave trade. His pacifist views went to the extent of refusing to supply drugs to warships during the Napoleonic Wars.[20]

The Tritton family had moved from a lowly yeoman background into brewing and banking. Like the Barclays the Trittons also began to drift away, and by the 1820s a new generation of a once exemplary Quaker family had found a new spiritual home in the Church of England.[21] The Gurney family told a similar story. Their links forged with London banking families placed them at the heart of the most eminent and influential metropolitan Quaker circles. Yet by the early nineteenth century, of the patriarch John Gurney's eleven children only four remained Quakers. Of those, the most famous was Elizabeth Fry, the prison reformer, yet none of her children stayed in the Society.[22]

While the austerity of Quaker life may have been an important ingredient in the rise of their prosperity in the eighteenth century, that same prosperity was able, in its turn, to corrode later descendants' attachment to the Society of Friends. It seemed, therefore, that the foundations for the future lay with intermarriage between business dynasties. At one level, this can be simply explained. Those who 'married out' (married a non-Quaker) were, until 1860, 'disowned' or excluded from the Society, so affluent families sought partners for their sons and daughters among Friends of a similar standing. The resulting family networks and ties embraced an extensive range of British economic concerns by the late eighteenth century – from textiles to pharmaceuticals, ironmasters to banking, and with a welter of smaller industries in between.

It has been calculated that between 50 and 75 per cent of the iron industry in England and Wales was in Quaker hands between the years 1700 and 1750.[23] Significantly, the wealthiest of these ironmasters had trading or family links with North America, but among the best remembered was the Lloyd family of South Wales and Birmingham, whose thriving metal industry expanded on the increased demand during Britain's various eighteenth-century wars (other Quakers found the dilemma over making money from conflict too disturbing). We have seen how, by the end of the eighteenth century, the Lloyds evolved into a banking family. Their name was linked, by marriage, to the Barclays and John Hanbury, the enormously successful Quaker merchant whose wealth was based on the lucrative tobacco trade to the Chesapeake (another quandary for the Friends, who had long denounced the twin evils of tobacco and the slavery which made its cultivation possible).[24] The Hanburys prospered on more than this, building up diverse interests in North America while acting as advisers on economic prospects there. The widening rift between England and the American colonies was, among Quakers, a matter of alarm that signalled commercial danger. As independence came closer, the Hanburys shifted these interests towards the West Indies and into banking. In any case, the family had already diversified at home, in the form of marriage with the Lloyds.[25]

In this way, Quaker losses in the wake of American Independence in 1776 remained small. They were able to withdraw their money and redirect their trade *before* the impending political and economic collapse for precisely the reasons that had helped them succeed in the first place. They were close to the pulse of American feeling via colonial Friends who had served to promote British fortunes and were able to warn of impending danger. Disaster was averted largely through the efforts of this international network.

Other short-term factors consolidated the fortunes of Quaker dynasties. Inheritance patterns ensured that wealth and assets were rarely passed on to a single son or daughter, but were divided among the next generation, usually on carefully devised grounds. This ensured that no one person could destroy the family well-being in a single generation.[26] More than that, and as we have seen, strict insistence on intermarriage secured that inheritance by diversifying family fortunes. It was a self-generating process of Quaker discipline and renewal.

Quaker networks were put under strain, however, by the broader pressures of cultural change during the course of the late eighteenth century. The pervasive sense of growing nationalism, first against America (1776–83) but more crucially against the French (1793–1815), transformed Britain, primarily in that a great deal of the nation's economic activities were diverted, directly or indirectly, towards the war effort. This posed serious problems for Quakers.[27] Birmingham Friends argued about the ethics of war production, but how could ironmasters like the Lloyds remain immune from the demands for massive investment in military hardware?[28] Quaker businessmen also faced moral dilemmas which could be fudged when the problem was physically out of sight. A number of crucial imports were produced by slaves on the far side of the Atlantic, but Quakers had been opposed to slavery from the late seventeenth century. However, so ubiquitous and complex were the commercial benefits of this produce that it became desirable to sidestep the issues surrounding such profit-making. Thomas Corbyn's trade to the West Indies had been with planters and the doctors who treated the slaves, but all prompted and helped by local Quaker contacts.

Less easily defined, but no less ambiguous for Quaker life, were the strains of material prosperity. There had developed an exceptional Quaker *haute monde* which was centred on their homes in the most fashionable areas of London, filled with the most desirable contemporary comforts and luxuries, but which also linked them to provincial Quaker communities. From Keswick to

Birmingham, from Norwich to South Wales and the West Country, this dynastic web became an élite network within a network, but in the move from an urban setting to landed estates, Quakers who had been pitched into the heart of rural England were sometimes drawn into the gravitational pull of the Anglican church. Many slipped through the net in this way; others were expelled for manifold theological or social lapses. It was a process which, within a few years, had managed to pull apart many of the families of the old élite. Sustained in their rise by Quaker networks, their old rationale began to disappear when those links no longer seemed important.

The question of how best to maintain the Quaker inheritance, to ensure that new generations remained within the Society, was troubling thoughtful Friends by the late eighteenth century. Some had come to accept that perhaps even the only way of guaranteeing their survival was to educate their children formally in Quaker ways. Networks were obviously not enough in themselves. Friends would gradually come to realise the value of successful Quaker schools.

6

Education

The most prosperous Quaker families have attracted more than their fair share of subsequent attention, but they do not provide an accurate picture of the Society's overall health. They were, after all, an unrepresentative élite: when they were at the peak of their power and fame, the Society of Friends languished. The responses to the annual *Queries* from London reveal a widespread discontent about Quaker affairs. During the eighteenth century there had been periodic efforts to tighten discipline, most notably by the appointment of elders to monitor local life. One of their tasks was to encourage suitable young Friends to put themselves forward as ministers, from which emerged a supervisory 'spiritual aristocracy'. But many Quakers were also concerned by outside changes which were threatening the Society itself. The promptings of the London Yearly Meeting for a return to essential simplicity were as much a denunciation of encroaching worldliness as they were a restatement of Quaker principles. In 1767 it was a 'matter of exceeding grief and concern to the faithful' to note that 'exemplary plainness of habit, speech and deportment . . . are now departed from by too many under our name'. A year later the point was made that those 'who prefer the gaiety, the vain customs, and fluctuating fashions of this world' were people who 'renounce wisdom for folly, duty for disobedience, and the reality of enduring substance for the flattering delusion of transitory enjoyments'.[1] Such exhortations were greeted by pessimistic responses across the country. The outcome was a decision in 1760 to launch a thorough review of the Society, but even though attempts were made to tighten its proceedings, the scrutiny did little to quell unease among English Quakers.

The most serious problem facing the Society of Friends was curiously one that many failed to notice: Quaker numbers were in decline. We have seen how material success and a changing social ambience exacerbated this trend, but it was also in part owing to their policy of 'disownment'. Whatever the cause, and notwithstanding the difficulty of assessing the exact numbers before the first Quaker census of 1861, the general figures seem clear enough. In 1859 the Quaker historian John Stephenson Rowntree estimated that in 1680 there were between 40,000 and 60,000 Friends in England and Wales, and perhaps 66,000 for the whole of Britain. A century later, however, this had fallen to less than half that number. At the beginning of the nineteenth century there were fewer than 20,000 in England and Wales.[2] It had become possible that the Society might even be consigned to the fate of so many other sects born of the English Revolution and become a mere historical curiosity.

Thoughtful Quakers realised that the Friends needed to change, but that a simple return to the habits of the late seventeenth century had little contemporary appeal. And this crisis, though focusing on both outward appearance and the internal discipline of the Society, went much deeper. It hinged ultimately on the issue of how or if the Society should engage with the world at large. Was its role to be that of an inward-looking, disengaged sect, interested solely in its own theology and conduct, or was it to confront outside challenges? At one level many had already taken this latter route in their commercial lives, yet even here there were points at which successful Friends had felt obliged to retreat from the harsher, more ethically troubling issues of trade.

Moral problems such as these rarely troubled ordinary Quakers, yet those struggling like their forbears to scratch a living found their lives transformed by the goods which came to Britain from all corners of the world: furs and pelts from North America; starch from the slave-grown rice of the Carolinas; tea and tableware from China; fish from Newfoundland; coffee from the Middle East and the Caribbean; chocolate and sugar (again, courtesy of the slaves) from Barbados and Jamaica; tobacco from the Chesapeake; even the potato, which for centuries had been the basic diet of the Indian peoples of the Andes. All these items began as the pleasures of the privileged, but were transmuted into 'essentials' upon which millions had come to depend. Even the poor were able to afford tea, sugar and tobacco.

Quaker life had been made easier by the removal or reduction of discrimination in the law, between the Toleration Act of 1689 and the Affirmation Act of 1722. The early Quakers had been regarded as a dangerous and subversive body, their ideals too democratic for late-seventeenth-century England. A century on, the Society was viewed at worst as a body of eccentrics for whom the state was, on the whole, willing to make allowances. This change in attitude had been aided by the success and influence of prominent Quakers, particularly those from the London élite who moved with such ease and confidence in mid- and late-eighteenth-century political circles.

Few were more highly regarded than Dr John Fothergill, medical doctor, scientist and associate of famous men on both sides of the Atlantic. Benjamin Franklin claimed that it was enough to address a letter 'Dr Fothergill, London' for it to arrive safely. Born into a Wensleydale farming family in 1712, Fothergill had been apprenticed to an apothecary in Bradford before eventually graduating in medicine from Edinburgh and settling in London as a physician. He was a successful research scientist, keen on botanical experimentation and cultivation, and imported exotic plants and seeds for these purposes, and for use in pharmaceutical preparations. Sir Joseph Banks thought that 'no other garden in Europe, royal or of a subject, had nearly so many scarce and valuable plants' as Fothergill's wonderful garden in Essex.[3] The link between science, medicine and horticulture was fundamental to the development of each discipline during the eighteenth century, and was a major factor in the establishment of Kew Gardens in 1759.

Dr Fothergill became a fellow of the Royal Society in 1763, but he was also a writer, editor, indefatigable correspondent and Quaker publisher, who maintained contacts in America (where his father and brother made ministerial visits), notably with Friends in Pennsylvania. He was especially close to Benjamin Franklin, their friendship beginning via their mutual scientific interests. Fothergill was well placed as a negotiator and tried to head off the impending break between Britain and America from 1774 to 1776. Throughout his life Fothergill was a central figure in Quaker affairs, indefatigable in the London Yearly Meeting, travelling to meetings across the country, and always willing to speak and write on the Society's behalf.

Fothergill was better placed than most to appreciate the Quakers' problems and he came to realise that education provided the key to the Society's future. He and others appreciated that the traditional schooling which Fothergill himself had received (the combination of private tutors, small private schools, apprenticeships, and in-house family or business-based instruction) was inadequate, both for the changing needs of society at large and, perhaps more importantly, to sustain a steady flow of educated young Quakers drilled in the ethics of the Society, and able to replenish the intellectual and theological vigour of Friends everywhere. The Quaker intellectual élite was also concerned that their own broadly based form of education had not been enjoyed by other Friends, far too many of whom remained formally ignorant, suspicious of book-learning, and unwilling to uproot themselves from the simplicities of rural or provincial life.

The issue was raised no fewer than twenty-seven times by the London Yearly Meeting between 1700 and 1740.[4] The response to a 1759 query revealed that there were twenty-one small boarding schools scattered round the country, in addition to numerous day schools. All told, there were only 630 Quaker children in attendance, not enough teachers, and few good scholars emerging from these schools.[5] Fothergill was not discouraged, hoping to see the introduction of education for 'the youth of our society' which would be as good 'as many think fit to give their dogs and horses'. The problem centred on those 'whose parents are not in affluence', and he worried that 'the inability of many Friends has been the occasion of keeping their children at home'.[6] He was seized with the issue, and a solution which served 'the very purpose' presented itself in 1777 when Fothergill was travelling in Yorkshire.[7] He heard of an ideal property at Ackworth near Pontefract: an old foundling hospital which had been derelict for the past five years, where foxes were reputed to rear their cubs in the deserted corridors.

Ackworth was a costly venture, but prosperous Friends, including David Barclay, subscribed handsomely towards the £7,000 needed to buy and maintain the buildings and 84 acres of land (curiously, part of the funding was raised from the strictly non-Quaker Navy Bonds). With Quaker financial expertise, such a hefty sum proved no obstacle.[8] Helped by William Tuke, the York tea merchant, who printed 1,000 copies of a plan for the school for use in the fundraising exercise, Fothergill's ambitions came to fruition when the new Quaker school opened in 1779, taking in children aged 7 to 13 and charging fees of £8 for each child per year. Some thought the fees too steep, but once the school was open and its merits plain for all to see, money began to pour in.[9] From Falmouth to Durham, Friends sent donations, annuities and bequests, and within twelve years of its foundation, the school had attracted some £17,000.[10]

Ackworth was organised initially from London and its purpose, according to Fothergill, was 'to provide a tender teachable disposition, inuring them to bear the yoke in their youth, which will moderate their desires, and make way for the softening influence of divine good-will in their hearts, fitting them for the fruitful discharge of every duty in life'.[11] But the key to success lay in the teaching itself. Quaker principles were to be 'diligently inculcated, and due care to be taken to preserve the children from bad habits and immoral conduct'. The syllabus was straightforward enough: 'That the English language, writing and arithmetic, be carefully taught to the sexes. That the girls also be instructed in housewifery and useful needlework.' Part of each day was to be devoted to silence and meditation.[12] Fothergill also insisted that all children undertake some form of manual labour, anticipating the ideal of nineteenth-century public schools in wanting to instil 'A sound mind in a healthy body'.[13] However, the ideal soon faded and, except for chores in the garden, manual tasks were left to the ground staff as pupils were thought to be at risk: 'moral evil is stated to have resulted to the children by associating with the labourers employed.'[14]

Ideally the Friends wanted the school to be run by a Quaker, or 'a sober couple, frugal, sensible and religious' who could manage the school while classes were taken by a younger colleague. The school was officially opened on 18 October 1779, with John Hill as treasurer and superintendent, aided by his wife Judith and teacher Hannah Little. The first pupils arrived from Poole. John Fothergill and his sister visited the school ten months later, and found 150 boys and 80 girls 'already moulded into excellent order, clean and attentive'. Boys were taught reading, writing and, significantly, accounts. Girls also learned needlework, spinning and housewifery. The curriculum soon expanded to include geography, history, science, Latin and French.[15] The school was designed very much as a family concern, with children acquiring the skills and habits they would need for stable family life.

Wealthy Quakers began to send their children to Ackworth. New pupils gathered in London and were escorted as far as Wentworth by a Friend, travelling for almost two days in an uncomfortable wagon. From there they were collected by the Ackworth 'conveyance': a cart pulled by a bull. We can only imagine what passed through their minds as they finally entered the bleak, flagged corridors of that large and forbidding edifice.[16] An early description by former headteacher Thomas Pumphrey told of the 'prison-like passage to the porter's lodge', thence on to the 'Great Passage, along which two or three oil lamps shed a gleam of dim light'. It was a building of 'thick massive walls, cold stone floors, vast empty halls, through which the echoes of every sound loudly reverberated, all looking chill, cheerless and desolate'.[17]

Quakers were not alone in wanting to develop a new system of schooling for their own particular needs, which would fit children for their preordained place in life. Girls would become wives and mothers; boys, the basic breadwinners. The need to encourage social and personal discipline was a recurring theme in the education debate, and was asserted in a number of new schools, beginning in the 1780s with Hannah More's Sunday schools 'to train up the lower classes in habits of industry and piety'. By the end of the century there were more than 1,000 such establishments across the country.[18]

Ackworth had much in common, then, with other schools, but it also aimed 'to establish young minds in Truth': to rear new generations, especially of poorer Quakers, in the culture of the Society of Friends. Fothergill also hoped that, in time, the school would provide 'a more learned education than we now can give'.[19] The school appeared to function smoothly, with monitors and inspectors from among the pupils reporting to the duty master. There was a conscious effort to encourage a sense of equality and harmony in the school, and visitors were invariably impressed by the composure and silence of pupils at the appropriate times of day. In fact the school attracted a stream of Quaker observers who were keen to see this educational experiment at work and to know the secret of Ackworth's success in the hope that they could repeat it in their own neighbourhood.

The Ackworth blueprint was copied in Ireland and America, and by the end of the century there were three Quaker boarding schools in Rhode Island, New York and Pennsylvania. New establishments in England followed at Sidcot, Wigton and Croydon (later moving to Saffron Walden), aiming to educate Quakers from all social levels.

All this was happening long before the introduction of compulsory schooling, although Sunday schools continued to provide the basics of popular literacy, linked to religious instruction, throughout the late eighteenth and nineteenth centuries. But Ackworth was doing much more: it tried to ensure that its pupils would remain Quakers. It was self-consciously a crucible for future relationships and family ties. In the words of the historian Hingston Fox, Ackworth 'promoted friendships and intermarriages, and was a chief cause in making the society like one large family'. This particular family, however, took very little rest. Like many pupils, John Bright's father spent five years there with not a single break or holiday.[20]

Life at the school was not as smooth or as disciplined as many of its early apologists suggested. Teachers and pupils alike posed an endless round of practical difficulties for the idealists who sought to mould the school. Fothergill's model schoolteacher proved hard to find, and even the posture of one member of staff dismayed him: 'I wish he could be under the hands of a Drill Sergeant – to teach him only how to walk'. In the school's rapid expansion there was a swift turnover of masters and mistresses. And pupils like George Swann were frequently reprimanded for less than Quaker behaviour. In 1783 he 'was found guilty of taking a Stick of Liquorice from one of his Schoolfellows'. A year later he was in trouble again, this time 'for disorderly Behaviour in the dining Room and we now think proper that he be ordered to eat his Meals at the Disgrace Table'. The punishment was not effective, and later that same year the entrepreneurial Swann was disciplined once more 'for taking Apples out of the Garden and selling them to his School Fellows'.[21]

The running of Ackworth was carefully monitored by the Yearly Meeting, and groups of Quakers were sent north to examine the discipline, which they felt 'should be inflicted with Coolness and Resolution without the least Appearance of Passion'. It soon became apparent to the investigating Friends that the children's scriptural grasp was weak and in 1816 Joseph John Gurney decided that each pupil should receive a bible on arriving at, rather than on leaving, the school.[22] The regime was physically spartan (though this was common to all boarding schools of the period), including numbing daily baths at 6 a.m. in an open-air spring, half a mile's walk from the school. Also in common with boarding schools everywhere, Ackworth thought it vital to keep pupils fully occupied throughout the day. And boys and girls were strictly segregated, right down to the eating arrangements.

Despite the inevitable teething problems Ackworth thrived. Moreover, the school became a regional Quaker headquarters, providing a venue for a range of gatherings from which a number of important initiatives were launched in the nineteenth century. At a reunion of former scholars in 1829, Samuel Tuke and Joseph Rowntree, prompted by the death of an Ackworth teacher and his wife's subsequent dependence on Quaker charity, discussed the creation of an insurance association. In 1831 their ideas culminated in the establishment of the Friends' Provident Institution in Bradford.[23]

As well as demonstrating the way to raise money for other projects, the school's design and layout also proved instructive. When William Tuke set out to found the Retreat, a modern mental hospital in York, he used both as a model, and took Ackworth's guiding principles as its own in the treatment of the mentally disturbed: 'By gentleness, kind and affectionate treatment, holding out encouragement and approbation to the deserving, exerting the influence of the fear of shame . . . to bring forward into the Society and its service a number . . . acquainted . . . with the discipline of wisdom.'[24] Among more austere Quakers, the plans and drawings of Ackworth School took their place alongside those of the interior of a slave ship as among the few pictures acceptable for Quakers to hang in their homes.[25]

William Tuke's wife Esther was especially interested in the education of Quaker girls and along with three women friends made regular visits to the girls' wing at Ackworth. Many girls were unable to attend the school for various reasons, and Esther Tuke determined to widen their prospects by establishing a separate school in York. The Tukes lived in a large house in Trinity Lane which offered ample room, so it was on New Year's Day 1785 that Esther and eight other Quaker women opened their own girls' school, hoping to instruct 'the Children in useful Needlework, Knitting, the English Language, Writing and Arithmetic'.[26] Fees 'for Board, Washing, and Education' were '14 Guineas a year, to be paid at Entrance, washing of Gowns and Frocks not included'. They sought from the start to impose a Quaker tone. So that 'plainness and moderation, consistent with our religious principles, may be attended to', it was requested 'that such apparel as is costly, or superfluous, may be avoided'.[27]

Yet Esther Tuke herself was far from dreary. She was a formidable woman who, in addition to her own two children, had inherited five from William's first marriage. A prominent and effective preacher throughout the North, she revitalised Quaker activities wherever she went.[28] Throughout her life she was especially keen to change the role of women within the Society of Friends, and was instrumental in establishing a separate women's section at the London Yearly Meeting. Her home offered a resting place for Friends travelling across the country and from North America. Though devout and loyal to Quaker fashion, she was also good fun socially, with 'a natural facetiousness which made young persons greatly enjoy her society'.[29] Yet she had a seriousness which impressed visitors and pupils alike.

Initially her school was run almost entirely by the voluntary efforts of local young Quaker women, whose energies and interests had few formal outlets but who found a worthwhile role in teaching and supervision (the only paid officer was the sewing mistress). The opening roll numbered seventeen girls but soon increased, and like Ackworth, the school was open 365 days per year, with pupils seeing relatives only when they travelled to York or attended local meetings. 'Simplicity of manners, and a religious improvement of the minds of youth were the principal objects', and all learning was directed to this end. Publications which 'unprofitably elate the mind and give a disrelish for the purity of gospel truths' were not allowed. The girls had to clean their own quarters and, at regular intervals, wait at table. Detailed attention was paid to reading and spelling; they also learned French, which from 1799 was taught by a Frenchman. Such lessons bore literary fruit in the love of and abilities in reading and writing displayed by former pupils in later life. Indeed, the literary achievements of Quaker women were to feature throughout the nineteenth century, particularly during the anti-slavery campaign.[30] Visitors to the school were struck by such an unusual and effective education for young women.[31]

The school had the added good fortune of attracting the services of the American Lindley Murray, the most influential grammarian of the nineteenth century, who had travelled to England because of ill health, settled in York and gravitated towards its well-established Quaker circles. Murray took a keen interest in the new school, agreed to teach grammar, and was persuaded by the other teachers to write a suitable textbook. When published in 1795, the profits from the sale of *Grammar* were devoted to Trinity Lane School, which in the early years greatly helped its marginal finances. Murray was an independently wealthy man who spent his time revising each successive edition of the book, which was to have a profound effect on teaching throughout the English-speaking world, but he did not make a penny from the hundreds of thousands of copies sold throughout the nineteenth century.[32]

Trinity Lane School began to attract the daughters of prominent Quakers, not only from the York area. In 1791, Abraham Darby of Coalbrookdale placed two daughters there, where they would be within reach of a grandmother in Doncaster who made regular visits to Quaker meetings in York. It is revealing that even such wealthy Quakers as the Darbys expected their daughters, in their spare time at school, to make shirts and collars for their brothers at home. The finished clothing was to be sent to the Lloyd family in Birmingham for subsequent collection. By the time the school closed in 1814, in times of wartime hardship, daughters of large numbers of prominent Quakers had been educated there.[33]

Wherever a Quaker school took root and flourished, it did so, initially at least, largely because of the efforts of a small band of dedicated Friends. But Fothergill, the Tukes and their supporters had demonstrated a personal determination which alone was not sufficient to guarantee survival. Prosperous York Quakers remained worried about the levels of ignorance among children of the urban poor and had founded a number of small, generally female-led schools to 'improve the moral condition of the rising generation'.[34] This was part of a much broader nineteenth-century concern about urban poverty and education which had given impetus to the foundation of Sunday, ragged and day schools, and had prompted Quakers to look outwards and to engage with society's major social ills. A reputation was thereby created for themselves as the nation's pre-eminent social reformers, spurred on by a religiously inspired conscience, and anxious to ameliorate the lot of their less fortunate fellow citizens.

Distinct from this was the persistent drive to establish Quaker schools and York remained an obvious location. Various proposals had come before regional meetings to consider the prospect of a boys' school, and even though finance was generally available, it was not founded until 1829. John Ford, headmaster of a Friends school in Rochester, was brought north for the purpose. His own teacher-training had followed the traditional route when, at the age of 14, he had left Ackworth and was 'articled for seven years of apprentice to Robert Styles, a schoolmaster at Rochester.' When he settled in York, in typical networking fashion he lived with the Tukes.[35] The school was initially located in Lawrence Street, later moving to its current site and taking the name Bootham School in 1846. By then the successor to Trinity Lane, the Mount School for girls, had been established, first in 1831 at Castlegate, then in 1857 at its present site in Dalton Terrace, under the direction of women who had taught at Ackworth. Yet for the Mount and Bootham Schools there remained the problem of securing the services of suitably trained teachers. Quaker networks were vital, for the wives, widows and daughters of Friends provided the mainstay of the workforce in its formative years. The Yorkshire schools also trained their own staff, granting entry to pupils on lower fees in return for future services. By the mid-nineteenth century, Ackworth was producing fully trained male teachers who moved on to various Quaker schools; the Mount was doing much the same, and employing experienced women teachers from other establishments. The reputation of the teaching profession, such as it was, remained low, however, as its returns were meagre, and its demands gruelling and sometimes harsh. For young women, teaching was seen as an unattractive alternative to marriage, shaping the image of spinsterly misery that clung to girls' teaching throughout the nineteenth century and beyond.

The content of nineteenth-century Quaker education began to change, incorporating newer disciplines, and broadening the education of both boys and girls. The latter remained more traditional, it became less narrowly focused, and included the sciences and maths. Samuel Gurney presented the first microscope to the Mount in 1852 and a telescope was set on the school roof. Natural science was part of the curriculum at Bootham from its early days. But perhaps more interesting was the arrival of a more formal religious education at both schools, though curiously not all were happy with this development. After all, religion 'was lived but not talked about', and any regulated instruction would necessarily demand approved texts, scrutiny of which would fall to the London Yearly Meeting.

In the years between the foundation of Ackworth in 1779 and the mid-nineteenth century relocation of York's Quaker schools to their present sites, the debate about education was transformed. The initial discussion, centred on Fothergill and his friends, about the use of education to preserve and advance the Quaker cause, had evolved into a realisation of the need for a clearer structure and curriculum, and a broad agreement that schooling ought to be more functional and purposeful, no longer confined simply to traditional Quaker principles. Britain was becoming an increasingly urban and industrialised society (by this time, children were travelling to their

York schools by train rather than carriage), and the Quaker debate comprised but one aspect of a general concern about how best to educate the nation's young. Quakers such as Joseph Lancaster, who had opened his first school for poor children in Southwark in 1798, played their own distinctive and important wider role, but it seemed increasingly clear that the majority could not continue comfortably to distance themselves.

The same question was asked time and again: what role should the Society of Friends play in a rapidly changing Britain? The other-worldliness of Quakers had become ever more striking and increasingly difficult to defend, particularly when so many were achieving conspicuous commercial success. Their achievements were most notable in the fields of industry, science and shop-keeping.

7

Industrialists, Scientists and Shopkeepers

Quakers had been prominent in the development of the Yorkshire iron industry from the late seventeenth century onwards, as they had been in the earlier industry of the southern Lake District and northern Lancashire, their products carried to markets and towns throughout the region by other Quaker merchants on trains of pack-mules.[1] Many of those metal goods subsequently passed into the holds of ships travelling to Africa and the Americas from the northern ports of Whitehaven, Liverpool, Lancaster and Preston (one form of currency widely used in bartering for slaves in West Africa was the iron bar). Their presence and influence was inescapable – indeed, it has been calculated that in the early eighteenth century 'Quakers owned or managed between half and three-quarter of the ironworks in operation', most of which 'were at least loosely interconnected by a complex series of partnerships and marriages'.[2] They were to the eighteenth-century iron industry what they would become to the chocolate industry one hundred years later. Moreover, the interrelated story of these ironmasters and their families reflects the major changes at work in the British economy as a whole. Industry itself was relocating: new specialised areas were satisfying a national and international market.[3] It is important not to overstate the role of Quaker pioneers in this process, yet their presence in a number of key innovative industries was significant in the broader shift towards such change. Moreover, many paths between interconnected areas of industry were paved by Quaker connections.

Quakers would transform a tiny traditional operation into a major regional or national enterprise. Metalworking, with its mining, small-scale smelting and casting, provided enterprising Friends with the perfect opportunity to exercise their entrepreneurial skills. In some cases a small business could develop into a massive pioneering company, with ramifications for the economy in general. Such a story can be told of the London Lead Company, whose origins lay in the late seventeenth century, a period marked by a sharp decline in lead mining. Two localised groups of Quakers – one in North Wales and Cumberland, the other in the North-East – moved into the business to form the Quaker or London Lead Company, and gradually spread their influence nationwide. (Their commercial success enabled Quaker shareholders to branch out into banking.) At each turn, the company sought the help, contacts and advice of other Friends: they bought the latest equipment (cylinders and engines, for example) from Quaker engineers; bills, orders and requisitions were signed not merely with the formalities of business documentation, but in the equally revealing Quaker vernacular, 'With due esteem, Thy Loving Friend' or 'thy obliged and faithful friend'.[4]

The founding fathers used other Quakers for the management and development of mining operations, finances were secured by Quaker bankers, and shareholding was in the hands of Friends. Company procedure was hampered in the early years by the need for directors to swear oaths, but the Affirmation Act of 1722 placed it on a secure Quaker footing. By 1705 the London Lead Company was soundly established with operations in Wales, the north Pennines, later in Derbyshire, even in Scotland and Ireland, and was to prove a major force in the metal-mining industry for the next two centuries.[5]

In addition to innovative and experimental production methods, the company pioneered an industrial paternalism which was to become a Quaker characteristic of the nineteenth century. Because it mined in isolated communities and was in effect the sole local employer, it was able to extend detailed control over the workers' private lives, providing churches, housing, schooling, welfare and shopping facilities (though trying to avoid the exploitations of the 'truck' system, where workers paid inflated costs at company stores). The London Lead Company was anxious to maintain regular employment for its workers, laying in stocks of raw materials, for example, to secure long-run employment, but as we might expect it demanded suitable behaviour in return. Workers could be dismissed for 'tippling, fighting, night-rambling, mischief and other disreputable conduct, or evidence of a thankless and discontented disposition.'[6] In 1708 the company was among the first to ban swearing, and their severe opposition to drink and drink-related offences was not unique to Quaker employers but was common to a number of early industrialists, all of whom were anxious to purge the labour force of its pre-industrial indisciplines.[7] Sick clubs and death clubs providing insurance cover were encouraged and received company contributions as part of that shaping of a working environment which was at once profitable to the owners and tolerable for the labour force.

When Abraham Darby, the era's most famous ironmaster, died in May 1717 he bequeathed to his large family a thriving business which was to become the centrepiece of a new English metalwork industry. Like so many other Quaker entrepreneurs, Darby came from humble stock. His father John was a farmer who also worked as a nailer and locksmith – a common enough combination in the Dudley region where they lived. Pig iron from the Forest of Dean, the upper Severn and the West Midlands was sold on to such farmer/craftsmen. Their operations were very small, often only a single forge which could be easily handled by one man and his sons. The finished metal products found their way via merchants to Bristol and London (and often from there, overseas).

John Darby put the young Abraham into a trading apprenticeship in Birmingham with Jonathan Freeth, who was active in local Quaker affairs. Abraham thus acquired workshop skills alongside a devotion to the Society of Friends, although from the first there was no clear divide between Darby's work and religion: his daily life was an example of his faith. After his apprenticeship, Abraham, now married to Mary Sergeant, the daughter of Quaker linen bleachers, became a manufacturer of malt mills in Bristol. There he moved among Quakers in the metal trades and, with the help of imported Dutch labour, and money and help from other Friends, he became a partner in the Bristol Brass Wire Company. Darby's determination to expand and to perfect new ways of iron-casting met with his partners' resistance, so in 1709 he switched his operations to an existing foundry at Coalbrookdale.[8]

Coalbrookdale had long been a productive coal region at a time when charcoal, traditionally used in iron-making, was becoming scarcer and therefore increasing in cost. The new site had ideal facilities: furnaces and forges, access to both charcoal and coal, and perfectly located water supplies to serve the works and to transport the finished product down the Severn.[9] By the time of Darby's arrival, the Coalbrookdale area had become a busy industrial region, albeit on a small scale. He took over and rebuilt a derelict ironworks, then began to process iron using coke (which he had previously used during his apprenticeship in the malt trade), thus avoiding the damaging sulphur impurities in charcoal. The end result was of a very high quality.

Throughout his years at Coalbrookdale Abraham remained an active Quaker, travelling to other regional meetings and organising local gatherings at the house he built there. When he died his surviving children were either sent to Quaker schools or apprenticed to Quaker masters, but when his wife Mary died a year later, the future of the children and the company looked bleak. Capital was raised by mortgaging half the works, and with a reorganisation of the shares, the company was placed on a sounder commercial footing. It was run by the sympathetic management of Richard

Ford, who had trained under Darby and was an astute businessman, well versed in the technology of the metal industry and keen to open new avenues of trade.

The company's products, mainly a great variety of pots, pans and kettles, were in great demand by merchants as far away as the South-West or Manchester. During this time the market continued to spread ever wider and eventually, via Bristol, overseas. What the company did not know, or at least raised no objection to, was the fact that a great deal of this export trade almost certainly went into the holds of Bristol's slave ships.[10] (One commentator was to remark of local metal pans in January 1760 that 'a large proportion was sent to the Guinea slave trade in Africa'.)[11] That massive flotilla of vessels plying from England's second port was central to the transfer of goods in exchange for slaves on the African coast, thereafter taking their human cargo to the Americas.

The Darby company gradually expanded its range of goods, including the unQuakerly manufacture of guns, while technical improvements, notably the use of a new steam engine, helped it thrive. Although the armament trade seems unethical for so devout a Quaker as Abraham II, the increased diplomatic and strategic tension in Atlantic trade in the 1730s made it virtually impossible to work the routes without armed protection against threats from the Spanish and the French.[12] In addition, the ships trading to and from Africa and the Americas used guns to cow their African cargo, and by the end of the eighteenth century, upwards of a third of a million guns were being sold to Africans each year in exchange for slaves. Coalbrookdale was but one of many places satisfying that demand.[13]

In 1745 Abraham Darby II took over management of the company and began to wind down its armaments business. (Quaker gun manufacturers, such as the Galtons of Birmingham, who refused to relinquish the trade were disowned.)[14] He experimented ceaselessly and greatly increased production of pig iron for use in the proliferating small metal industries of the Midlands, where forges were turning out wrought-iron goods in growing volume.

In this way, Darby gradually shifted focus away from Bristol and by the mid-eighteenth century he was rapidly modernising and expanding his Coalbrookdale plant. To his contemporaries it presented a spectacular sight, familiar enough today but utterly amazing at the time. Abraham's daughter described the scene to her aunt in 1753: 'the stupendous Bellows whose alternate roars, like the foaming billows, is awful to hear; the mighty Cylinders, the wheels that carry so many different Branches of the work, is curious to observe'. The entire site, a compact hive of noise and activity, day and night, was set against beautiful rural scenery, the spectacle of which was to impress Arthur Young on his travels in 1776. The surrounding countryside he found to be 'too beautiful to be much in unison with that variety of horrors art has spread at the bottom; the noise of the forges, mills etc, with their vast machinery, the flames bursting from the furnaces with the burning of the coal and the smoak of the lime kilns, are altogether sublime'.[15] When the American Quaker Jabez Maud Fisher visited in the same year, he was astounded by the sight – 'we are presented with all the horrors that Pandemonium could shew' – yet he had to admit that 'These Iron Works, for Perfection, for Extent and Convenience are superior to any upon Earth'.[16]

Abraham's business thrived, but his family life was blighted by tragedy. The deaths of several children and the early death of his first wife were harsh even by eighteenth-century standards, but throughout he remained resolute in his faith and his painstaking commitment to the business. The Darby home welcomed visiting Friends and associates, and, through the usual intermingling, ties of friendship blended with mutual commercial interests: investments were made and deals were struck; marriages reinforced such links.[17] When Abraham II died in 1763 he left a flourishing concern. Too early to speak of the Industrial Revolution, his era was none the less marked by small-scale and sometimes crude technical and mechanical developments that increasingly depended on the production of high-quality metal products, and which Coalbrookdale was able to supply in abundance. Within such parochial and regional developments were the seeds of that eventual revolution.

Each new generation of the Darby family brought fresh perspectives to the management and progress of Coalbrookdale. Abraham II was succeeded by his son-in-law Richard Reynolds (at 28, already a widower with two small children), a Quaker who had served his apprenticeship with Joseph Fry in Bristol. Like his predecessor Reynolds pressed on with experimentation. He replaced wooden with metal track on the company's railways, and developed links and partnerships with a number of other Quaker ironmasters. He amassed considerable wealth, investing much of it in real estate, but more importantly it enabled him to become in effect the Coalbrookdale company's banker. It was an evolving pattern: acquisitive Friends financed their own and other industrial and commercial ventures by lending at below the market rate, confident that their investments were safeguarded by the ethical standards and rigorous scrutiny of the local Quaker community. Like the Darbys before him and successful Quakers a century later, Reynolds paid special attention to protecting the interests of his workers by constructing homes for them, establishing schools and Sunday schools, and seeking to create as congenial an environment as possible. As his sons grew to maturity they were introduced to the varied work around the company, and each sought to keep in touch with technical and commercial developments in industry generally. In this way the company became involved with Boulton and Watt, whose engines were providing Coalbrookdale's power by the 1780s, but it was Abraham Darby III's construction of the famous Iron Bridge at Coalbrookdale between 1777 and 1779 which remains its most memorable and easily recognisable achievement.

The company sought to continue to operate on ethical lines, refusing to profit from the market booms created by various wars when armaments were in demand, taking steps to establish a 'fair price' for their products when such demand might push prices high, and realising the need to avoid involvement in the slave trade.

And the Friends in charge gave generously to a wide range of charitable causes, though often anonymously to avoid any acclaim for their benevolence.[18]

As the Darby–Reynolds family expanded through marriages, new generations and yet more links, the spread of the network of Quakers became both familial and industrial. The Coalbrookdale Quakers were particularly close to and had investments in the companies of the ironmasters in South Wales, who in their turn had ties with Quaker brewing and banking interests in London, who came to be linked to the Gurney family of Norwich. It was a remarkable dynasty of successful Friends.

Quaker-dominated metal industries also included brass-making in Bristol, which was established in the early eighteenth century by a group of local Friends with family and business links mainly in Wales, London and the Midlands. Again, the determination to provide satisfactory conditions for workers went hand in hand with industrial progress. Success in one enterprise invariably led to experiments and subsequent success in another (sometimes related) industry. The Champion family of Bristol, for example, diversified from brass-making into pottery.

The eighteenth century saw a massive increase in the production of domestic tableware, led initially by the imports of Chinaware by the East India Company. The English pottery industry sprang up around the china-clay deposits found in Cornwall, and derived from the skills and enterprise of the Quaker William Cookworthy, who was born into a poor Devonshire weaver's family in 1705. Following an apprenticeship to the London apothecary Silvanus Bevan, William was dispatched to establish a shop in Plymouth, and as his business prospered he continued to teach himself a range of skills. Moving around the West Country, partly on business, partly pursuing his duties as a Quaker, allowed Cookworthy to acquire an intimate knowledge of local trade and resources. He experimented with clays and stones until he perfected a form of porcelain which seemed as good as the Chinese variety. With the help of skilled men from the local region and Europe, he developed a fine manufacturing system in Plymouth and Bristol. (He was eventually driven out of business by the emergence of the more aggressive manufacturers of the Potteries.)[19]

Joseph Fry of Bristol is best remembered for his successful chocolate business, but for a time he was inspired by Cookworthy's success to consider the pottery industry. He also dabbled in soap manufacture in association with another Bristol Quaker, Mr Fritt, through a company which would eventually become the giant Lever Brothers. But the most successful of all Quaker chemical companies was established by Joseph Crosfield, a descendant of old Cumbrian and Lancastrian Quaker stock. Crosfield had served his apprenticeship to a female grocer in Kendal before working for Samuel Fothergill, whose Warrington shop was a retail and wholesale tea business, and who had clients in America. Crosfield made regular business trips to the growing port of Liverpool for stock and used his Quaker connections there and in Warrington to emerge as a prominent local Friend and the head of a large family. He was a man with an eye for commercial openings and in 1799 went into partnership with colleagues in Liverpool to purchase a sugar refinery in Lancaster (it did not matter, presumably, that the sugar was cultivated by West Indian slaves). The business thrived despite setbacks, and even though the port of Lancaster was edged out of the maritime limelight by the rapid rise of Liverpool. Eventually the company, and the Crosfield's family, made the inevitable move to Liverpool in 1818.

One of the Crosfield sons, also called Joseph, was apprenticed in 1807 to Anthony Clapham, a Quaker chemist and apothecary in Newcastle who also moved into soap and chemical manufacture. When Joseph junior completed his apprenticeship he returned to Warrington to establish his own soap-making business. With his father's advice and money, and with the expertise acquired in Newcastle, the 21-year-old set up in Bank Quay in 1814. Warrington was an ideal starting place: it had excellent river and canal links to Manchester and Liverpool, Merseyside was already a centre for chemical manufacture, it was close to chemical deposits in Cheshire and the coalfields of south Lancashire, and was on the very edge of the burgeoning cotton industry (whose expanding population was in need of soap products). Joseph's early business days proved insecure, partly because of post-Napoleonic War dislocation, but he weathered the storm with the help of the financial support of his father and other local Quakers. Such arrangements were not charitable donations, but sound commercial investments made by Friends with spare capital who were keen to help, yet no less keen to strike a canny deal. This pattern repeated itself as money was directed to fledging soap and chemical concerns, and the new investors were incorporated into the business in various roles.[20]

Joseph's brothers, drilled by their father in the Quaker ethics of frugality and sound business activity, went their own commercial way, establishing grocery concerns in Liverpool which specialised in wholesale tea, coffee and tobacco. It was natural enough that the sons of a Quaker merchant should turn to the mainstay of the remarkable boom in late-eighteenth-century shopkeeping, yet they chose to ignore the fact that the products they sold were brought forth by the sweat of imported African slaves in the Americas (except for tea, but that too was made palatable by the addition of slave-grown sugar).

Joseph Crosfield's Warrington soap business thrived (even though the overall number of manufacturers contracted through rationalisation from 971 in 1784 to 304 in 1834), as the expanding population used some of their spare cash to clean themselves, their clothes and their homes as never before. Crosfield invested in improved plant and new systems by using both his profits and a sympathetic bank for loans and advice. He continued to cast around for other commercial openings, investing in the grocery trade, corn-milling, chemical manufacture, glass-making, cotton manufacture (a disaster), the new wave of joint-stock banks and, inevitably perhaps, the railway companies. As his success mounted, he invested even further afield in Europe, Central and South America, and later in Indian tea.

Not surprisingly Crosfield was of a reforming political bent, supporting the Quaker radical John Bright, particularly in his campaigns for the removal of trading restrictions.[21] But his most significant public efforts went into good works in Warrington, where he established schools, a Mechanics Institute, libraries and a bible society. Throughout his life he was of course active within the local and regional Society of Friends, but before he died quite suddenly in 1844 at the early age of 51, his last words, written on slate (he was too ill to speak), were about business: 'I look for very liberal aid to George [his son] in arranging with the bank.'[22]

Business was a preoccupation secured by, among other things, fruitful family links from one generation to another. The sons of Crosfield junior made the most of their inheritance so that a generation on, their fledgling soap business had become a hugely successful example of late-Victorian prosperity. The modernised and expanded plant disgorged a range of products for the home and overseas markets which greatly profited the founding family and their shareholders. Yet only one of his three sons, George, remained a Quaker. His two brothers, Morland and John, married outside and became Anglican, although they displayed their Quaker upbringing throughout their lives, never more strongly than in their denunciation of drunkenness. The Warrington company continued that tradition of industrial paternalism through sick funds, long-service pensions, other welfare schemes, company-financed day trips and the acceptance of workers' representation within the plant.[23] However, this system was tested to the limits by any significant increase in the size of operations. Paternalism worked best when the grandees knew the names of most of their employees; when the workforce was measured in their thousands (by 1913, there were almost 2,500 at Warrington), it inevitably lost its way. Quaker commercial success could contain the seeds of its own downfall: just as it lured new generations of prospering employers away from the austere world of the Society of Friends, so it could drive a wedge between master and worker by the sheer scale of production. This was to happen later in the confectionery trades.

Much of this Quaker success may have been carried forward by the changing consuming habits of the British people, but how was any entrepreneur, Quaker or otherwise, able to predict what they would want or could afford *before* the patterns of consumption were established? Quaker commercial alertness and imagination very likely played a role, for the Friends' contacts, nationwide and beyond, enabled ideas, experiments and prospects to be shared and compared. One venture always seemed to lead to another along the Quaker network. We cannot be sure what drove these particular men of imagination – what enabled them to develop or persist with a particular idea that others believed to be less rewarding or promising – yet so many of those who persevered were Quakers.

Benjamin Huntsman, pioneer cutler of Sheffield, was born of a German family and apprenticed to a Doncaster clockmaker. His manual dexterity quickly singled him out as a man able to handle rudimentary machinery, but he realised that any improvement in such machinery would require a better form of steel. With this in mind, Huntsman moved to Sheffield in 1740. After endless experiments and failures he succeeded in producing the kind of steel which, despite initial resistance from local cutlers, played a significant role in the development of the town's trades. Yet even in such a highly technical field, the question of domestic consumption was never far away. These improvements in tempered steel, among other things, revolutionised cutlery production, which in turn changed the face of domestic British life. Strange as it may now seem, knives and forks became part of everyday household life only from the mid-eighteenth century onwards, gradually replacing the common habit of eating from a dish with a spoon and bread.[24] This was made possible by the work of Benjamin Huntsman, who felt unable to accept the offer of a Fellowship of the Royal Society. Despite his success, he retained a humility that sat comfortably with many of the early Quaker industrialists.[25]

Huntsman's career typifies that of many Quaker innovators *en route* to success. He had tackled the problems of metal production because as a clockmaker and locksmith he felt dissatisfied with the quality and limitations of existing metals. The Quaker tradition of self-improvement, rigorous apprenticeship and detailed record-keeping bred an intellectual and commercial curiosity which spilled over into related or even distant fields. Huntsman's craftsmanship edged him towards metallurgy. Cookworthy's chemistry and science led him to china clay and porcelain. Crosfield's youthful contact with chemicals and soap prompted a lifetime's attachment to developing that new industry. But in all these cases, and many besides, such men needed more than a Quaker upbringing to capitalise on any commercial potential. They required the broader network of a religious community that sustained and protected its members, and an acceptance by outsiders that they were a trustworthy people whose business ethics were unimpeachable.

Quaker entrepreneurs came from the most unlikely, remote and unpromising recesses of British life, but shared this common identity shaped by the Society of Friends. Their curiosity about the world at large extended to the work of the seventeenth- and eighteenth-century shopkeeper, which generally involved a great deal of business trial and error. Producing what customers required was not simply a matter of repackaging goods from the wholesaler. Shopkeepers devised their own products, breaking down and reassembling different sugars, combining and mixing various tobaccos, blending teas, roasting and mixing coffee beans, varying one blend then another until they discovered the right formula. Any advertisement, of tea for example, would stress their own distinctive mix as a form of commercial motif, and Quakers turned to tea and coffee retailing in large numbers.[26] This experimental approach characterised the early days of the chocolate magnates, and was in essence a rudimentary scientific system of testing, rejecting, adapting and proving to discover an elusive formula that might then yield anticipated riches.

Often, however, the end result of Quaker intellectual curiosity has been remembered only in scientific or technological rather than commercial history, as was the case with clock and watchmakers. George Graham, a Cumberland-born Quaker, is best remembered for his work at the Royal Observatory at Greenwich, which proved valuable for its major contribution to not only the development of modern time-keeping, but also the evolution of mechanisation itself. The training and skills of the watchmaker had much in common with those of the engineers of early industrial mechanisation. By the late seventeenth century a clutch of Quaker watchmakers in London had become the pre-eminent practitioners of their craft and were in great demand by the wealthy throughout western Europe. Daniel Quare was the watchmaker to British royalty (and his daughter married into the Bevan apothecary empire).[27] In tandem, small-town Quaker clocksmiths throughout England were plying their skills in the creation and repair of modern timepieces. Theirs was a skill of major importance and application, with major implications for the new technology developed for maritime navigation.[28]

It is often difficult to distinguish those men who were driven by intellectual curiosity rather than profit, but to suggest a divide between the amateur and the utilitarian professional is to misunderstand the nature of the natural sciences as they evolved in the seventeenth and eighteenth centuries.[29] Quaker scholars and scientists ranged from those who seemed merely to potter in their gardens, analysing flora and fauna, through to scientific botanists whose findings were important for medicine, pharmacy and even commerce. We have seen how Dr John Fothergill pursued a well-established Quaker interest in botanical/horticultural work; both George Fox and William Penn had promoted the concept of the garden as a practical forum for learning and instruction. Indeed, all the new medical organisations of the seventeenth century created gardens in which they could cultivate ingredients for medical purposes. This process was expanded by the growth of empire, the consequent establishment of botanical gardens worldwide, and the transfer of exotic species from the edges of colonial settlement to the gardens of Britain – Oxford from 1621 and Kew from 1759.[30]

Quakers were well placed to develop this interest in part because they denied themselves most other contemporary recreations. By

1. The Gracechurch Street Meeting, *c.* 1770: the Quaker leadership

2. Teaching Geography in an early Friends school, from a drawing by J. Walter West

3. Elizabeth Fry, the most famous prison reformer, reading at Newgate

4. The London Yearly Meeting, *c.* 1840, by Samuel Lucas.

5. The key to this painting shows an impressive gathering of leading Quakers including Jonathan Backhouse (14), Samuel Tuke (17), William Allen (18), Samuel Gurney (21), and Joseph John Gurney (23)

6. Joseph Rowntree, aged 42, 1878

7. Joseph Storrs Fry, *c.* 1905

8. Cadbury's Bournville model village

9. Rowntree's New Earswick model village, 1910

10. The girls' dining room at Cadbury, 1910

11. Mixed tennis: a rare exception to the company segregation rule at Rowntree

12. The Cocoa Works at Rowntree, Haxby Road, York, 1896

13. Advertising Rowntree's Elect cocoa on a Thames barge at the turn of the century

14. The Anti-Slavery Society Convention of 1840 by B.R.Haydon. Quakers dominated the movement throughout. Thomas Clarkson addresses the meeting and William Allen is seated bottom left

15. Cyrus Clark (1801–66) and

16. James Clark (1811–1906), founders of the Quaker shoe industry in Street, Somerset

17. The Friends' Meeting House in Street, 1717–1849, from a watercolour by Aubrey Clark, son of Cyrus

18. Allen and Hanburys' Bethnal Green factory in 1873

19. The Huntley and Palmers biscuit factory in Reading, 1851

20. The entrance to the factory in 1867

21. A Palmer family party, 1870

22. Quaker ironworks: The Upper Works at Coalbrookdale, an early view by François Vivares, 1758

23. Coalbrookdale in the 1840s by W.W. Law

24. The Iron Bridge, 1780, ink and watercolour by Michelangelo Rooker

the end of the seventeenth century they had come to accept the pleasure of floral decoration and had produced 'a quite disproportionate number of botanists, plant collectors and nurserymen'.[31] Though they disliked the use of colour in their dress and their homes, they were at ease with the natural beauty of a cultivated garden. Some Quaker botanists then made the natural progression to the development of a more serious interest as their business lives gave them access to samples, cuttings, seeds and bulbs from overseas. Peter Collinson of London used his family's trading connections to collect items from America, his enthusiasm having been prompted by correspondence with botanist Friends there and by a spate of publications on the subject in the early eighteenth century. Collinson was also in touch with scientifically minded men in Europe, passing on ideas, papers and information back and forth (a role he furthered through his membership of the Royal Society). He became especially friendly with Benjamin Franklin and Dr John Fothergill. From such networks there emerged a culture of scientific enquiry through an international pooling of information and experimentation, much of it taking place in Collinson's garden, which was transferred to Mill Hill in 1749, later to become part of Mill Hill School.

As we have seen in the case of Thomas Corbyn, the London apothecary and merchant, Quaker doctors were keen to learn about the latest botanical findings, although there was no strict divide between the two scientific worlds. Indeed, a number are remembered for their work in both fields. William Logan, a Bristol physician, drew heavily on his correspondence with his more famous botanist brother James in Pennsylvania. Dr John Fothergill was both doctor and botanist, who sought to transfer plants and trees to new regions of the world in the hope that they might take root locally and become commercially viable. So began the process which underpinned British commercial well-being in the seventeenth and eighteenth centuries, most spectacularly with the case of sugar cane into the West Indies, and in the nineteenth century the development of the tea industry in India.

What did they have in common, this array of industrialists, scientists and shopkeepers, save their membership of the Society of Friends? Their culture nurtured the belief that they could rely only on each other, and behind this self-reliance lay a deep-seated curiosity secured by communal strength and trust. It formed a nexus of personal and social circumstances which reached back to the early days of persecution and social upheaval. These sectarian qualities were to germinate, in more tolerant years, into a flourishing enterprise culture which branched into a host of directions. From ironmakers to doctors, or soap manufacturers to botanists, all traced their success as much to their Quaker origins as to their spark of individual genius or enterprise. But many were beginning to realise that this growing prosperity, which had depended upon networks rooted in mutual trust and secured by the Society of Friends, was not necessarily an end in itself.

PART III

The Consequences of Capitalism

8

The Quaker Conscience

The Quaker conscience emerged from a faith tempered by painful experiences of the seventeenth century; thereafter the word 'sufferings' entered the Society's vernacular. It was not surprising, therefore, that Quakers developed a powerful sympathy for those in similar circumstances and directed much of their public efforts towards the relief of persecuted peoples. From their early days they had been as concerned about the welfare of oppressed Friends as they had been about the spread of their faith, and from the late 1650s undertook to record and document such sufferings throughout the country.[1] Even when the worst phase of persecution had passed, Quakers continued to encounter discrimination until well into the early nineteenth century. Understandably they never lost the sense of isolation and vulnerability which shaped Quaker introspection; Friends turned to each other for spiritual and practical help as a defence against a hostile outside world.

The Quaker instinct for change, inspired initially by their own condition, was naturally attracted by parallel demands for reform, and by the late eighteenth century they had begun to play prominent roles in a number of campaigns. They brought to their chosen causes what Joseph John Gurney called a 'clearness of conduct'.[2]

The objects of their efforts ranged widely from prison reform to slavery, but any Quaker involvement was inevitably marked by a systematic organisation and an attentive eye to detail, propaganda and influence: they were businesslike. Indeed, the word 'business' was used repeatedly by these reformers in their various campaigns, most notably against slavery.[3] Yet their influence can be only partially explained by this methodical approach. In matters of conscience and morality, Quakers came to be respected for their plain-speaking and truth-telling, which was fired by their antagonism to inhumanity and institutional cruelty, whatever its form. And there was plenty to catch the Quaker eye.

The Society of Friends was committed to a belief in the sacredness of human life and an acceptance of the worth of all, irrespective of gender or colour. Quakers were alert to injustice in its many forms, few of which had failed to attract the attention of George Fox and fire his anger. His targets ranged from the obvious (excesses of the ale house and popular culture) through to the less noticeable (unfair trading, the inadequacies of teaching, shortcomings in family life), and he assailed practices (the exploitation of working people) which scarcely raised an eyebrow elsewhere. He was on more popular ground in denouncing the iniquities of the legal system, for few social issues seemed more in need of Quakers than the horrors of imprisonment.[4] Fox complained long and hard to Parliament and others, and demanded an end to the more outrageous penal punishments, including flogging, transportation and public execution. He also called for a more humane treatment of the less fortunate, demanding public housing for the disabled, widows and orphans, and beggars, proposing that the expense be borne by using the proceeds from fines and tithes, and converting public buildings, churches and even Whitehall into almhouses. Fox's ideas were not designed to endear him to the wealthy, but none the less provided a framework for the developing Quaker conscience.[5]

So severe had been the early persecutions that Quakers had become preoccupied with looking after their own ranks, yet their social compassion extended beyond the most conspicuously deprived groups. Workers also deserved decent treatment and Quaker employers were urged to pay fairly and promptly, and to provide adequate working conditions. The terms of apprenticeships received particular attention, understandably perhaps, since this was a traditional route in the education of their young men. Quakers were also directed to 'Lay no more upon your servants ye would be willing should be laid upon you, if ye were in their place and conditions'. Even shipping merchants and captains were asked to care for their crew – and their passengers.[6]

The issue of poverty, which pervaded seventeenth-century England, was tackled by Quaker philanthropists through proposed retraining schemes. The ideal Quaker devoted time and money to the subject, but the main aim was to promote self-help: to empower people to overcome their own problems. Quakers insisted on this even among prisoners. After all, they themselves had kept busy in jail, and Friends assumed that the time-wasting of idle hands was one of prison's most destructive outcomes. Most of their outlines for social reform centred on the provision of useful work; the old, the infirm, the unemployed and imprisoned were all assigned appropriate tasks where possible.[7] A number of local initiatives created workhouses where charity went hand in hand with self-improvement. Such ideas were ahead of their time, however, and did not resurface until the early nineteenth-century drive to cope with the new and varied problems of urban and industrial poverty.

Throughout the developing Quaker conscience ran a persistent refrain of humane compassion. In the words of John Bellers in 1695, 'It is not he that dwells nearest that is only our neighbour, but he that wants our help also claims that name and our love.'[8] It was broadly based and had no real boundaries, but addressed itself to myriad issues – many parochial; others (such as slavery) of global significance. The protection that Quakers sought for themselves extended to other persecuted minorities.[9] But the monitoring of this conscience by the Society of Friends inevitably led to friction between principles and practical self-interest. The strict code of individual discipline demanded close scrutiny of Quaker conduct, and questions were asked of Friends whose interests or behaviour seemed to offend on such matters. This was especially troublesome for those whose business dealings touched on moral issues of slavery and warfare, for example. Successful Friends needed to tread a delicate line as instructions concerning any transgression were quick to follow from the local meeting or its officers. We have seen how this operated in business matters, but such pressures from within the community could be applied to a wide range of issues. The Quaker conscience embodied the Society's ideals; they were not a private concern or a matter of individual choice.

Throughout the first century of the Society's existence, Quakers wrote about, spoke and agitated for the oppressed and defenceless. Though their best-remembered reforming zeal belongs to the late eighteenth and early nineteenth centuries, its ethical roots reach back to the formative days. Few were more obviously downtrodden, more despised and rejected, than the slaves shipped into the Americas. Quakers were among the first to be alerted to the problems of slavery and to the moral dilemmas of involvement with economies which flourished on the back of it. In the rush to convert the West Indian islands to fruitful production, a small number of seventeenth-century Britons complained about the horrors visited on the imported Africans. Morgan Godwyn was one, arguing in 1680 that '*Negro's* are Men, and therefore are invested with the *same Right* . . . that being thus qualified and invested to deprive them of this *Right* is the *highest injustice*'.[10] George Fox was equally distressed by what he saw on his travels to the Caribbean and America. That equality of humankind, fundamental to Quaker philosophy, was offended by the relegation of the slave to the level of beast of burden: bought, transported, inherited and consigned to a lifetime's bondage. In Barbados in 1671, Fox was keen to see slaves converted and trained up 'in the fear of God'; Friends there preached to them, to the consternation of local slave-owners, though were at pains to tell them 'to be subject to their masters and governors'.[11]

Early strictures against slavery did not always prevent Quaker dabbling. Some Friends in the New World found it hard to distance themselves from the source of such ready material prosperity; others, however, were eventually persuaded of the errors of their ways. One such was Dr John Lettsom, born into a slave-owning family on Tortola in 1744, who freed his slaves on return from his education and medical training in England in 1767.[12] The profits which flowed from slavery never swayed the Society of Friends, and at regular intervals throughout the eighteenth century objections to it were recorded. In 1727, for example, it was resolved that Quaker involvement 'is not a commendable nor allowed practice, and is therefore censured by this meeting'. But dealings with slavery could be indirect or even hidden. Indeed, so pervasive were its benefits that it must have seemed impossible to avoid. Who could resist adding sugar to their tea or coffee? None the less, Quaker businessmen were urged to 'be careful to avoid being in any way concerned in reaping the unrighteous profit arising from the iniquitous practice of dealing in negro, or other slaves'.[13] The London Yearly Meeting had to repeat the warning in 1758 that they should not participate in a trade which was so 'evidently destructive of the natural rights of mankind'.[14]

Quakers, then, were pioneers and pacemakers in the national drive against the slave trade which culminated in its abolition in 1807. They were the first to petition Parliament against it, they regularly preached and published on the subject, and when the Abolition Society was established in 1787, nine of the twelve founding members were Quakers.[15] Friends throughout the country formed a national network of contacts and sympathisers who were able and keen to advance the cause in their region, and these links extended to North America, where abolitionist Quakers, especially in Pennsylvania, were readily recruited.[16] After 1787 the campaign drew its strength across urban Britain, often with Quakers providing the initial energy even in towns such as Liverpool and Bristol, where slave trading seemed vital to the local economy.[17] Again, what gave their drive its hard edge was insistence that the organisation be conducted on business lines: methodically, systematically, with a careful recording of their transactions and finances.[18] Thus did the ethos of the counting house enter the world of reforming politics.

Anti-slavery was the most spectacular and the most successful of all Quaker political campaigns, though their success ultimately lay in popularising abolition through petitions, tracts and public meetings. In this and other matters of reforming conscience, Quakers were carried along by the rising tide of evangelicalism. Born within the Anglican church, it was most forcefully expressed by the first leaders of the Methodist movement and sought to shake up contemporary religious apathy. Even though it was socially conservative, it released a progressive energy which gave birth to a host of philanthropic initiatives from the mid-eighteenth century onwards. The face of urban British society was disfigured by a range of man-made social problems – poverty, ill health or child labour, for example – all of which attracted such attention, but evangelicalism was also a movement which disturbed existing churches and sects. The Society of Friends found itself shaken most notably by the challenge it posed to the Quaker quietist tradition. All this was taking place at a time when a small band of eminent Quakers, including the Gurneys, were drifting away from the Society, borne along by the complications of their wealth and the seductions of other faiths. The whole process was compounded by a group of American evangelical Quakers preaching mainly in London in the early nineteenth century.

These complex forces transformed the very nature of the Quaker conscience. Their philanthropy became more open – more aggressive, even – and Friends were more willing to work with others outside the Society if necessary, but what brought success was a combination of prosperity and networking. The Society of Friends comprised an organisation of literate, highly educated people with access to the printed word, able to publish as they wished, and who in the exercise of their faith were accustomed to public meetings, speaking and organisation. This structure, the very fabric of Quaker life, was ideally suited to political campaigning.

William Allen, one of London's most prominent Quakers, was a scientist and pharmacist whose company, Allen and Hanburys, was famous for its high-grade products. 'I never profess to sell cheap but trust the quality of the articles will recommend them to those who are judges in our business.'[19] Fiercely insistent on prompt and fair dealings, Allen was the model Quaker businessman, but much of his energy and commitment was devoted 'to promote the comfort and happiness of our species'.[20] When the British slave trade was abolished in 1807, Allen turned to the African Institution which was founded to establish new trading links and replace the commercial ties of slavery. He was also committed to educational reform (supporting Joseph Lancaster's scheme to educate poor children) and published *The Philanthropist* from 1811 to 1817. For more than twenty years Allen also held a financial interest in Robert Owen's co-operative venture in the mills at New Lanark, despite sharp differences with Owen himself. Here was a Quaker whose reforming energies led him to a great variety of philanthropic interests, from the major international issue of the slave trade and Africa to small-scale parochial efforts, such as poor relief in Spitalfields. But his conscience was an extremely public one and often controversial, all of which was made possible by his status and wealth. It was far removed from Quaker quietist origins.

This engagement with contentious public issues was in part a consequence of the new wider sensibility about social and human suffering, prison reform being a good case in point. Quakers had long concerned themselves with the subject, but when in 1812 some Quaker friends of William Allen visited Newgate Prison, they were appalled by what they saw, particularly in the women's section, and took the matter to Elizabeth Fry. Born into the wealthy Gurney family, Elizabeth had been reared in a cultured world, but her life was changed in 1798 by the visit to Norwich of the American evangelical Quaker William Savery. His words sparked her transformation from fashionable young woman into plain Quaker. Unhappy with the frivolity and emptiness of her life in the propertied class, she began to direct her attentions to the deprived and needy. It was a process of self-discovery which continued after her marriage in 1800 to Joseph Fry, the London tea merchant, with whom she had eleven children. Despite family preoccupations, and the succession of Quakers who descended on their home, especially for the London Yearly Meeting from May to June each year, Elizabeth adopted an increasing number of causes: the poor, schools for them, visiting the sick, health care. But in 1812 the sights of Newgate made her a prison reformer.

When Elizabeth was finally able to devote time to the cause in 1816 (during the previous four years she had given birth to her ninth and tenth children, while her seventh had died), she set about transforming the female wing. A school was established for the children; the women were given simple instruction in sewing and knitting. Quaker merchants provided the materials and the proceeds from the sale of finished items went to the inmates. All prisoners were divided into groups, each monitored by a matron, and were instructed about cleanliness. Decisions were taken by a vote and there were healthy doses of bible reading. Elizabeth had become a respected preacher and public speaker, and her words and posture were more than enough to calm the unruly women: 'A way has been opened for us beyond all expectations to bring the poor prisoners into order; already, from being wild beasts, they appear harmless and kind.'[21]

Fry's work made her famous. In 1831 she was summoned to give evidence before Parliament, where she took the opportunity to lay out her plans for penal reform. Her case was made more convincing by the fact that her own experiments had worked, though part of their success stemmed from her own formidable presence. She quelled the usual disturbances among women on the eve of transportation (she visited 106 convict ships leaving for Australia between 1818 and 1843), she calmed the condemned on the eve of execution, but perhaps most importantly her ideas were effective and influential. The organisation of prisoners into small supervised groups undertaking useful employment proved that something positive could be achieved where others had merely looked despairingly at a 'criminal class'. But she paid a price. The problems she encountered were partly responsible for her nervous collapse in 1819. She eventually recovered and renewed her work, but her husband's business failure and bankruptcy in 1828 led to his inevitable disownment from the Society of Friends. It was a personal and family humiliation which caused Elizabeth great pain, though she and her husband were comforted by the kindness and support of individual Quakers. But her work continued. Her prison reform was promoted by 'Ladies' Committees' throughout Britain and even in America; later, she turned her attention to hospitals. Towards the end of her life, Elizabeth Fry had become perhaps the country's most famous Quaker, her advice and correspondence sought by, among others, the King of Prussia and politicians from around the world. She has always been associated with her prison work, yet her importance transcends the details of that and her other social concerns. She proved instrumental in helping to change the very nature of Quakerism in shifting it from quietism into engaged public campaigning that challenged contemporary social ills.

The need for prison reform continued long after the death of Elizabeth Fry in 1845, but her work had put the issue firmly on the political agenda. What had begun as one woman's determination to help the unfortunate was transformed into a significant international organisation comprising committees, policies, public debate and activity, and all the apparatus of an effective pressure group. The backing of wealthy patrons had greatly helped, but it had begun to dawn that, in tackling social problems, private benevolence might not be enough. Personal philanthropy, individual effort or contributions seemed mere gestures when confronted by the unfolding problems of early nineteenth-century British life. Thus the Quaker conscience began to adapt itself, but so too did the Society of Friends. Many of the old habits of Quaker life were clearly no longer effective. They faced a number of problems, none more serious than the continuing decline in membership (down to around 16,000 in 1840). The severe style of plain Quakers was increasingly at odds with the changing world; the Society appeared to be both archaic and unchanging in an age which took pride in the rapidity and profundity of 'progress'. As Quaker numbers dwindled, realisation grew that the Society should become more responsive to the times of Queen Victoria and less influenced by those of Charles II.

The Society suffered a number of inevitable defections and splits in the process (though nothing compared to the divisions and breakaways experienced by American Quakers in the early nineteenth century), but the lobby for tradition seemed unassailable: secured by ties of family and friendship, reinforced by business links, and maintained by the education received in Quaker schools. Yet in the pages of new Quaker periodicals the arguments for change refused to go away, and was expressed most forcefully in 1859 by John Stephenson Rowntree in his book *Quakerism, Past and Present*. John established his name as a reforming Quaker just as his brother Joseph took over the small family grocery business in York.[22]

John Rowntree's analysis portrayed the Society as an unbending sect, tied to ideals and rituals of a long-lost era, and excluding the very people it had set out to help: the poor and the deprived. Over the years Quakers had found commercial, financial and educational success, and had driven out those who fell by the wayside. It had become commonly accepted that worldly achievements commanded the most respect.[23] Though the meek might inherit the earth, it was the materially successful who had come to dominate.[24] The book revealed that what underpinned the Society of Friends was the assumption that the Quaker way of life was a route to such success. It comprised in effect an élite of preselected personal and social qualities which, while replenishing itself from generation to generation, had proved itself incapable of maintaining popular support. A wide base to the Society would have undermined that success. Yet John Rowntree and others realised that the Friends needed to add to their numbers and to revitalise their collective tone if the Society was to be anything more than a minority group with a guaranteed but tiny following.

The most self-destructive Quaker convention was the exclusion of those who 'married out'. Between 1800 and 1855, almost 4,000 members (one-half of the total number who married) were lost to the Society in this way. Of 852 boys who passed through Ackworth School, 304 had married out. This haemorrhage of membership was potentially fatal to the Society.[25] It was moreover completely unnecessary, except as a reminder of an exclusionist philosophy which was itself inappropriate to the mid-nineteenth century. Only a group indifferent to its own decline could afford to ignore such evidence, yet the problem had been eclipsed by the presence of the business élite within the Society. It was reassuring to point to the famous and the prosperous in Quaker ranks, and to feel that the Society continued to be a force for good in their philanthropy.

Those anxious for change had begun to flex their muscles, notably in the provinces. The old Joseph Rowntree of York had been the moving force behind the relaxation of the marriage rule, which was agreed to in 1858, a few months before his death. There followed a liberalisation of the dress code, but such reforms failed to staunch the decline in membership. To make matters worse, many departures were voluntary, the social restrictions being at odds with the style of life that Victorian prosperity made possible. The growth of such industrial and commercial wealth, shared (indeed, created) by a number of prominent Quakers, generated a tension within the Society that was as old as Quakerism itself, but was accentuated by the widening gulf between its steadfast attachment to old habits and the ever more gaudy face of society at large. At their extreme, Quaker habits appeared risible: the refusal, for example, of one old magnate to accept the ease of a comfortable chair even in old age. Still less did it seem a virtue worth boasting about. Such a flinty interpretation of life held little attraction.

Not all fell into these polarised categories of the unbending versus the alienated. The Society is as well remembered for those prospering Friends who remained steadfast but who used their wealth to benefit others. It was a new breed of Quaker magnate and few were to do this with more lasting effect than the chocolate manufacturers. Such businessmen were notable for trying to bring about improvement in the workplace, though Quakers were not the only Victorians wishing to do so. Contemporary life abounded with stories of industrial and social experiments conducted by captains of industry of the most diverse kind. Some like Robert Owen were inspired by a secular radicalism; others like Sir Titus Salt came from severe nonconformist traditions, which they expected their grateful workers to follow.

These reformers had plenty of scope in which to implement their ideas. Of all the popular and durable images of nineteenth-century Britain, few are as stark as the pictures of working-class industrial life. For all their sense of caricature, such images contain an element of reality which no amount of counter-factual analysis can hide. These conditions, especially in the first half of the century, disturbed many; moreover, Victorians were less easily shocked than we might be today. Paraded before them (via surveys, pioneering journalists and commentators of all kinds) were distressing stories about the degradation and poverty of their fellow subjects in all parts of the country. The price of Britain's undoubted rise to industrial greatness was being paid by the working people. How to break the cycle of misery, how to use the power and rewards of industrial life for the betterment of most rather than a minority, became a perennial theme in social thought and action. It was an issue that concerned Christian and atheist, socialist and Conservative. What was to be done about the poverty of those in and out of work? What could be done to ameliorate working and living conditions? How could the Quaker conscience bring something distinctive and useful to the manifold problems facing industrialising Britain? And how could so small an organisation of dwindling numbers achieve anything worthwhile in a society whose population was expanding?

There was one group among them: the increasingly important

band of nascent industrial magnates, whose wealth and standing could help their workforces and dependent communities. And their fortunes might, if applied in the right directions, have an even wider application for social good. There was a new and increasingly powerful process of modernisation at work within the Society of Friends, and it flowed from the drive and resources of this new breed of self-made industrialist.

9

The Modernisers

The statistics in John Stephenson Rowntree's book *Quakerism, Past and Present* remain a starting point for all subsequent discussions about the decline in Quaker membership.[1] As we have seen, he estimated a sharp decrease between 1680 and 1800. Numbers continued to fall from 16,227 in 1840 to 13,859 in 1861. Thereafter, however, membership began to level out and then from 1871 to 1901 to increase by almost a quarter (although the overall population grew by 43 per cent).[2] Quakers were not alone in feeling perplexed about the changing nature of their following. Victorian Christians of all sectarian sorts saw shifting patterns of support which demanded explanation and prompted the Religious Census of 1851.[3]

The story of the Church of England forms the context for the progress of dissent itself. Ensnared by political and theological divisions, buffeted by the successive waves of evangelicalism from the late eighteenth century, it had struggled to maintain the loyalty of the English people. The three main dissenting groups of Baptists, Congregationalists and Methodists flourished but experienced similar internal frictions. The Quakers also felt the seismic wave of evangelicalism which in places tore apart the local meeting and dispatched the so-inclined into the arms of the Anglican church or other neighbourhood chapels. Yet these broader patterns of faith and religious disputation provide only one element in the story of nineteenth-century Quakerism. The fate of the Society of Friends was very much of its own making, and this central issue formed the basis of John Stephenson Rowntree's analysis.

We have seen how the policy of disownment ensured that a regular flow of Quakers left their ranks, taking their new spouses into the arms of other, more sympathetic churches. Between one-quarter and one-third of Quakers had been expelled in this fashion during the years 1800 to 1855. In the words of Rowntree, it was an 'act of suicide' unparalleled anywhere in church history.[4] Once the rule was relaxed in 1858, membership began to increase for the rest of the century. Rowntree's research and modern historians confirm that the Quakers had been the architects of their own downfall; that until 1860 their numbers had declined because of the strict application of this rule in a more flexible society which allowed ex-Quakers room for social and religious manoeuvre.

This offers an explanation as to what happened to Quakers between 1800 and 1860. Something like 700 emigrated while, in the same period, deaths outnumbered births, but the main loss was via expulsions and resignations to the tune of 2,400 Friends.[5] This was at a time when the level of recruitment of new members remained relatively low. By 1852 there were perhaps 9,000 Quakers who continued to attend meetings but who were denied full membership of the Society because of whom they had married.[6] Yet there were some instances where affairs took a different turn and where local meetings established a style of a more benign and tolerant nature. This was the case in York.

By the mid-nineteenth century, York was established as one of the nation's leading centres of Quaker activity. Its roots were not as old as, for example, the West Country's, and Bristol in particular, but the rise and dominance of a small coterie of powerful and wealthy families transformed the York meeting, just as their economic success was to transform the city itself. Esther Tuke had been appointed a minister in 1778 and set about revitalising the meeting. She preached in and around the city, and indeed across the country, enthusing large numbers of people (she spoke to 1,000 people in Berwick Town Hall in 1785) and creating a ministry which was continued by her daughter and stepdaughters. We have seen how these women played an active role in a range of local initiatives, including the opening of Trinity Lane School (later the Mount School) for girls and, with William Tuke, the establishment of the Retreat mental hospital in 1796.[7] However, such work was distrusted by those clinging to the old quietist traditions of the Society, who were suspicious of the application of intellect to religion: 'It is the frequent device of Satan to transplant the religion of the believer from the *heart* to the *head*.' Instead they remained attached to the writings of the early Friends; Barclay's *Apology*, in particular, was 'the sheet anchor of our principles'. This insistence that inner spirituality was the only way to find God, clashed with more earth-bound, socially responsive trends in the Society. Quietism opposed evangelicalism, disapproved of the increased wealth of some Friends, and insisted that all should live in isolation from the world and eschew the very missionary and philanthropic work that characterised much Quaker effort of the early nineteenth century.[8]

The religious, intellectual and social life of York's meeting was at variance with these tenets, which was made more apparent by the wealth issue. A flourishing attachment to intellectual interests, combined with the trappings of material prosperity, created a changed environment for an increasing number of York's Quakers. With the reorganisation of English local government in the early nineteenth century, for example, cities were incorporated and the repeal of the Corporation Act in 1828 removed the problem of oath-swearing. Quakers therefore found themselves eligible for local office. In York in 1830 a Catholic lord mayor performed duties alongside a Quaker sheriff. Thereafter Friends quickly swarmed through the committee and council meetings of the City of York, and by mid-century were fully integrated into local government. They formed a radical presence, but generally remained wary of a more formal attachment to party politics.[9] In retrospect, those Quakers who emerged to take their position alongside that city's most prominent citizens are perhaps best remembered for the way they used their new status to good social effect, but this meant, of course, an edging away from the more traditional quietist style. With each local or national campaign, these Friends inevitably became more integrated into a world from which they had once stood aside.

Early Quaker engagement with the wider world is typified by the anti-slavery movement. Indeed, as we have seen, the abolition movement beginning in 1787 was essentially Quaker in origin. Friends in York took up the cause, aided by the presence of William Wilberforce as a local MP, and were gradually drawn into open politics in supporting his candidature via the ballot box and financially. Quaker printer William Alexander produced local anti-slavery publications, and at a local level female abolitionists were often crucial in the organisation of anti-slavery activities: committee work, public meetings, petitioning and publications.[10]

By the 1820s and 1830s, therefore, Quakers had taken steps towards political activism, which, although facilitated by the toleration they now enjoyed, was made possible by their material prosperity. They advanced as part of the newly enfranchised middle class, and went on to create prospects and opportunities for other Friends. It is interesting to note that as Quakers in York thrived the nature of the local meeting changed from its eighteenth-century incarnation as a petit bourgeois gathering, closely involved with artisan trades and shopkeeping. As the nineteenth century progressed, to take two simple but telling examples, more York Quakers employed servants, and not a single one in the eighty years to 1860 was unable to sign a formal register – they were a highly literate group.[11]

The emergence of such a powerful upper-middle class transformed the meeting's style and doctrine, but what happened in York was unusual. In Bristol, where a powerful Quaker élite did not develop, the meeting was denied an injection of leadership and dynamism, and consequently declined. In York numbers increased, contrary to the trend in other parts of the country, even though some of the demographic problems troubling the Society as a whole were in evidence. There was a relatively low birth rate among Quakers at a time when Britain's population in general was expanding at an alarming rate. Quakers tended to live to a ripe old age, itself possibly due to the superior material conditions they enjoyed, but Quaker women in York tended to marry when they were older, in effect losing a number of their childbearing years. This pattern was also true for prospering middle-class women as a whole. But the York meeting admitted more converts than most (by contrast, in the thirty years to 1863, the Bristol meeting lost 256 members), and seemed reluctant to disown members (in Bristol 406 were disowned in the period 1780–1860, compared to York's 112). It admitted almost as many new Friends as it expelled existing ones.[12]

Quaker activities in York were creating new working opportunities for other Quakers: the Retreat hospital, the girls' school at Trinity Lane, a school for poor girls in the city, the Bootham School, and, most striking of all, Rowntree's shops and manufacturing. Moreover, affluent Quakers were able to employ others in various domestic roles in their homes. And all this was parallel to the benign climate that characterised the local meeting and enabled Quakerism to function in a more flexible fashion than was the case elsewhere. Of course, York had its own share of unreconstructed Friends, but the élite (though they would have denied the label) had steered the community towards a more modern way of conducting its affairs. It was no accident that the most persuasive analysis of their problems, Rowntree's *Quakerism, Past and Present*, had come from within their ranks, nor that the author belonged to the thriving confectionery family.

Prosperity did not lead to the departure of successful Friends from the York meeting, partly owing to the influence of Quaker matriarchs within powerful local families, with their attachment to philanthropy, education and public service, who ensured that new generations grew up dedicated to the traditions of local Quaker life. York became a very distinctive Quaker city comprising a network of institutions – a hospital, schools and businesses – centred on the local meeting house, and in their turn connected to the leading families. York itself continued to be dominated by small businesses, shops and domestic employment, remaining resistant to the massive industrial and urban changes transforming other parts of Yorkshire. But it proved an ideal environment for that small band of imaginative and energetic Friends who were keen to improve themselves, to help others in the Society and to bring benefits to the broader community. Though their strength lay in the extent of their commercial success, it was securely anchored by their influence over local religious affairs and their ability to edge the meeting into a more responsive mode. The combination of economic power and a sympathetic meeting proved a fertile breeding ground, yet what would have happened without the latter? Would the local magnates have been forced out or opted for another church? What unfolded in York was the continuing rise of Quaker business success, the consolidation and viability of their varied activities, and the evolution of a local meeting which, until mid-century at least, was accommodating to the needs and interests of the dominant families. The meeting had modernised itself just as the emergent magnates were modernising the economy of the city at large.

The experience of York Quakers was an object lesson for other regions. They had thrived owing to an atmosphere 'of harmony, leniency and tolerance' which stood in stark contrast to affairs elsewhere.[13] The unique latitude they had been given, especially in terms of public conduct, resulted in a flowering of Quaker activity. This, in turn, attracted other Quakers to the city – not all prosperous, of course. Many were humble working people, more in keeping with the Society's traditional roots.[14] York had signalled to the Society as a whole that the urge to humanitarianism and the determination to educate both Quakers and non-Quakers marked the emergence of the Friends as an important social force in nineteenth-century Britain. And the role of Quaker women was crucial, not only as the helpmates of their more publicly active menfolk, but also as political activists in their own right. In embarking on their public reforms, Friends in York inevitably drew closer to other political and church groups in the city without the loss of their own ethical standards. But the conundrum remains: would any or all of this have been possible without that wealth which came to characterise York Quakers?

As they became ever more prosperous, despite periodic downturns in the local economy, the associated social status aligned local Friends into closer dealings with other middle-class groups. They shared not only common economic interests, but a desire for a tranquil and stable environment, hence their involvement in a host of civic activities in which they had previously been marginal. In the years between the French upheavals of the 1790s and the mid-nineteenth century, local Quakers emerged from the exclusivity of their sectarian shell.

Victorian Quakers were in effect becoming increasingly like their fellow citizens: harder to distinguish at first glance or hearing and wanting to be treated as such, rather than as a separate group. Cartoonists continued to portray any hint of puritanism in general by dressing their Quaker caricatures in the severity of the old code, but many Friends had begun to move away from this (particularly younger offspring of the prosperous) long before it was formally proposed in Quaker circles. Promoted by the radical Joseph Sturge in 1857, changes to the dress code did not come about until 1860, when it became optional. It was a campaign which benefited greatly from Sturge's unimpeachable standing; he was a man who had prospered in the corn trade and who had toiled long and hard, both within the movement and as a reforming MP, for a range of social changes. His attack on the Society's self-defeating introspection and the refusal of many to come to grips with the problems of the changing world of mid-Victorian Britain helped to win the day (although he did not live to see the introduction of the dress reforms).[15] Sturge also railed against the penalty for 'marrying out'.

He believed that it was cruel and unjust to those who had done no wrong, and that it severely damaged the Society. The ensuing debate was fierce and protracted as never before.

The 1850s had proved a decade of deep divisions; passions ran high, not so much in disagreement about this or that issue, but about the very basis of Quaker belief. Each proposal for reform took the Society back to first principles, thus any debate about a specific subject often became a more fundamental one about the words and actions of the founding fathers, and the precise interpretation of scripture. To compound the worries of traditionalists, there was the concern that any change would move the Society ever closer 'to the World'. Assimilation corroded the principle that Quakers were an elect group set apart from others. If they were to be merely one among many denominations, what was their rationale? The proponents of change, however, stressed that each element of difference in dress, language and marriage habits had lost its justification. It took no leap of the imagination to see how the younger generation were unhappy with the conflict of growing up in a world where enhanced consumption allowed them an ever greater variety of material pleasures, in stark contrast to the plain colours of clothing and subdued leisure moments of their faith. For people who claimed to pay no attention to 'outward forms of religion', the insistence on plainness as a badge of Quaker devotion seemed contradictory and perverse.[16] Moreover it appeared beyond doubt, especially in the case of the marriage restrictions, that these conventions had long since become counter-productive. However ancient their justification, the old rules and styles were sapping the Society's vitality and eroding its numbers; persistence with them would lead to inevitable self-destruction. Without this challenge to Quaker 'peculiarity', and the liberalisation pushed through after the painful debates of the 1850s, the Society would have been doomed to a slow demise.

The changes introduced by 1860 placed the Society on a different path for the rest of the century. The decline in membership was arrested and eventually reversed, though the Society always remained small. Members were primarily middle class, often traders, and it was from this broad base, via manufacturing, that the great Quaker magnates emerged in the second half of the century. The structure of this membership was inverse to the general population, 70 per cent of which were working class. The largest single group in the Society was drawn from 'Class I' (the most prosperous), and these upper reaches exerted a disproportionate influence over the meetings, not only because of their greater wealth and education but also in that they had the time to attend to religious affairs more assiduously. Poorer Quakers were too busy scratching a living to be active. The meetings did have their share of humble Friends, but they rarely got in the way of the middle-class-orientated local and national organisation that became the Society's distinguishing feature.

Many commentators from within and without the Society remarked on its middle-class nature. Quakers were part of a growing section of the community whose prosperity and influence became a prominent feature of mid- and late-Victorian life. They were at once architects and beneficiaries of the trend, and like other such groups it was inevitable that Quakers would involve themselves in social and political affairs, whatever the Society of Friends formally decreed.

Even in the early nineteenth century Quakers had been known to flex their political muscles, especially in defence of their local interests. For all the formal disapproval, Quakers had from their early years pressed Parliament for improved treatment, normally via petitions demanding the liberties and rights of other citizens. They also tried to persuade prominent statesmen and politicians using direct interview, and this 'taking tea' with the great and the good came close to being in awe of them. It was said of Elizabeth Fry, who had entertained the King of Prussia over lunch, that 'Her weakness was that of her generation, the idolatry of rank, wealth and title'. In a similar vein Cobden remarked in relation to Sturge, whom he greatly admired, 'The only fault I find with our "Friends" is their inveterate propensity to run after Emperors and

Kings.'[17] Yet such assignations with the famous attest as much to the Quakers' ability to secure such audiences as they do to their political tactics.

We have seen how, from the 1830s, provincial Quakers began to occupy positions of local power in alliance with other middle-class groups to effect political change. From such positions Quakers were able to embark on new national radical politics in pursuit of their own interests and on behalf of those social reforms dear to their heart. This progression provided the route for Joseph Pease, who became the first Quaker MP in 1833 (a number of ex-Quakers had already been elected).[18]

Quaker feathers were more thoroughly ruffled by the radical activities of Joseph Sturge and John Bright. The subjects of Sturge's work, initially black emancipation and then amelioration of the condition of the former West Indian slaves, tended to negate any worries about the vigour of his politics. How could anyone be concerned about so worthy and just a cause, particularly one which had been Quaker in origin and inspiration? But Sturge's associations with the Chartists in the 1840s provoked great discomfort, as did the activities of John Bright in the Anti-Corn Law League. At the controversial edge of contemporary politics, these issues were at once divisive and to many dangerously subversive. Both men were severely criticised at various meetings. The fact that many agreed with the principles involved was not the central issue, for these high-profile Quakers were running the risk of dragging the Society into fierce and potentially damaging public argument.

Piecemeal and often reluctantly, Quakers found themselves involved in formal politics. The education debate – for example, should the Anglican church have a dominant role in the development of British schools? – inevitably raised Quaker hackles. But by the mid-nineteenth century they had long since lost that political naïvety which had once hampered their affairs. Their sympathies tended to be Whig (later Liberal) like other members of their class; for much of the century Quaker Tories were political eccentrics. Parliamentary Quakers tended to be more interested in philanthropic reforming matters, their worthy, high-minded speeches were famous for rapidly emptying the House. But they were also notable for their wealth – hardly surprising, perhaps, given the necessary costs and qualifications for any Member of Parliament. (The only Quaker MP of modest means was Joshua Rowntree, a Scarborough lawyer.)[19] Like the Quaker élite in general, these MPs were often interrelated by marriage.

It would be wrong, however, to consider this nineteenth-century drift into formal politics solely or even generally in terms of Parliament. Quakers were most effective in their own bailiwick: they held important positions, influenced local committees and organisations, took part in municipal affairs, and promoted those philanthropic causes which we tend to regard as national issues. This was all made easier and more effective by the economic power of local leading Friends.

Quakers are perhaps better remembered for their philanthropy rather than politics. As we have seen, this humanitarism reached back to the early days and was sustained by a unique culture of egalitarianism which informed the Society throughout. As in matters of commerce and business, Quakers came to play a role out of all proportion to their numbers, and contemporaries were in no doubt that the Friends were crucial to the dynamism and success of a great deal of Victorian philanthropy. Once again this image rests on the shoulders of the wealthy, who gave huge amounts of money to their favourite causes, and established ventures of lasting fame and influence (some, including the various Rowntree Trusts, surviving to the present day). But it was a deeply ingrained principle involving men and women of all sorts, most of whom worked anonymously for their chosen cause. Though we might readily call to mind famous Quaker charitable foundations, it is less easy regarding the armies of women, for example, who toiled away, often in miserable conditions, to bring relief, improvement and education to the less fortunate. Once again, this work was not unique to Quakerism (philanthropy became an emblem of the Victorian middle class), but the Friends involved do stand out.

Despite their reputation, Quakers were by no means united over the issue. Those who clung to the quietist tradition tended to resist the idea of public engagement with social issues, with all the attention it would attract. Prosperous Friends, however, could hardly turn their back on the needy, not least because, as their wealth became more conspicuous, they were besieged by humbler folks seeking relief. But philanthropy offered them more than the chance to do good works, as 'the generous use of wealth justified them in the possession of it'. More than that, as their charitable ventures themselves prospered (some had massive endowments and large numbers of staff) they became vested interests in their own right, which could distract Quakers from the very problems they intended to address. To outsiders, many Quaker philanthropists seemed to fall victim to the vice of those in general: love of fame and praise.[20] For every Friend who protected the secrecy of their benefactions, there were others happy to accept plaudits for their work. But affluent Friends found it difficult to resist the charitable demands made upon them. Prominent families inculcated in their young a sense of obligation, that their good fortune placed a duty on their shoulders. Standing in the community was assured among other Friends not so much by a Quaker's wealth but by what he did with it. From one dynasty to another – the Gurneys in Norwich, the Rowntrees in York, the Cadburys in Birmingham, the Frys in Bristol – eminent family members discharged that duty.

The Quaker political presence was most influential in the campaigns for slave emancipation. Though slavery in the British West Indies ended in 1838, it continued to thrive in the USA until 1865, and in Brazil and Cuba until the late 1880s (not to mention indigenous slavery in Africa, India and Asia), and Quakers continued to lend their considerable prestige and money to the crusade against it. The Anti-Slavery Society, founded by Sturge in 1839 and still in existence, involved itself in a host of campaigns in Britain and abroad. From the outset the Quakers ran into shoals of political problems: the issue of equality seemed straightforward enough, but its repercussions were far from simple.[21] The first campaign to end West Indian slavery ran the risk of seriously damaging a range of British commercial interests, including shipping, banking, insurance, manufacturing and British ports, quite apart from the planters' own concerns. Similarly after emancipation, when demand grew for the removal of the sugar duties which kept prices artificially high in Britain, campaigning Quakers were forced to accept that to allow a cheaper product into the home market was to give a fillip to those countries continuing to use slave labour in the cane fields. Quaker free-traders thus found themselves opposing such a change which would have benefited Brazilian slave-produced sugar. The free market was rarely a morally neutral one.

Economic self-interest versus ethical and theological outrage swirled around the subject of slavery throughout the nineteenth century, drawing Quakers into a complex, highly publicised and bitterly divisive political debate which many of them disliked and resisted. Moreover, their public posturings exposed them to accusations of double standards: why feel aggrieved about the conditions of distant slaves when ignoring the sufferings of the most blighted of British workers?[22] This accusation of 'telescopic philanthropy' was levelled many times against those who waxed indignant at foreign problems while remaining apparently unmoved by domestic concerns. Sugar duties were eventually removed in 1846 as part of the broader drive for free trade, but the bitterness surrounding the argument survived, pitching Quakers against each other for years to come. In the short term, slave-grown produce continued to arrive in Britain and left protesting Friends with the only option of boycotting its purchase.

There were other features of the anti-slavery movement which disturbed Quakers. The Royal Navy was used to patrol shipping lanes in the Atlantic and Indian Oceans to stop slave ships, using force, or the threat of it, to impose British policy. But how could Quakers sanction the use of military power even for abolition? Once again they were drawn into a highly contentious debate inside and outside Parliament, their quietist instincts inevitably relegated in the drive against slavery. As with other issues, it proved impossible to pursue their traditional humanitarian concerns without engaging in the messy world of public politics.

The broader issue of free trade also involved the Anti-Corn Law League. This campaign was committed to ending the duties on corn, thereby lowering the price of food, and naturally attracted a number of prominent Quakers. Their support was grounded in sound economics allied to the attractive claim that cheaper food was socially desirable for the nation's poor. The sentiment was couched in terms which held traditional appeal for Quakers: the Corn Laws were part of 'Old Corruption' – the Church, the landed classes and the Establishment. Here was a reform movement through which Quakers, particularly manufacturers, could promote economic self-interest in alliance with the social good, not for the first or last time. Cheap bread for the common people went hand in hand with expanding markets at home and overseas.

The pillars of the Anti-Corn Law League comprised the Quaker manufacturers of the North, while Quaker money from various sources greatly helped its campaigns. Yet again, those same men were often reluctant to contemplate parallel demands for improvement in factory conditions. Their time, effort and money were diverted to other good causes which (not coincidentally) benefited their economic interests. Quaker insistence on freedom naturally involved their right to secure these interests untrammelled by the intervention of outside agencies. They believed they were in the best position to regulate and care for their own workers; self-interest could be to the greater good of their employees and the nation at large.

The older tradition of prison and penal reform launched by Elizabeth Fry continued to attract a small band of Friends but rarely received the sums lavished by Quaker magnates on other social campaigns. Quaker women were drawn to the late-century campaigns against prostitution, especially the Contagious Diseases Acts of 1864 and 1866–9 which authorised arbitrary medical checks on women suspected of being prostitutes. More strident and more predictable was the Friends' involvement in the temperance movement from the 1830s, despite a long tradition in the brewing industry, in the belief that drink was the root cause of other social problems. Quaker money and support enabled the movement to flourish in the teeth of well-heeled commercial opposition. Temperance steadily gained ground throughout the Society of Friends, helped by its elevation into a moral campaign – the very stuff of traditional Quaker politics. However, life was made uncomfortable for that band of Quaker brewers whose business interests were gently but firmly criticised at various meetings. But as the century advanced, the sting of the temperance movement was removed not so much by their own success as by the general decline in levels of drunkenness. The demon drink had become less of a social ill by the end of the century.[23]

Throughout the nineteenth century social reformers sought to alleviate problems by raising the quality of British working-class life, but not solely in terms of material conditions. There was, for example, a widespread feeling among the propertied class that ignorance and lack of even the most basic education were crucial factors in the impoverishment of millions. There was also concern that an ignorant labour force posed a serious threat to domestic harmony. As the franchise was progressively extended in 1832, 1867 and 1884, it seemed more important to educate working people to render them fit for their role in a highly urbanised and increasingly democratic society. But this impulse is more complex than it appears at first glance.

The arguments had begun in the late eighteenth century, when it was thought that the provision of Sunday schools would deflect working-class demands during the years of the French Revolution. The founders of those early schools were keen to raise a new generation of Britons on a conservative and religious diet of simple truths and precepts, more likely to encourage obedience and loyalty than curiosity and dissent. Quakers were slow to respond to the challenge of the Sunday-school movement, partly because of their quietist traditions. While other sects used Sunday schools to recruit new members, Quakers remained hostile to such activity until the

1840s. Thereafter, their First Day School Association, under the guidance of Joseph Storrs Fry, flourished: 17 schools in 1847 had increased to 288 by the end of the century. The bulk of those establishments catered for adults, not children. There were, in fact, more pupils in those schools than Quakers in the Society of Friends.[24] As with previous forays into education, the backbone of this movement consisted of the voluntary efforts of Friends who forsook the comforts of home, enduring miserable conditions in cramped rooms to educate poorer fellow citizens. Of course, the schools' backers and teachers often took the opportunity to promote other Quaker issues, most notably temperance, though it was recognised that some principles, particularly pacifism, might prove counter-productive. Among the more prominent backers were the Quaker chocolate magnates, their reward being promotion of their products in the schools' official newspaper.

Self-interest alone does not explain Quaker support for the First Day Schools. There was a widespread and genuine horror at the ignorance and irreligion at the heart of urban Britain. The urge to improve the lot of the unfortunate permeated the efforts of the teachers in the movement, although other forces were at work: concern about the stability of such a society and that other disruptive voices might win over the urban poor. But among Quakers, example and duty played a part. The hierarchy, particularly the powerful magnates and employers, came to expect a social commitment among their colleagues. Younger Friends were urged to adopt these causes under the watchful eyes of their elders and employers. A worthy idea spread easily and rapidly throughout the Society, and few issues seemed to be so desirable as the First Day Schools. These institutions encouraged the effective spread of popular literacy before the coming of compulsory education, and even though they may seem only marginal to the story of Quakerism itself, it must be reiterated that they were important in the schooling of tens of thousands of Victorian adults.

Pacifism, perhaps the most memorable of modern Quaker ideals, also had its immediate intellectual and social roots in the course of the nineteenth-century movement. It evolved an ideology and rationale that proved remarkably durable, and was to find its most memorable expression during the major conflicts of the twentieth century. Originating in the post-Napoleonic years, it drew strength from the Friends' rejection of violence, which again went back to the early days of their own suffering. But Quaker pacifism flourished, like so much else in Victorian society, on the back of their other successful campaigns, and through the advocacy and wealth of a number of famous families and commercial dynasties. Once more, successful Friends were expected to contribute to the cause even if they did not participate wholeheartedly in the campaigns of the various peace movements.

As Victorian society evolved, so too did confidence in and the efficacy of social reform. In the earlier years of Victoria's reign it had been easier to feel confident that individual effort would relieve a chosen problem, but by the 1880s the first effective wave of modern social investigation had begun to reveal the true extent and depth of especially urban problems in Britain which had remained stubbornly immune to philanthropic attack throughout the century. This process of investigation was part of a well-tested tradition, reaching back to the fictional portrayals of Dickens, among others, and the mid-century journalism of Henry Mayhew. Each successive late-Victorian survey undermined the old certainty of Quaker philanthropy (and of most other philanthropists, for that matter) that charity provided the obvious answer. How to replace it with something more effective was a question which was to tax British social policy thereafter – indeed, right down to the present day. And in seeking answers to those problems, successful Friends were once again at the heart of the matter. And it comes as little surprise that much of their success was based on chocolate.

10

Chocolate

Of all the exotic commodities that Europeans encountered in the Americas, few seemed less appealing than the humble cocoa bean. The Aztecs had used it to produce a bitter drink with spices, vanilla and chillies – one of the luxurious habits of the court of Montezuma. It was also a means of exchange, tribute and taxation; a 'tolerable good slave' could be bought for 100 beans. At first the conquering Spaniards disliked the chocolate drink, but they and other Europeans were won over when it was mixed with cane sugar, itself transplanted from islands in the Atlantic into the Americas and cultivated by imported African slaves. This additive also made palatable two other popular European drinks of the late seventeenth century: tea and coffee.[1]

By the 1590s polite social rituals had emerged around chocolate drinking in New Spain, and it quickly found a niche in fashionable European circles. The resulting demand persuaded planters and their backers to develop production in other regions of the world, and cocoa was transplanted and cultivated in West Africa, the Philippines, Indonesia and throughout the West Indies.[2] Chocolate drinking, in common with other exotic importations, began as the luxury of the prosperous before becoming a widespread passion of the masses. It was helped to this mass popularity in England by the work of a small band of Quakers in the eighteenth and nineteenth centuries.

Chocolate may have first found favour in Spain and in Spanish colonies, but the eventual break-up of this New World empire enabled other Europeans to import it from their own colonies and to consume it at home. The Dutch shipped cocoa to Amsterdam from their Caribbean islands and Venezuela. After 1655, the English began to import it from the newly conquered island of Jamaica, but in the development of domestic taste, fashion and fad also played an important part. Chocolate would initially take hold in royal and courtly circles. From there the habit passed quickly to those propertied groups keen to confirm their economic status by copying their social superiors. In Amsterdam, merchants had been among the first to start drinking chocolate; similarly in London, it found a place in the coffee shops which sprang up in profusion in the City from the 1660s onwards and served the surrounding mercantile community. It seems to have been first advertised in London in 1657: 'in Bishopsgate, in Queen's Head Alley, at a Frenchman's house, is an excellent West India drink called Chocolate to be sold'.[3] Seven years later Samuel Pepys, always willing to sample the latest offerings, went 'To a Coffee-house, to drink jacolatte, very good'.[4] After 1660 cocoa was taxed, and dealers had to display emblems above their doors proclaiming their authority to sell it.

Like tea, coffee, sugar and tobacco, chocolate took its place in the apothecary's shop. There developed a lively scientific debate, in Spanish and later in English, about its supposed medical and scientific benefits. One proponent claimed that it had the 'wonderful faculty of quenching thirst, allaying hectic heats, of nourishing and fattening the body'.[5] Various Spanish authorities on medicine had earlier claimed that chocolate was good for the chest and the stomach, relieved catarrh, and it was alleged to be an aphrodisiac. The early manuals which described how to concoct and consume the drink referred to it initially as a medicine. Thomas Gage, an English Dominican who had lived in the Americas, claimed in

1648 that he had enjoyed perfect health having drunk four or five cups per day for twelve years, 'not knowing what either ague or fever was'. There seemed to be few complaints that it could not cure or alleviate. In the words of one author of the 1660s, chocolate 'helpeth Digestion, Consumption and Cough of the Lungs, Plague of the Guts and other Fluxes, the Green-Sickness, Jaundice, and all manner of Inflammations . . . It Cleanseth the Teth, and sweeteneth Breath, provokes Urine, cures Stone and Stargury, expells Poyson, and preserves from all infectious Diseases'.[6] Such exaggerated claims were periodically made by scientists, doctors and apothecaries for most of the new tropical produce throughout late-seventeenth-century Europe.

The growing taste in London for chocolate and other tropical staples could be satisfied because the British now controlled their own colony of Caribbean islands and were able to populate them with armies of African slaves. But the cocoa bean never became a major export crop from the British West Indies mainly because sugar rapidly came to dominate the economy, and planters found their money and efforts best invested in its production. Despite the enthusiasm, drinking chocolate at first failed to match the popularity of coffee or tea. In part this was because it was too awkward to concoct, mainly because of its large butter-milk fat content, and time-consuming (ideally prepared overnight). None the less, by the early years of the eighteenth century, fashionable shops sold 'chocolate mills' for whisking the crude product with other ingredients, and the drink had secured a small but fashionable niche in public places of entertainment, and in more prosperous private homes.

The technique of removing the butter milk was not devised until the early nineteenth century by C. J. Van Houten in Holland, and there quickly followed the manufacture of more easily made drinks and slabs of eating chocolate. But until then, compared to most other such staples, the volumes of imported cocoa were small. As late as 1837 it stood at a mere 5,000 tons, much of which was consumed by the Royal Navy, yet by 1914 that figure had grown to

50,000 tons. Quaker involvement in all this seems at first to have been accidental.

The story begins in Bristol, which played a significant role in England's Atlantic trade in the early eighteenth century and where ships returned from the Caribbean with cocoa destined for local consumption.[7] In 1753 the young Joseph Fry, having completed an apprenticeship to a local apothecary, set up as one himself. He was from a Wiltshire family of long-established Quaker stock and forged close commercial links with other local Friends. His business prospered, thanks to his 'affable and courteous manner and sound Christian principles'.[8] Quakers always assumed that the commercial success of Friends was due to their godliness, however there may have been different factors involved, not least the assistance of other Friends.

Like all contemporary apothecaries, Fry stocked cocoa as a medicine but its consumption for pleasure gradually increased. He had a formula for manufacturing tasty chocolate, though he was not alone in this and faced competition from the more popular chocolate of Walter Churchman, who had been active in the business in Bristol since 1721. A decade later, Churchman had patented a water-powered machine 'invented for the expeditious, fine, and clean making of Chocolate to greater perfection than any other method in use'. His company prospered, but in 1761 it was offered for sale 'blind', because Churchman's manufacturing system 'being a Secret cannot be exposed to view'.[9] Fry took the risk, bought the business and the patent, moved the whole concern to a new site in the town, and in 1795 introduced a Boulton and Watt steam engine to the process.[10]

Fry's business expanded, greatly assisted by its location. The raw chocolate was shipped straight into his home town; close by was the fashionable town of Bath where the routines of propertied leisure were punctuated by sessions of drink and conversation. Local consumption gave Fry the start he needed, but his market quickly expanded: within three years of buying Churchman's business he had agents selling his produce in fifty-three towns. His younger brother William moved to London to manage their metropolitan chocolate warehouse, and in 1777 Joseph moved into premises where the company remained for the next 150 years.[11] This chocolate-based prosperity enabled Fry to diversify his interests, but always with the help and partnership of other Quakers. As we have seen, he involved himself in china manufacture and soap production; he was also successful in the printing industry, devising a hugely popular typeface and forming a family publishing business for two of his sons.[12]

In 1795 the chocolate business was taken over by Fry's son, Joseph Storrs Fry, who further expanded and modernised the process. He used outside experts to advise on the best manufacturing systems and placed great reliance on advertisements to persuade the public that his product was of the highest quality. However, his finances were insecure, partly owing to expansion, partly to his other business deals, notably brewing in Bristol with a Quaker cousin. Fry needed capital and fortunately there were Friends to hand with access to it. In 1805 he took a partner, Henry Hunt, who invested £1,000, raising his commitment in 1814 to £6,800, equal with Fry. The two men appeared not to have got on, and after Hunt's departure in 1822, the business flourished. It imported ever more cocoa, and sales of chocolate rose steadily. Fry incorporated his three sons and by 1822 the company had become J. S. Fry & Sons, which remained its famous trademark thereafter.

The company was relatively static for the remainder of the 1820s and 1830s, however. Little investment was made and money seems to have been withdrawn possibly to launch various Fry children in marriages and businesses of their own. But from the mid-1830s, when the next generation of Frys took control, the company changed direction again. It began to advertise heavily in newspapers (this was the age of rising mass literacy, cheap print and the growing social importance of words and images), modernised its factories and expanded its outlets in London.

From the mid-nineteenth century, though chocolate was considered a luxury product, Fry and others were able to increase the

British demand for it: between 1841 and 1868 per capita consumption doubled. Fry's accounted for a substantial part of all the cocoa imported into Britain (30 per cent in the 1820s; about 23 per cent by mid-century), converting the raw material into an expanding range: in the 1820s it made eleven products; twenty years later, twenty-eight. Much of this consumption can be accounted for by the apparently simple shift from drinking chocolate to drinking cocoa, made possible by technical changes in the processing. Each new range was designed to overcome the problems of earlier brands but was also cleverly marketed to appeal to the foibles of Britain's changing tastes. These products were also promoted as healthy foodstuffs. The most expansive market was at the cheaper end, within the reach of working people, and as the cost of chocolate products fell, sales to lower-income groups (whose real incomes were, in any case, increasing) rose steeply. In 1771, Fry's best chocolate sold for 7s 6d per pound; in the 1850s, its popular brand but not the cheapest sold for 11d per pound.[13]

Eating chocolates had been perfected in Europe, mainly in France and Switzerland, where the products and presentation were altogether more sophisticated and fanciful. In Britain, however, most 'sweets' were as their name suggests: boiled-sugar derivatives. They were manufactured by innumerable small-scale local firms, most of whom were infamous for their adulteration.[14] Fry's made its first venture into eating chocolate around 1850, producing simple sticks and drops before developing more complex products such as chocolate nuts, crystallised fruits and cream-centred chocolates. In this, the English followed the example of French and even adopted French names for their produce, effectively cashing in on their reputation for quality and presentation.[15]

Fry's sales figures rose from £102,747 in 1867 to £1,866,396 by 1914. Chocolates were but one type of many items of luxury consumption as an expanding population found itself with the cash to spend on more than life's essentials. Most of Fry's produce was sold in Britain, though a steady flow reached the overseas dominions. Europe and North America proved difficult to penetrate, not least because of their established chocolate industries. There was plenty of business at home, however, and Fry's greatly expanded its labour force from 193 employees in 1867 to 5,000 in 1914, all in a complexity of buildings on the increasingly cramped Bristol site. It took on the appearance of a mini-industrial city with ancillary buildings to service each and every aspect of chocolate manufacture.[16] Unlike many other food manufacturers, the claim of Quakers that their produce was pure and unadulterated was likely to be believed.[17] But Fry's was not alone in promoting the benefits and pleasures of chocolate. Curiously its two main chocolate rivals were also Quakers: Cadbury of Birmingham and Rowntree of York.

We have seen how York's Quakers had long played a major role in the social and cultural life of that city; the same prominent Quakers were involved in a host of local enterprises. The Rowntree chocolate company originated in the Tuke family, founders of the Ackworth and Trinity Lane Schools and the Retreat mental hospital. In 1725 Mary Tuke had established a shop in York, first in Walmgate and later in Castlegate. In 1746 she was joined by her 14-year-old nephew William Tuke as apprentice, who inherited the business on her death in 1754.[18] Tuke became close friends with another Quaker shopkeeper, Joseph Rowntree of Scarborough, who had established his business at the age of 21. The ties between the Rowntrees and Tukes were reinforced, as we might expect, by marriage as well as mutual business interests, but the Tuke children found their attentions drifting to London and banking, so they needed managers to run the York business. They took on a Rowntree son, Henry Isaac, who had served an apprenticeship at his father's shop in The Pavement, York. In July 1861 the Tukes announced to their customers 'that we have relinquished the manufacture of cocoa, chocolate and chicory in favour of your friend H. I. Rowntree . . . whose knowledge of the business in its several departments enables us with confidence to recommend him to the notice of our connexion.'[19] Rowntree's first task, however, was to reassure customers that his produce was of the highest quality. The Genuine Rock Chocolate introduced by his predecessors would continue 'in its integrity and purity'. Rowntree continued, 'My special attention will be directed to this branch of the business with a view to the introduction of such improvements in the manufacture as may present themselves.'[20] In fact his company was to go much further. It positively sought out the commercial and manufacturing secrets of others in order to steal a march on its rivals in the highly competitive chocolate market.

With one salesman, a dozen workers and annual sales of £3,000, in 1861 Rowntree was by any standards a modest concern, perhaps only one-twentieth the size of Fry's in Bristol. Rowntree used the pre-Van Houten manufacturing system but remained adamant about selling drinking chocolate of the highest quality. He stuck to his Quaker principles, refusing to take the short cuts of other food manufacturers, and in promoting his produce was resolutely opposed to making exaggerated or false claims. In 1862 he moved to new premises in an old city-centre foundry bought for £1,000.

However, Henry Isaac Rowntree's abiding interest was the Society of Friends and much of his creative energy was invested in their activities and not those of his company. By 1869 he was in financial trouble and agreed to bring in his brother Joseph as a partner. Educated at Bootham, Joseph had also served an apprenticeship at his father's shop, and his decision to join Henry was as much to head off the great Quaker shame of bankruptcy as to seize a business opportunity. It was a move which ultimately transformed the company, for Joseph was to revolutionise it by his bookkeeping skills and sales instincts. He was 'serious-minded, attentive and meticulous', qualities which yielded quick results. Lines were increased and expanded, and Rowntree was keen to respond to customer demand. But initially at least, Joseph remained unsympathetic to advertising, preferring to write directly to customers with information about new products.

Business however remained uncertain throughout the 1870s, but when Joseph set out to London in March 1872, ostensibly 'in search of workmen', he embarked on a development which fell some way short of the elevated ideals of Quaker business conduct, though it was ultimately to the company's benefit. He placed an advertisement in London newspapers.

> To cocoa and chocolate makers.
> Wanted immediately,
> A FOREMAN who
> thoroughly understands the manufacture
> of Rock and other Cocoas, confection
> and other chocolates.
> Also several WORKMEN used to the trade.
> Good hands will be liberally dealt with.

Setting himself up at a central London address, Rowntree began to interview, or rather interrogate, the applicants. He wrote down meticulously detailed notes of what they said about themselves, their colleagues, their work experience, the processes, machinery, costings, packaging and the workplace. He also paid them for the production recipes they handed over from their current employers. It is an extraordinary story of recruitment-cum-industrial espionage.[21]

Rowntree's first and major catch was James French, an experienced foreman from the Taylor Brothers' chocolate factory in London. Hired on a three-month trial period at 20s per week, French also received a 'present' of £5 'for his receipts'. Robert Pearce, a friend and workmate of French, was also hired for £2 per week, 'he imparting all his knowledge'. Another of the Taylors' workmen, William Garrett, was important in that he had 'the receipt of Unsworth's Cream Cocoa', and he provided names of other skilled men. Rowntree gradually pieced together a complete picture of how the Taylor Brothers manufactured their chocolates: who serviced and repaired the machinery, who roasted the beans, which ingredients were used, the times taken and the alternatives tried. Henry Thompson, a man with twelve years' experience in chocolate manufacture, had served under a man with thirty-five years' experience. Thompson was offered 30s per week and given 'a lump sum of £10 for all his receipts and knowledge'. Later Rowntree decided not to hire him for reasons that are unclear.[22]

Unbeknown to the Taylors, their company proved a rich recruiting ground. In April 1872 Joseph Rowntree went back to London to interview other men who had been recommended by French, concentrating this time on the machinery of production and the specifications required by their various customers. This information was received in tandem with an engineering report by Thomas Neal, comparing York's practices with the processes he had seen at other chocolate manufacturers.[23] By the early summer of 1872 Rowntree had a reasonably accurate picture of the costs, finances and profits of the Taylor Brothers' factory.[24]

Joseph Rowntree began to look further afield for similar help. He travelled to Birmingham, Bristol and London again, and was especially keen to talk to French workers who had been employed by Cadbury. From Paris he acquired detailed information about the machines used in local chocolate production. In London that September, Joseph Rowntree was once more actively picking the brains of experienced chocolate men. He also began to pay attention to the public details available about his British and European competitors, collecting their printed price lists and other ephemera, including packaging and flyers.[25] French, German and Dutch companies were far in advance of their British colleagues, and in the mid-1870s Rowntree began to take more interest in their activities, visiting their factories, recording what he saw in very great detail, and collecting their packaging and advertisements.[26]

Rowntree's most rewarding technique seems to have been the morally dubious approaches he made to employees from other companies. He talked to Cadbury's workers in Birmingham and was by now making regular visits to London to buy trade secrets. He always paid, but the sums ('I gave him £3 for his recipes', no doubt attractive to working men) were small for such valuable information.[27] In this way he had managed to gain access to Fry's recipes, and the processes used in the Taylors' London factory continued to be bought from current and past employees.[28] Sometimes other companies' recipes were volunteered at a price, and experienced workers with other chocolate manufacturers had begun to approach Rowntree for employment, but he wanted more than experience: 'Has he any special knowledge of value?'[29]

Joseph Rowntree was playing a dangerous game. After all, other bigger, older and more refined companies might adopt the same tactics towards his own. But his activities are revealing of a more fundamental issue. Here was a prominent Quaker, upon whom praise has been lavished in high-toned abundance, who spent part of the formative years as head of his company actively poaching from other businesses. Not surprisingly he was alert to any such misdemeanours among his own workers in York, but it is curious that those commentators on the man and the company have simply overlooked this remarkable episode.

Rowntree's accumulation of this information did little to relieve directly his company's precarious state in the 1870s. Commercial salvation came not from success in a fiercely competitive world, but via co-operation (a cartel, in effect) between the main Quaker confectioners. Rowntree believed that the best way forward might be some form of agreement or association with Fry and Cadbury.[30] It was a move which was to transform the history of Rowntree and of the City of York.

Cadbury's chocolate company in Birmingham had, like the others, humble Quaker origins. Richard Tapper Cadbury, originally from Exeter, had served an apprenticeship as a draper in Gloucester before working first in London, then in 1794 in Birmingham. Cadbury set up business in a former inn in Bull Street, and married Elizabeth Head from Ipswich in 1796 (the couple went on to have ten children). He became a prominent Birmingham Quaker, known to his contemporaries as 'King Richard', and involved himself in a host of social reforms and good works. When he retired from his drapery business in 1828, it passed to one of his sons, Richard Head Cadbury. In his turn, the younger

Richard had apprenticed his son John to a Quaker in the tea trade, first in Leeds, later in London. Given money to establish his own business, John Cadbury had returned to Birmingham and in 1824 began as a tea dealer and coffee roaster in the house next to his father's drapery. Among his very first customers were two people who bought some cocoa.[31]

Seven years later, in 1831, John Cadbury took over a warehouse and embarked on a career as a chocolate manufacturer. A lively, energetic man, though one restrained by rigid Quaker principles (he refused to sit in a comfortable chair until he was 70), Cadbury was as active in philanthropy as in business. He insisted on following to the graveside the coffin of the area's first cholera victim in 1832 at a time when most other people fled in panic from the epidemic's casualties. The highly paid bearers, smoking to ward off the disease, were followed 'by Mr Cadbury, in a broad-brimmed hat and flowing Quaker frock-coat'.[32] In a city troubled by a complexity of contemporary urban ills, this exemplary man left his mark on a number of issues which engaged people of a social conscience. Yet Cadbury also had a sharp eye for commercial possibilities. He was one of Birmingham's first businessmen to use plate-glass windows in his shop, attracting people simply to gaze at its contents, and he even employed a Chinese worker in full national costume to weigh and pack his tea. By the early 1840s his range of eating and drinking chocolates had increased dramatically. Like the other Quaker manufacturers, Cadbury took great pains to rest 'his claim to the public support on his determination to maintain a character for the thoroughly good and uniform quality'.[33] In an age of widespread food adulteration, honesty and wholesomeness were no mean qualities.

In 1847 Cadbury moved to a new factory in Bridge Street that was able to accommodate more than 200 employees, and he was joined in the expanded venture by his brother Benjamin. Their new Homoeopathic cocoa, promoted like the products of other Quaker chocolate manufacturers in the genuine belief that it had health-giving qualities, began to sell in growing quantities, pushing aside the older but continuing trade in tea and coffee. By mid-century, Cadbury's chocolate business had begun to attract attention. In October 1852, *Chambers's Edinburgh Journal* carried a long and flattering account of the company and its processes, describing how the raw material from the former slave islands of Trinidad and Grenada was transformed into commercially attractive edible chocolate and cocoa.[34] The whole concern was mechanised and clean, which formed a sharp contrast to the prevailing filth and gloom of Birmingham's other industrial sectors (even the Cadbury factory chimney was filtered to prevent adding to the city's infamous pollution). No less striking was the workforce, selected for its 'moral character' but in return granted excellent conditions of service and fringe benefits, including holidays, trips, educational courses and savings schemes. Given their employers' beliefs, they were also encouraged to abstain from tobacco and alcohol.

The company's finances were flagging, however, but revived from 1861, thanks to the efforts of two of John's sons, Richard and George Cadbury (the latter having served time at Rowntree's grocery business in York). This combination of two very different men, though united in their attachment to the Society of Friends, had a remarkable effect on the business. When they took over the company from their father, like Rowntree in York they faced that most dreaded Quaker failing: financial disgrace. Some of the company's produce was unsatisfactory, it was now the smallest of the country's thirty or so chocolate manufacturers, and it was a fine-line decision whether to stay in the business or to invest in something else. At this point Cadbury adopted the Dutch cocoa-processing machine, two years before Fry's in Bristol. With the butter extracted from the cocoa, their products became more palatable and more easily managed by consumers. Drinking chocolate could be made in the home as easily as tea. Cocoa Essence, launched in 1866, proved immediately popular and successful, and became the foundation for the company's subsequent commercial prosperity.[35]

Cadbury promoted its new product heavily, stressing its medical benefits and distributing samples to doctors. It was advertised on London omnibuses, and met all the objections fortuitously being raised in Parliamentary debates, and the Acts of 1872 and 1875, concerning food adulteration. These brought Cadbury a huge amount of unplanned but wholly favourable publicity. The company paid increased attention to the presentation and packaging of its produce in a series of designs where taste was sharpened by intelligent artwork and commercial acumen. It spread its sales network across the country, and into Europe, North America and the dominions in the 1870s.

The three Quaker chocolate manufacturers were clearly very similar. They were all active members of the Society of Friends and committed to good works in their home towns. They knew each other, had trading connections and shared many industrial and commercial interests. They also *felt* that they had much in common.[36] Thus it was in 1872 that Rowntree, while securing manufacturing secrets from other companies, wrote to Fry and Cadbury to suggest that they co-ordinate prices and restrict discounts given to shopkeepers. These early moves took formal shape in an agreement in 1889 about shop displays and inducements given to retailers. In 1895 the accord was extended to prices, but such arrangements were not designed to curtail each other's commercial freedom.[37]

One problem they all faced was traditional Quaker hostility to new trading methods, especially the growing emphasis on aggressive and colourful advertising. Most of the men at the heart of these companies had emerged from the Quaker shopocracy, where the style was unassuming and dull. Even when Rowntree had grown into a leading York company, those at the helm continued to view themselves as shopkeepers in the old tradition – as late as 1875, Joseph Rowntree described himself simply as a 'master grocer'. Like so many other trading Friends, they had built up a clientele who were happy with the service and the quality of goods received. It took a leap of the imagination for such men to realise that advertising, or 'puffery' in the vernacular, could add anything of value to their well-tested and proven trading practices: a shop well stocked with high-quality goods had seemed to offer the best route to commercial success. Advertising had for many years been closely associated with the dubious fringes of quackery and adulterated products, a world where the advertisement was more important than the product itself. Quakers found it hard to overcome the feeling that it was in some indefinable way an unprincipled, very unQuakerlike conduct of trade.

On the other hand, Quaker industrial management was well ahead of most contemporaries. Rowntree was particularly insistent on managing its business and controlling its labour force in a dignified, principled fashion, and avoided industrial confrontation, which was regarded as little better than the conflict Quakers renounced on principle. Rowntree provided welfare facilities for its workers well in advance of most employers, but expected and generally received a loyalty and honest commitment from the workforce in return. This was the classic world of the Victorian paternalist, best exemplified by the Quakers but by no means restricted to them. The industrial and commercial landscape was dotted with (often nonconformist) magnates who created these communities on the back of pioneering and successful businesses. It was a world which today seems archaic and distant, yet it was more commonplace than we might imagine, certainly until the 1870s. Moreover, such paternalism proved to be a remarkably effective management tool.[38] Certainly Rowntree had no reason to feel that its Quaker-inspired system was in itself lacking or failing to deliver.

Not all Quakers took the view that advertising was crude, often mendacious and sometimes wrong-headed. They could after all turn matters on their head and capitalise on their reputation for honesty in business. Both Fry's and Cadbury felt able to publicise their chocolate products much more vigorously than Rowntree. Indeed, their commercial prominence, led by Fry's, in the course of the late nineteenth century was directly related to their greater willingness to advertise. Fry's had been doing so in newspapers from the 1830s. In 1866 the company invested a hefty £2,000 for such purposes.[39] The Cadbury business was revived by a combination of new production techniques and their advertisement. When also in 1866 Cadbury introduced its new Cocoa Essence, it was promoted as 'Absolutely Pure: Therefore Best', to other Quakers' irritation. This product and the associated publicity proved enormously successful and brought the company back from the brink of commercial demise. Fry's tried to make up the ground lost to Cadbury by introducing its own Cocoa Extract in 1870, but it failed to make such an impact largely because the company did not launch a similar promotional campaign. But in 1883, Fry's launch of its Concentrated Cocoa was accompanied by vigorous advertising which stressed its purity and wholesomeness. Within six years it had established itself as one of the company's leading lines.[40] Even more significant in the long term was the fact that Cadbury's rising fortunes, based on its Cocoa Essence, enabled the company to relocate operations to Bournville on the outskirts of Birmingham.[41] In all this, significant differences between the various Quaker chocolate manufacturers had emerged. Cadbury had shown a technical and promotional flair which was notably missing in York. It was clear enough that quite distinct commercial and entrepreneurial cultures could spring from similar Quaker origins in the same industry.

For much of the late nineteenth century the real competition was between Fry's and Cadbury. For example, Fry's was the first British company to introduce milk-chocolate products, linked again to a powerful advertising campaign. Cadbury came late to the field, but with its Dairy Milk chocolate soon became the market leader.[42] All three companies had, by the end of the century, become wedded to essential and eye-catching promotional activity. Fry had set the tone with its early emphasis on healthy and reliable goods, but the industry's publicity was part of a much broader transformation in the world of food advertisement in general. Chocolates were now promoted as safe and beneficial to an increasingly sophisticated and anxious British consuming public, and appeared with the alleged plaudits of medical approval wrapped around their boxes and tins. Advertisements were festooned with either the imagery of medals, trophies and certificates that had been awarded at various international exhibitions, or even the ultimate sanction of royal or aristocratic approval. Fry resorted to using the services of a London advertising agency. In 1870 the company spent less than £5,000 on promotion; by the end of the century that had increased tenfold.[43]

Rowntree lagged behind the other two magnates partly because Joseph had refused to share their early enthusiasm for cocoa essence, but mainly because of his resistance to the idea of a more up-to-date and assertive marketing strategy. But Rowntree's fortunes were revived on a massive scale by a stroke of good luck. In 1879 Joseph Rowntree picked up on the interest in fruit pastilles made by French confectioner Claude Gaget. After initial setbacks, Rowntree began to sell its own version in 1881. They were an immediate success, prompting further factory and workforce expansion. Again, the emphasis was on quality produce – a combination of old ingrained Quaker instincts and the necessity to beat off French competitors.

Even with the confidence and income born of this new success, Rowntree remained a finely balanced concern when in 1883 Henry Isaac died young. At each stage of the company's history, when money or support was required, other Quaker relatives or associates could be relied upon for assistance. Gradually a new generation of managers and younger relatives moved into responsible positions, and Joseph Rowntree, as head of the company, delegated power and influence to them as it expanded. Under the influence of this more hard-headed younger intake, the company began to take seriously its marketing needs, but always against a resistant distaste from Joseph himself.[44]

Rowntree's pastilles inflated its profits in the 1880s, but Cadbury and Fry's surged even further ahead, thanks to their investment in cocoa essence. Rowntree was eventually forced to follow suit and invest in the Dutch machinery necessary to produce its own variety.

There were new premises in the middle of York and new machinery, but the business remained relatively small-scale and with low profit margins. Joseph was even heard to complain that he wished he had remained in his father's grocer's shop. However, in 1890 Rowntree made a major shift, copying Cadbury's move to a greenfield site by buying a 20-acre plot to the north of the city. True to his Quaker modesty, Joseph Rowntree worried aloud that the move might bring personal riches which he did not want – for himself or his children. Yet he also recognised that such wealth might give him the power to satisfy the traditional Quaker urge to do good works. It gave him the chance to reward his workers with not only an adequate living wage, but also a working and social environment that would elevate them from the cramped, mean conditions so characteristic of urban working life. Like Cadbury at Bournville, Joseph Rowntree realised that, if the move to the new site succeeded, he had a great opportunity to become a social reformer as well as a successful businessman.

By the early 1890s Rowntree had relocated to its new site, with raw materials and produce brought to and fro on an extension line of the North-Eastern Railway. It was perfect timing, for this proved to be a decade when the British people consumed chocolates and cocoa as never before. Per capita consumption more than doubled and Rowntree's sales quadrupled. In the process, a small family concern blossomed into a major national organisation. Whereas Rowntree employed a mere 100 people in 1879, that had grown to 1,613 twenty years later, most of whom were young women. Though remaining smaller than both Cadbury and Fry, Rowntree had become one of the nation's largest employers, and inevitably the greater informality of the old company's working arrangements had to be changed. The traditional paternalism of Rowntree management and the anticipated deference in return was out of place in the new, harsher environment of such factory operations. Labour disputes surfaced which had been unimaginable under the old regime and were to Joseph's incomprehension. It was as if the world were shifting on its axis: the Quaker qualities of personal care and attentiveness began to crumble before the anonymity of large-scale manufacturing.[45]

A new code of industrial and management practices were introduced, though were not always trouble-free. Directives on time-keeping, discipline and punishments, for example, were laid down in a rather autocratic style by a management which had naturally grown accustomed to having their way, for all their worthy intent. Whenever concessions were granted (increased pay or fewer hours), the company expected to make savings elsewhere. In effect, the 1890s witnessed a modern company bursting from the cocoon of its old Quaker self, but many remnants of its previous form clung uncomfortably to the new expansive business. Few were more obviously influenced by the past than the grand old man of the company, Joseph Rowntree himself.

Though willing to see his industrial practices change, Rowntree remained reluctant to follow the inevitable path to modern marketing, but after seeking advice from another major Quaker company, the Reckitt chemical company in Hull, he inaugurated a sales team. The first batch, which grew only from fourteen to thirty-three between 1890 and 1897, sallied forth with a bag of samples, a list of customers and the good wishes of the company. The younger Rowntrees began to overcome Joseph's inbred resistance to advertising. Whereas he had authorised £100 in the late 1880s, by 1892/93 the company was investing £4,000 in promoting its wares. Joseph continued to try to rein in such activities, despite the successes of competitors and (perhaps because of) the national drift to large-scale, increasingly gaudy publicity for each and every article of consumption, but the company carried on regardless. One of the first motor cars in York was bedecked with a large mock-up tin of Rowntree's Elect cocoa. At the 1897 Oxford–Cambridge boat race, a barge festooned with adverts for the same product followed the teams.[46] Quakers elsewhere had been less hesitant. Huntley and Palmers biscuits, for example, established their reputation through the power of clever merchandising. In the years when Joseph Rowntree maintained his crusty rearguard defence of the old order, the attractively packaged biscuits (in tins designed and manufactured by yet another Quaker company) had found their way into the remotest corners of the globe. Indeed, these tins became sought-after items in themselves, and remain collectors' items for those interested in Victoriana.[47] Brand images and design iconography, together with the promises and patter of the salesman, had become as important as the goods themselves.

Advertising worked, if the products were good, and Fry's prosperity was closely linked to careful promotion. Initial emphasis had been placed on the medicinal qualities of its chocolate products, but Fry's felt the pressure from the emergent power and success of its two competitors in the 1880s and 1890s. As each company's ploys and products seemed to bite deeper into their rivals' markets, they resorted to more costly advertising. By 1910 their respective budgets stood at £69,000 for Fry's, £119,000 for Cadbury and, surprisingly, £127,000 for Rowntree. Yet even within Fry's, where qualms about marketing had been overcome long before Rowntree, the Quaker instinct lived on. Fry publicly claimed in 1910 that a good company could not be built on advertising alone. Quality merchandise and consumer trust formed the foundation for successful business. And Joseph Rowntree recognised further, while sanctioning the move towards a more aggressive marketing strategy, that the core of the campaign should in addition concentrate on fair-dealing.[48]

At the heart of these companies lay the precepts of the founding fathers of the seventeenth century: in one particular industry in three different cities (and we could replicate the story in other areas of business), traces of traditional Quaker commercial ethics survived. But adjustment to the material successes of the modern world placed great strains on their faith and lifestyle. Some Friends had resolved the dilemma by simply quitting the Society; others remained 'plain', clinging to the formal trappings of simple dress and language, and in their refusal to bow to modernising trends becoming ever more striking, unusual and even eccentric. The chocolate families exemplified a third way, in seeking to adapt. Styles changed across the generations as different family members went their separate routes, but largely within the chocolate dynasties their Quakerism endured, despite being qualified by the commercial and industrial imperatives of a modernising business.

In the years before the First World War, these companies had become massive concerns. By 1910 Fry's sold chocolate to the value of £1,642,715, Cadbury £1,670,221 and Rowntree £1,200,598.[49] These figures in fact represent a relative decline for Fry's, which had dominated the market throughout most of the previous half-century. Moreover, unlike its rivals, Fry's continued to work from its original city-centre site in Bristol. Inside the company there was a feeling that it was being held back by Joseph Storrs Fry II, the man 'who dominated the management from 1867 until his death in 1913'.[50] A plain Quaker of conservative habits, he worked hard throughout his life at good causes, for the Society of Friends and for his company. However, he was not an innovator. He resisted the efforts of younger family and company members to confront the challenges of a changing market, and was slow to recognise competition. He was similar to Joseph Rowntree in that both men were devout Quakers of the old school, alert to social problems, keen to promote the interests of their workforce and hesitant to embrace commercial tactics. The major difference was that Rowntree granted an independence to younger relatives and junior colleagues which led to modernisation within the company. He delegated, handed over areas of responsibility, listened to new advice and sometimes reluctantly followed it.[51]

All three businesses had by the early years of the twentieth century grown too large for their traditional family-based structures. They were reorganised (at different times) and became public companies, but maintained and extended family investments and interests. Care was taken, for example, to ensure that the Rowntree family and other Quakers were securely lodged in positions of power and responsibility throughout its corporate hierarchy.[52] It remained to be seen whether the challenges of the market could be met without corroding the Quaker spirit which had inspired and shaped these companies from their inception. They now employed armies of workers and dominated their local economies. Their products had helped to transform the key social habits of millions of people worldwide, especially in the dominions. Wherever British people travelled, settled, traded or visited, they took chocolate with them. Cocoa sustained explorers of the Arctic regions and was supplied to millions of men in all theatres of operation in the First World War. Rowntree publicised the fact that a tin of their Elect cocoa saved a soldier's life by deflecting a bullet, and that the military continued to enjoy its produce in many countries.[53] The chocolate companies controlled distant regions from the Caribbean to West Africa, which were the sources for their raw materials, and they commanded transportation systems to ferry these materials and the end products back and forth. When Joseph Rowntree was a child, York had no railway; by the time he retired, his company had its own line. When war began, and foodstuffs and shipping became the close concern of ministers and the military, the chocolate magnates involved themselves in high-level discussions about strategies for food supplies. It was all far removed from the founding fathers serving across the counter of a local shop.

Joseph Storrs Fry II, George Cadbury and Joseph Rowntree, for all their success, were committed to using their worldly wealth to good ends, rather than allowing it to undermine their families' attachment to the Quaker way of life. It gave them an opportunity to establish social and welfare reforms of a kind few others could even envisage. At a time when radical politicians and reformers at Westminster and in cities across Britain were speculating on how best to tackle the manifold problems of urban and industrial life, the chocolate magnates were able to effect change.

They embraced the well-tested nineteenth-century tradition of philanthropy from both sides of the Atlantic, but there *was* a difference between these Quakers and other millionaire benefactors.[54] Most others were above all else individualists: men who were edged towards such activities by personal factors – some religious, some secular. Quakers, however, came from a culture in which public service and good works were part of the warp and the weft of their beliefs. From the 1650s, charity and benevolence had been a fundamental characteristic. Indeed, the history of Quakerism in Britain is highlighted by such acts which left their mark on the development of British society. Chocolate magnates devised paternalistic schemes of employment and then built 'model villages' to house their workers, all well ahead of provision at that time. They championed workers' leisure facilities and self-improvement, and funded social welfare programmes on an unusual scale. The impetus for all this belonged to a Quaker tradition that reached back to the words of George Fox.

11

Quakers as Employers

Few images of Victorian life remain more durable and popular than the bleak caricatures of the Industrial Revolution. Whatever historians have done to refine and modify them, these views persist. Yet even from the very early days of industrial change, certain employers sought to run their businesses without generating the worst forms of contemporary hardship and exploitation. This was an uphill struggle, for the economy seemed to respond best to an aggressive, almost anarchic thrust for expansion in which little thought was given to working and living conditions. Not surprisingly, from the first, the Quaker conscience had been drawn to these deep-rooted problems. Curiously, however, of all the social questions that attracted their attention in the nineteenth century, factory conditions did not figure large.[1] But as the economy matured, a new breed of Quaker magnate was able to effect major change in the lives of their labour forces.

Quaker employers may have belonged to the broader tradition of industrial philanthropy, but their immediate inspiration was the ethical code of the Society of Friends.[2] Though few ran their businesses in precisely the same way, they all displayed unmistakable Quaker characteristics. They had a Foxite distrust of earthly rewards, were uneasy with their wealth, and felt the need to put their success to good use, particularly for the growing numbers they employed. Yet they were rarely able to forge a sense of fraternity with the workforce. Try as they might to help, most ran as tight a commercial operation within their plants as possible. They expected others to work as hard as themselves, hours were invariably long and pay was generally low. Many continued to live frugally and expected others to follow their lead. Moreover, of that generation of Quakers who became leading industrialists in the nineteenth century, many had known hard times in their early days. Either they had been born into much less comfortable circumstances, or had been forced to stave off financial and commercial disaster only by dint of application, perseverance, and the financial support of other Friends. As is often the case with self-made men, success had not come easily, which tended to confirm their expectation of others to keep their collective noses to the grindstone.[3]

These magnates of the late nineteenth century saw their businesses transformed in their lifetimes. At first, owners would know all their workers, helped out when they faced problems and generally kept themselves informed about their employees' affairs. Such familiarity inevitably disappeared as their operations grew and new structures added layers of intermediate management applying increasingly complex rules with a firmness laid down by the Quaker bosses. The entire Quaker industrial approach was suffused with a strict paternalist tone which stood in contrast to the tougher regimes elsewhere. In the world of successful Victorian industry, there was no mistaking Quaker principles at work.

We have seen how rapid growth in the late years of the nineteenth century took hold of the Quaker chocolate companies. In the 1860s Fry's was far and away the largest employer with 193 members of staff; Rowntree had 12 and Cadbury 20. Thirty years later the three companies employed 4,500, 2,683 and 1,613 respectively.[4] A similar revolution took place in the Reading biscuit company, Huntley and Palmers. The 41 employees in 1846 increased to almost 1,000 twenty years later, and by the 1890s stood at more than 5,000.[5] At Street in Somerset, where the Quaker Clark family developed its thriving shoe-manufacturing concern which had been based initially on out-work, the founder James Clark had begun in 1829 with one employee, the village shoemaker. He soon acquired a handful more and by 1841 employed 24 in Street and 14 in Glastonbury. In 1855 he claimed to employ 800, mostly recruited within the region.[6] The Reckitt chemical company in Hull, which began life as a small starch business, had almost 5,000 workers by the early twentieth century.

As new industrial techniques were introduced, the nature of the work and the size of manufacturing plants were transformed. The decision to shift operations to custom-built modern factories was often to cope with growing demand, but it also provided Quaker employers with the opportunity to rethink the working environment. Cadbury was the real pioneer, developing its new factory in 1879 and launching its associated town in 1893 at Bournville outside Birmingham on rational, efficient and, as events soon proved, commercially viable lines. Built on a 15-acre site ideally located for rail and canal links to other parts of the country, everything was 'arranged for well-studied convenience'. Not surprisingly, 'Order and regularity prevailed throughout the factory'.[7] The lessons were not lost on York rivals Rowntree, and in 1890 it too purchased a 20-acre site on the edge of the city. The 1890s saw a gradual relocation to what henceforth became known as the 'Cocoa Works'. In Hull, Reckitt was also blessed with a large site on which it was able to build a more modern factory.

This drift to large-scale production saw a further delegation of day-to-day management, often to non-Quakers. It was impossible to find enough Friends for supervisory roles (in any case, they tended to occupy more senior positions). The Quaker owners and upper management thus found themselves effectively at a remove from their workers as a result of their own success. Furthermore, this expansion of the workforce proved a fertile breeding ground for the emergence of organised labour.

Late in the nineteenth century, trade unions were not welcome in many Quaker plants, partly because of the traditional employers' response, but mainly because they were contrary to the Quaker way of doing business. Unions were at once an obstacle to their idea of industrial philanthropy and an assertion that workers had a legitimate voice in local affairs. Quakers were no different from other Victorian bosses in feeling that they alone knew how best to run the business. They were always willing and keen to listen to individual pleas or arguments, but were unhappy to concede the right to collective bargaining. Unions undermined two tenets of Quaker business ethics. Firstly, they suggested that employees needed representation despite the sympathy of Friends towards workers' interests. Secondly, unionisation created sectional divides which tugged at the Quaker sense of an organic working community. At the end of the century, when Quaker employers led by Rowntree began to pay systematic attention to the union question, they did so as much from the need to revise management strategies in the wake of new labour demands as from a sense of revitalised paternalism.[8]

The culture of long hours for low pay was not exceptional. The working day at Huntley and Palmers in 1850 stretched from 6.30 a.m. to 6.30 p.m., with forty minutes for breakfast and an hour for lunch, finishing at 2 p.m. on Saturday: a 58½-hour week which was eventually reduced in 1872 to 54 hours. Not until 1918 did it go down to 48 hours. Another Quaker biscuit company, Carr's of Carlisle, offered a 63½-hour week, though again time was allowed for meal breaks.[9] Cadbury reduced the working day to 10 hours in the 1890s; Rowntree brought down their working week to 48 hours in 1895. Other Quaker employers slowly followed over the next decade or so.[10] But these reductions and the granting of local and national holidays resulted from twentieth-century legislation, union deals and agreements in particular Quaker businesses. Most of these companies were under no pressure from the wider labour market to change their ways. They had little trouble with recruitment, and as they expanded they came to dominate the local economic hinterland. They offered steady work in a reasonable environment at a time when employment was often hard to find.

Changes in the methods of wage calculation also reflected the transformation from workshop to factory production. The founding fathers had decreed what should be paid to their small band of employees, adjusting salaries according to personal circumstances, but such an arbitrary system meant that employees could find their wages going up or down for reasons they were unable to fathom and rarely allowed to query.[11] As staff rolls increased rapidly, pay structures had to change. Labour matters were handled by professional personnel officers; wages were organised according to age, experience and skills, with bonuses for reaching targets or degree of difficulty. Where appropriate, piecework was established but with an eye to business efficiency as much as fair payment. Thus by the 1890s, the Quaker companies were in keeping with modern terms of employment regulated by agreements which were made known to everyone, even if they had been imposed rather than negotiated and agreed.[12]

What convinced Quaker magnates of their approach, however, was not so much the moral strength of their position but its commercial results: managing the labour force decently was good for business. It is hard to view their successes, notwithstanding the occasional periodic blip, as a flawed style of management. When they moved into this phase, new comprehensive welfare schemes were introduced. What inspired such plans? Was it a repositioning of traditional Quaker instincts, or was it merely good business sense?

Employers, too, had started to come together in associations to promote their joint interests. Quakers had their ready-made network, but (as in the case of the chocolate manufacturers) it was a co-operation often qualified by the need for commercial confidentiality in the face of competition. From mid-century, employers had sought to undermine the power which skilled workers had been able to exert over production. As long as manufacture of any kind depended on such men, they could impose a day-to-day control over proceedings. New machines and procedures enabled management to wrest this back, reducing swathes of industry to dependence on semi- or unskilled labour, and consolidating their authority over the entire manufacturing process. In all this they had begun to pay careful attention to the science of work studies. Employers, not workers, began to dictate the nature, structure and rewards of local labouring practices. In return, however, they began to experiment with industrial welfare within and around the workplace. The Quaker companies saw this as a natural extension of a much older philanthropic tradition in British social history, but it also offered, among other things, a chance to come to grips with the consequences of rapid growth. Such welfare programmes also gave them an added advantage in the increasingly complex world of labour management, a good example of which can been seen in the York factory of the Rowntree company.

Joseph Rowntree had witnessed an explosion in employee numbers, and he was more aware than anyone that the 'informality and mutual loyalty' between himself and the workers had disappeared. The men he placed in charge, in a carefully devised management structure, imposed strict rules of work discipline with a dispassionate application. The resulting conflict on the shop floor was alien to Rowntree's Quaker principles and he spent a great deal of time pondering how best to avoid or resolve it.[13] As the company grew, those lower down the chain of command began to take decisions which had once been the preserve of the patriarch and sons. All this was taking place within a context in which Rowntree sought to create a congenial working and social environment: 'Healthy conditions of labour are not luxuries to be adopted or dispensed at will. They are conditions necessary for success. In keen competition the vigour and intelligence of the workmen are likely to be a determining factor.' These conditions were the best that contemporary design could provide. To sustain female workers, large numbers of whom were young teenagers, Rowntree employed a team of women welfare officers, and all workers were strictly segregated by sex. As a matter of policy, both Rowntree and

Cadbury dismissed most of their young men when they reached the age of 21, as did Huntley and Palmers. The confectionery industry was reluctant to employ costly adult workers when they could make do with more poorly paid youths or women. However, Rowntree would often feel compelled to find work for a young man if his father was an employee. But that, and the cavalier award of sick pay, rises and benefits, served to create a sense of injustice among the workers. Not until 1903 did the company place the structure and award of wages and benefits on a fully systematic and public basis.[14]

As part of the drive to promote business success through ethical management, Rowntree launched the *Cocoa Works Magazine* in 1902. Its columns take us directly to the heart and mind of managerial Quakerism at work.[15] In its first edition, Joseph Rowntree wrote that it was no longer possible for him personally to keep in touch with his 2,000 employees – hence the magazine. The directors hoped that 'in combining social progress with commercial success, the entire body of workers must be animated with a common aim'. The company had gone to great trouble 'to make the conditions under which work is carried on favourable to the health by proper ventilation, heating and cleanliness', and it had provided a number of improving and pleasant social and recreational amenities. The benefits, Joseph Rowntree claimed, went far beyond the York factory: 'The example of such . . . tends to improve the general conditions of labour in the country.'[16] But the greatest beneficiaries were local employees. The magazine listed a catalogue of facilities and organisations: a library; savings schemes and hospital funds; clubs for singing and music-making, angling, bowling, football and cricket, gardening, photography, cycling, and gymnastics for girls. There were dress-making evening classes; material could be bought by weekly instalments and sewing machines hired from the company.[17] Rowntree organised annual trips to Blackpool, that seaside Mecca of working people throughout the North of England. It promoted the Cocoa Works Domestic School to train female workers in 'domestic duties' which had been neglected because they spent so much time in the factory. But over and above such specific amenities, the management used the magazine to promote their social philosophy of punctuality, personal cleanliness, clean living and no smoking, of education and general application to work. In his 1905 Christmas greeting, Joseph Rowntree reminded his young workers 'of the need for cultivating intelligence and of acquiring habits of industry and thrift'.[18]

Rowntree established an old-age pension scheme in 1906, payable from the age of 65.[19] It is worth recalling that eligibility for the first state pensions in 1908 began at the age of 70. To ensure that workers were healthy and remained so, Rowntree followed the lead of Fry's and Cadbury in appointing a company medical officer (himself related by marriage to the Rowntree family). When it was shown that most absenteeism was caused by dental problems, given the workers' access to cheap chocolates and sweets, a full-time works dentist was appointed.[20]

By now, a whole new hierarchy of control and decision-making had emerged: large numbers of clerks, teams of commercial travellers, female secretaries, engineers and chemists were all trained up in return for an anticipated lifetime's loyalty. (The pattern was similar at Fry's and Cadbury.) In an echo of the company's Quaker origins, the more senior the rank, the more active an employee was expected to be within the wider community.

All new workers were issued with the company's rules and regulations. The mothers of prospective female employees were interviewed and their daughters' welfare discussed. Employees who left without good reason were not rehired. The whole process ran smoothly thanks to an efficient record-keeping system which, while common in other big businesses, came naturally to Quakers. While care in recruitment and training may now seem commonplace, it was unusual for the time. Such matters were usually left to the foremen and shop-floor management, but those old patterns from an earlier, smaller-scale industrial system could not survive much longer. Rowntree and Cadbury paralleled each other not only in changing the nature of chocolate manufacture, but also in creating a management system more appropriate to the broader needs of modern British industry.

The new factories at York and Bournville thus initiated a process 'of centralised hiring, training, job security and welfare benefits [which] represented an investment in an efficient and cooperative workforce'.[21] Those in secure and permanent employment were the lucky ones, however, as a major pool of temporary workers was brought in for seasonal work. For all the company's benevolence, it had few qualms about terminating the contracts of women when they married and, as we have seen, those of many young men when they reached the age of 21. The confectionery industry as a whole depended on the availability of casual but experienced labour which could be recruited at short notice. The welfare programmes were designed in part to secure loyalty and hence better returns.

Rowntree pensions, which depended mainly on investment from company funds, rested on Joseph's belief that fear of poverty in old age created dissatisfaction at work, so any promise of security would, he argued, create happier employees.[22] This went beyond mere Quaker instinct. The discussion about the nature and origins of urban poverty had particular resonance in York. In 1901, Seebohm Rowntree, a company director and Joseph's son, had published devastating findings in *Poverty: A Study of Town Life.* Based on an 1899 survey of 60 per cent of York's population, his conclusion that almost one-third of the population lived on or below the poverty line *even when in work* confirmed what these people knew from bitter experience and what others had long suspected: that millions received inadequate wages. Among those who inevitably slid into poverty were the old.[23] More telling, however, was the discovery that the poorest British citizens could do little to alter their own circumstances; that it took resolute determination, planning, hard work and good luck simply to survive. Any call to self-improvement and individual effort was met with frustration and despair.

There was enough detail within this survey to confirm many of the old Quaker antipathies towards drinking, gambling and smoking. The feckless habits enjoyed by large numbers of poor people seemed to contribute to, if not cause, their circumstances. Joseph Rowntree periodically used the columns of his company magazine to denounce such behaviour. At Christmas in 1907 he advised his workmen that there was 'absolute agreement among medical men that smoking among youths, during the years when they are growing, is distinctly injurious'.[24] But the importance of *Poverty* went far beyond its specific findings. The debate it prompted was only the latest variant of one which stretched back to the founding Friends of the seventeenth century. One important identification of the survey was the problem of poor housing. York may not have had the large working communities living in jerry-built accommodation that was so common to the industrial heartlands, but the city had its own distinctive black spots with all the consequences for ill health and inherited poverty via the family life cycle.

Joseph Rowntree had taken to retreating to Westow, a small village 11 miles outside York, whenever he wanted to study or write. Though he rarely spent more than a few weeks there each year, he began to ponder the benefits of such a life. Notwithstanding the real problems of rural and agricultural poverty, he was quickly won over. The publication of *Poverty* helped to confirm his growing sense that he ought to take steps to create a new kind of environment for his workforce. With this in mind, in 1901 he bought 123 acres of land bordering his factory site to the north-east of York.

Rowntree was not the first magnate to use his wealth to such ends. Utopian communities had sprouted on both sides of the Atlantic for a century and more. From Robert Owen at New Lanark to Sir Titus Salt at Saltaire, there were plenty of famous examples. As early as 1846, Northern Ireland Quaker John Grubb Richardson had founded Bessbrook, a community built to house workers in his linen mills. He had been influenced by the ideas about urban planning advocated much earlier by America's founding Quaker William Penn. This lively intellectual and practical debate had witnessed the foundation of a number of pioneering towns with varying degrees of success, the most spectacular and successful of which being those constructed on the very edges of colonial settlement: Adelaide, Wellington, Dunedin, Christchurch and Canterbury. But it was the advent of modern town planning in the 1880s which gave the process a fillip, notably in the creation of Port Sunlight by William Lever on Merseyside in 1887. In 1893, George Cadbury launched his own initiative at Bournville.[25]

From the outset, Cadbury's aim in constructing cottages for his workers was to alleviate 'the evils which arose from the insanitary and insufficient housing accommodation supplied to large numbers of the working classes, and of securing to the workers in factories some of the advantages of outdoor village life, with opportunities for the natural and healthful occupations of cultivating the soil.'[26] Joseph Rowntree was interested in Cadbury's experiments at Bournville, and the two Quakers corresponded with each other about the project. Cadbury wrote to Rowntree, 'Thy letter is most interesting. It is a great pleasure to think of Bournville Village as a happy home for many generations of children where they will be brought up amid surroundings that will benefit them spiritually, mentally and physically'.[27]

Seebohm Rowntree's survey had underlined the ubiquity of dire urban problems. Three years after *Poverty* was published, the site plan for the model village of New Earswick outside York was drawn up. For all the conscientious intent of creating a new environment, it was also a commercial venture. The houses were not so much ideal as 'decent': 'artistic in appearance, sanitary, well-built, and yet within the means of men earning about twenty-five shillings a week.' The tenants did not have to be Rowntree employees.[28] It soon became clear, however, that even the cheapest rents, devised to cover the building costs only, were beyond the means of the very group that Joseph Rowntree was targeting. Thus less elaborate homes were constructed and offered at even lower rents, but from the first the village comprised a range of different types and prices of housing. Built on unmade roads on the edge of the city, with no street lamps or public transport, the development appealed initially to families with a pioneering spirit. Gradually it acquired all the familiar landmarks of community: schools, a community centre, sports fields, a nursery, and even trees and verges were added to the roadside. Yet Rowntree's primary aim to provide housing for the lowest income earners was never realised, even though it remained the main concern of the controlling trust in its first twenty years.[29] By the end of that period there were 2,000 residents, and some 850 of them worked for Rowntree.[30]

Like other Utopian social experiments, New Earswick sprang from the best of motives. It was a well-meaning attempt to offer a humane alternative to some of the most serious social problems facing urban Britain, to provide a small-scale alternative way of living, and to enable working people to improve their material lot by harnessing their own efforts to the investments of well-intentioned magnates. But it could never have moved beyond the local and limited. The story of Rowntree and the City of York provides a striking example of the nation's contrasting fortunes. Here was a leading international company that was able to command resources worldwide, create employment for thousands, and influence the social and dietary habits of millions. Yet the financial might of so large a concern seemed to make little impression on the social ills of the small city which was its home base and headquarters. If the strength and benefactions of such powerful patrons fell short, what other forces could be called upon? The conclusion which many drew from, among others, the Rowntree experience in York was that only centralised state intervention could offer the financial and political muscle to tackle these problems.

The enormous cost of Rowntree's varied and expanding welfare services for employees was calculated in 1908 at 0.8 per cent of the gross selling price of its produce. Joseph Rowntree continued to devise new schemes, including profit-sharing, improved sick-pay schemes, holiday pay and convalescent facilities.[31] Yet it is not to diminish the motives or achievements of Rowntree, Cadbury or other industrial philanthropists to suggest that their pioneering welfare projects should in fact be judged as contributions to a new style of industrial management, rather than as exercises in Quaker-inspired benevolence. These confectioners had after all become leading companies by the First World War: Huntley and Palmers ranked 33rd among the nation's largest manufacturing employers, Rowntree 80th, Fry's 51st and Cadbury 57th.[32] The individualistic paternalism which had been at the core of Quaker company affairs had been superseded by a more ordered and regulated style that was tempered by such welfare provision.

Despite the large scale of their operations, Quaker magnates tried to maintain a distinctive moral tone at work. The Rowntree family insisted on decorous behaviour to and from the factory, and used supervisors to monitor it, recruited workers from what they considered to be 'respectable' homes, and campaigned aggressively against gambling, especially on the premises, but mainly to no avail. They refused to employ married women in the belief that they should care for hearth and home; single mothers were never employed. Men who had to marry their pregnant girlfriends were not entitled to the customary three-day honeymoon holiday. Nor would anyone absent through venereal disease qualify for sick pay. This residual paternalism, in particular the refusal to allow time off to attend York races, was resented and formed a major element in the mounting friction between workers and management before the First World War, but was merely one aspect of a national rise in working-class militancy during the same period. Though Quaker companies had resisted trade-union organisation, when employees ultimately voted for representation they would accede to popular demand.[33] Long before the upheavals of war, the magnates had been drawn into formal discussions between management and unions throughout their own industry, and often against their better instincts. These bosses now found themselves conducting their business far removed from their own communities; discussing prices, wages, conditions, hours and benefits with officials they had never met before.

These industrial and employment changes were a microcosm of

the challenges faced by the Quaker movement as a whole in the same years. How could a small sectarian and ethical organisation, accustomed to one-to-one dealings, cope with the unprecedented amassing of wealth and legions of employees in an international market, itself governed by complex and often uncontrollable forces of finance, raw materials and geopolitical upheaval? Like their eighteenth-century forebears, Quaker millionaires strained to abide by the stricter, 'plainer' tenets of the Society of Friends. Some found themselves held back, sometimes catastrophically, by the inordinate attention they paid to moral and social rather than business matters; their other-worldiness was often redeemed by the attention of family or Quaker partners to more prosaic matters. When the biscuit magnate William Isaac Palmer died in 1893, his benefactions were so enormous that relatives had to intervene to rescue his estate. More wisely, both Rowntree and Cadbury organised their philanthropy on the systematic and rational basis that had characterised their business lives.[34]

Along with the shoe manufacturer William S. Clark, the confectionery Quakers remained fundamentally 'plain'. Despite lavish wealth they clung to a humble lifestyle, and worried greatly about its effect on their descendants. They struggled to encourage or support all good works and saw nothing inconsistent about their lives. The long hours, low pay and casual labour posed few ethical problems for them, as they were down to market forces which had to be dealt with in providing the reasonably priced high-quality goods for which they had developed a distinctive reputation.

Other Quakers found it impossible to remain Friends while pursuing successful business careers; some remained Quakers, but displayed precious little benevolence towards their workforces. (Those involved in textiles paid lower wages than the industry as a whole and even withdrew the benefits they had once given.) Once again, the children of certain successful Quakers drifted away from the family faith, taking their wealth with them.[35] And while it is tempting to point to Rowntree or Cadbury as typifying Quaker business ethics, it is important to be aware of the more unpleasant and aggressive story of Bryant and May in precisely the same period. Two of the sons of founding father William Bryant remained nominally Quaker (the other two became Anglican), but in their relation to weaker partners, most notably Francis May, displayed to employees and in their own self-interest few of the redeeming qualities we have seen among other Friends. The best-remembered highlight of their turbulent stewardship of the company was the match-girls' strike led by Annie Besant in 1888 and the subsequent formation of the first women's trade union. The company did albeit slowly introduce that raft of welfare provisions we have seen elsewhere, but again we need to recall that such changes were part of the general evolution of managerial tactics throughout British industry.[36]

It became a Quaker truism that the third generation of wealth swept the grandchildren away from the Society. Since the eighteenth century, many families had been lost from it, but much of that had been down to the Society itself. We have seen how strict marriage rules, disownment and contracting Quaker numbers affected membership. There is even evidence to suggest that wealthy eighteenth-century London Quakers were happier to see daughters married *outside* the Society than to remain spinsters within it.[37] After this period, legal changes in the nineteenth-century removed much social and political discrimination, which allowed successful Friends to move into a range of institutional positions once denied their forebears. Prosperous Quaker families gravitated away from their traditional geographic centres as they moved into homes more befitting their wealth; their children and grandchildren slid into the seductive embrace of Anglicanism. None the less, many ex-Friends remained deeply influenced by the moral traditions of their families. Those 'good old Quaker principles' were, for example, promoted by the Lancashire Crosfields in their chemical business long after leaving the Society, as well as Carr's biscuits in Carlisle and Peek Frean in Bermondsey.[38]

Quaker successes of the nineteenth century have often been described in terms which today need some qualification. There were many other entrepreneurial and manufacturing rags-to-riches stories of men who were not Quakers, though it is true that many sprang from nonconformism. Nor were these Friends unique in devising welfare programmes for their workforces and communities. Indeed, their ideas were shaped as much by new ways of thinking and writing about the science of management as they were by the old tenets of the Society of Friends. Too often the philanthropic industrial Quaker has been cast in the role of the selfless, almost saintly character anxious to do his best for his fellow men and women. In truth, what they set in place made good business sense and was reflected in the remarkable success of their companies. It is also important to note that the sites of two of these businesses, York and Reading, revealed significant urban and industrial problems. Seebohm Rowntree used family money and Quaker concern to spell out the true extent of poverty in York. A decade later and using similar techniques, Arthur Bowley unearthed evidence in Reading that one working-class family in four and almost half the town's children lived in poverty. Yet both were considered to be models of what Quakers could achieve. The degree to which Quaker business activity may have contributed to local problems remains one of the most perplexing paradoxes for any critical observer. Working for Friends was in many respects better than working for many other late-Victorian employers, but their dominance of a labour market was no guarantee against social ills. The challenge lay in tackling that poverty in the midst of Quaker plenty.

12

Poverty and Social Change

As nineteenth-century Britain rose to be the world's leading industrial and commercial power, the economic benefits seemed to bypass large sections of the population. From one generation to another, millions remained rooted in a poverty which seemed impervious to any attempts at improvement. Ignorance and ill health too, and the complex ramifications of all three, had long attracted the attention of Quakers and others of conscience, yet for all their philanthropic efforts the problems deepened. Moreover, the statistically minded Victorians were able to document and tabulate its extent more thoroughly and more subtly than previously. Modern social investigation stemmed from an interest in the causes of poverty which was centuries old, but which by now had come of age. From the 1830s onwards it was assumed that the 'facts speak for themselves'.[1] When they did, they often told a terrible story.

Statistical societies in major cities and a multitude of Parliamentary inquiries were scrutinising Britain's myriad social ills. Those involved with such work often approached the task via a firm attachment to reform, sharing a widespread belief that any such proposals would be greatly assisted by the facts and figures of their investigation. But there was also a strong commercial dimension at work; a feeling that the long-term economic well-being of the country to some extent depended upon social improvement. The numerous instances of prominent businessmen and reformers working together in local surveys formed the backbone of the 'statistical movement'. This was especially striking in the case of Manchester: not only an emblem of the nation's early industrial progress, but also home to its manifold problems.

The nature and direction of social enquiry shifted dramatically under the influence of Charles Booth. Born into a devout Unitarian, commercial Liverpool family, Booth had been committed from his early days to such work and social reform. Turning his back on his beliefs in charity and his family's religion, he embarked on a life of secular endeavours which, after his move to the capital in 1875, focused on the East End of London. Through long conversations with early socialists and direct contact with a group of working men from the area, Booth determined to anatomise the nature and processes of poverty itself. He and his associates began in Tower Hamlets in 1886. As the project expanded, so too did his team of gifted and committed workers, and their complex exhaustive findings were published as *The Life and Labour of the People of London* in seventeen volumes between 1889 and 1903.[2] The first study concentrated on poverty itself, forming what *The Times* in 1891 called 'The grimmest book of our generation'.[3] Booth's publications went on to examine issues such as wages, housing and health, and shifted attention towards the extent of these problems by suggesting that one-third of the population lived on or below a 'poverty line' which he himself had devised. As the century drew to a close, more and more evidence was coming to light that being poor was not so much a consequence of individual frailty and personal weakness, but one of complex social forces such as low wages.[4] What troubled some, however, was the fact that Booth's London-based evidence might not be true of other parts of Britain.

One admirer of Booth's work was Seebohm Rowntree, who later confessed, 'I thought to myself . . . "Well, one knows there is a great deal of poverty in the East End of London but I won-der whether there is in provincial cities. Why not investigate York? . . . "'[5] He was a scientist by training and inclination, and had been curious about whether poverty could be measured scientifically. He had also made it his business to mix with the people of York, like his father Joseph. (Joseph Rowntree published a surve, on the problem of drink and licensing in 1899.) Seebohm was a teacher in one of York's adult schools and a frequent visitor to local working-class homes. It was a role which he felt derived from his Quaker background: 'the true Christian is the humblest', he scribbled in a notebook. He told one of his classes, 'You cannot live in a town like York, with its poverty, its intemperance, its vice, without a sense of responsibility being from time to time borne in upon you.'[6]

Other critics had been clamouring for the attention of the socially concerned. In 1890 General William Booth of the Salvation Army had published *In Darkest England and the Way Out* on the subject of poverty, which sold 200,000 copies. Seebohm Rowntree read the book and used it in his classes. Three years later, Andrew Mearns issued *The Bitter Cry of Outcast London*. The subsequent national press debate prompted suggestions that life in provincial cities was in fact worse than anything so far revealed in London. To add to this crisis, a series of government and Parliamentary reports into specific black spots spelled out further details about the nation's social and industrial ills. The discussion about how best to tackle poverty was given added urgency by the rise of the early socialist movements offering their own solutions. Rowntree was by no means hostile to these socialist theories – indeed, a number of prominent figures visited his family home. Their ideas, in conjunction with the flood of literature about the subject in general, pricked his conscience and persuaded him to act.[7] Thus it was in the spring of 1899 that this prosperous York Quaker began his study.

York's mere 75,812 souls comprised a medieval city which had been virtually bypassed by the Industrial Revolution, except for the railways and chocolate manufacture, yet there was a side that visitors rarely saw, but which was bound up with its few dominant industries. The process of collecting data about local poverty was difficult and protracted. Vital details about wages were hard to come by as men were reluctant to divulge their salaries, and their womenfolk were often ignorant of the amount. Fortunately Rowntree had access to his own company pay rolls and was given all he asked for by the local railway company. His 1901 survey *Poverty: A Study of Town Life* was based on statistics collected from 11,560 families (a sample of 46,754 people). Rowntree openly acknowledged his debt to Booth's work and encouragement. It was remarkable that their findings from utterly different urban environments were broadly similar.

Rowntree's study divided those living in poverty into two classes: those in primary poverty, whose wages were inadequate even for the basic essentials of life (10 per cent), and those in secondary poverty, whose earnings would have been sufficient but for 'other expenditure, either useful or wasteful' (18 per cent).[8] The data defined its recurring phases as working people passed through childhood, middle age and old age, and it underlined the specific problems facing women in their childbearing years. But as we have already seen, perhaps Rowntree's most revealing discovery was that one-half of the men in primary poverty were in regular work.[9] It must have been unnerving for a director of the city's main employer to show that 'the wages paid for unskilled labour in York are insufficient to provide food, shelter, and clothing adequate to maintain a family of moderate size in a state of bare physical efficiency'.[10]

Poverty had a profound impact on a broadly based political readership that ranged from socialist to Liberal, and challenged a host of preconceptions about cause. Drink, gambling and fecklessness of all sorts may have played a part, but Rowntree proved that many problems of the poor were not of their own making. Furthermore, the study was accessible and manageable: a single volume, compared to Booth's multiple massive tomes. There were many other more popular studies available, but the quality of Rowntree's book lay in its crisp exposition of facts and argument.[11]

Rowntree's analysis confirmed that for those in primary poverty the old solutions simply did not work. The traditional Quaker virtues of self-help and thrift among those affected, and philanthropy on the part of the prosperous, could never touch, let alone cure, the residual problems of the abjectly poor. A number of critics resisted this conclusion, preferring to concentrate on secondary poverty to illustrate that personal weakness was the route to perdition, but most observers grasped the fundamental political significance of Rowntree's work.

One such was the young Conservative MP Winston Churchill. In December 1901, at dinner with the Liberal politician and author John Morley and other luminaries, Churchill was urged to read *Poverty* with the comment, ''Tis sure to be on the table at the Carlton.' He was greatly moved by the book and promptly 'set out to bring it to the attention of those whom it might otherwise have passed by'.[12] He reviewed it for a military journal, ostensibly to explain poverty among military recruits, and remarked, 'Although the British Empire is so large, [the poor] cannot find room to live in it . . . they would have had a better chance of happiness, if they had been born cannibal islanders of the Southern seas . . . this festering life at home makes world-wide power a mockery, and defaces the image of God upon earth.' Over the next month, Churchill frequently wrote and spoke about the effect that Rowntree's work had had on him. It was, he said, 'a book which has fairly made my hair stand on end'. To another correspondent he noted, 'I see little glory in an Empire which can rule the waves and is unable to flush its sewers.' Churchill worried that 'people who have looked abroad have paid no attention to domestic matters, and those who are centred on domestic matters regard the Empire merely as an encumbrance'.[13] The effect of Rowntree's study on this rising young statesman was only one of many strands of experience that edged him towards social reform. Crossing the floor of the House and becoming MP for Oldham served to confirm Churchill's assessment that some form of state intervention was necessary to secure a decent standard of living for poor British working people.

When Churchill joined the Liberal Government in 1906 he soon found himself in league with that other political giant Lloyd George, a man of humble origins and equally clear in his mind of the need to lay the political axe to British poverty. Since his first election to Parliament in 1890, Lloyd George had singled out this issue, and all the social forces which lay behind it, as a regular target. When in 1908 Lloyd George was promoted to Chancellor and Churchill was President of the Board of Trade, the two men embarked on wide-ranging fiscal and social reforms. The famous People's Budget and its related social-welfare legislation provoked a short-term constitutional crisis in the resistant House of Lords, but the reformers won the day. The 1911 National Insurance Act made basic state provision for unemployment, old age and sickness. For all its shortcomings and flaws, here was the foundation of a new social philosophy which was to dominate British life for the rest of the century. The state had taken upon itself the task of providing a safety net for those who seemed unable to care for themselves, albeit in the form of at first a minimal and meagre provision, but the principle had been won. The nation had moved a long way from that fierce Victorian belief in charity as the sole means of alleviating distress and engaging the efforts of the propertied classes.

Seebohm Rowntree's *Poverty* was a book with a *fin de siècle* significance which argued the case for pushing aside the ideals of the nineteenth century and seeking new modes of arranging social life.[14] Parallel evidence of the need for change included the rise of organised labour, demands from the suffragettes, the simmering troubles in Ireland, all in addition to domestic economic uncertainty. This volatile political and social climate in Britain spawned many critical assessments in the form of articles, books, and a veritable torrent of reports, inquiries and government statistics. Rowntree had also offered a model for other researchers, and the subsequent detailed case studies that poured forth from across the country confirmed his broad conclusions. Moreover, researchers who embarked on different topics often found themselves returning to the central question of poverty. Surveys of income levels, unemployment and foreign investment were unable to avoid the shadow that the poor cast across their findings.[15]

Doubts about securing personal wealth at the expense of the public good encouraged the birth of 'New Liberalism', from which came the post-1906 political reforms. Churchill's *Liberalism and the Social Problem* of 1909 bore all the hallmarks of Rowntree's influence: 'No view of society can possibly be complete which does not comprise within its scope both collective organisation and individual initiative . . . I look forward to the universal establishment of minimum standards of life and labour, and their progressive elevation as the increasing energies of production may permit.'[16] Rowntree's message percolated down to people who had not even read it. It became in effect refracted light, its ideas affecting the lives of those the book itself could not reach, though subsequent cheap editions did help to widen its audience. Rowntree himself promoted the book vigorously; he travelled incessantly, giving lectures throughout the country and winning over the powerful to the idea that low wages were the key.[17] He also befriended Lloyd George, even though, as men, they were as different as could be imagined: Rowntree, the quiet and studious Quaker, deferred to the flamboyant and eloquent brilliance of the Welshman. Yet both were outsiders. Neither belonged to the dominant class or religion of the nation whose principles and legacies they both sought to correct. Lloyd George was a visitor to Rowntree's York home and was known to wave a copy of *Poverty* before his audiences during the years 1907 to 1910. Later, the two men would work together on various reforming projects.

Rowntree's style of clarity and brevity appealed to Lloyd George, and proved instrumental in the latter's establishment of a committee to scrutinise the issues of land, land tax and housing. The committee included Rowntree as a member and used the methodology he had devised for his York research. It proved a massive undertaking that occupied most of his time (along with a research staff of seventy) between 1912 and 1914. When his father Joseph Rowntree, the architect of the chocolate company's success, received the second volume of the committee's report on land in spring 1914, he remarked with unconscious prophecy, 'How we must hope that no untoward gale will come and wreck the safe voyage of the ship that has been launched.'[18] Lloyd George was poised to launch a major campaign for land reform – which had long been a favourite topic, since British landowners seemed to form the unreconstructed obstacle to the answer to so many contemporary problems – when this and all other questions of social reform were swept aside by the start of the First World War.

Seebohm Rowntree's growing expertise on land shifted the focus of his interests. He undertook comparative research in Europe, one result of which was his conviction that trade unions were crucial. Without them, 'the great improvement in the lot of the workers during the last seventy or eighty years would have been impossible'. He also thought that the development of garden cities would create a healthy move towards a more widespread and diversified agricultural system, with increasing numbers of people working at their own small holdings.[19] As we have seen, his ideas were actively pursued by the Cadbury family in Bournville and his own family at New Earswick near York.

In the years before 1914, Seebohm Rowntree issued a steady stream of publications to press home his evidence and arguments about the condition of rural England, and its relationship to the nation's social ills in general. This position was far removed from the detached Quakerism of two generations earlier. Rowntree's interests may have broadened, but he remained wedded to his home town. After all, the chocolate company provided the wherewithal to spend time and employ the staff on his various projects. His father Joseph determined to make similar work possible by the creation in 1904 of three charitable trusts, using half his personal fortune for the initial funding. One was designed specifically for the development of the model village of New Earswick, the others to finance the investigation of various social problems. Like his son, Joseph wanted not only to investigate or remedy a problem, but also to get at 'the cause of things'.[20]

In the York factory, we have seen how father and son sought to ensure that the working and social environment was as congenial as possible, viewing these costly ventures as sound business sense rather than regrettable concessions to the labour force. Their business was, in effect, New Liberalism in microcosm, standing in stark contrast to the unbending resistance to workers' demands that pervaded much of contemporary British industry. Seebohm Rowntree, as head of the Labour Department, kept in touch with the factory floor via a number of 'social helpers' or supervisors who reported directly to management about the social welfare of the labour force. The purpose was 'to make employees feel that they are more than mere parts of an industrial machine, that someone in the factory cares for them as human beings'.[21]

These ideals might seem unexceptional to modern eyes, but before 1914 they were remarkably unusual and far-sighted. Yet as Seebohm well knew, such solicitude was worth nothing if wages were inadequate, and having spent so much time illustrating the problem in the city itself, he could hardly have ignored the question in his own factory. By reviewing each worker's wages at three-monthly intervals (they were paid on a piecework rate) the company tried to ensure that employees did not fall below a minimum-wage level. Those who did were moved on to different work or encouraged to increase their output. Those who could not were dismissed or encouraged to find jobs elsewhere. (Like Quakers who were disowned for their failings, workers not up to the task were removed.) But this whole process hinged on whether the basic piece rates were in themselves fair. Again, Rowntree established periodic checks to this end – indeed, it became an indication of a department's efficiency to test what proportion of employees secured more than the minimum wage.

Rowntree's wages policy necessarily left no room for the culture of collective bargaining which had become commonplace trade-union activity elsewhere in British industry by the early years of the twentieth century. The company's ethos was one of 'fair' treatment of employees, based on a complex internal structure of productivity and profit-making: a 'fusion of philanthropy and efficiency'.[22] Despite Seebohm's convictions, Joseph Rowntree remained wholly sceptical of trade unions. In the enlightened world of his booming factory there seemed little point to them, but as the ranks of employees swelled, relations and old loyalties, particularly the deference between master and worker, began to change. The wider context altered too, with the post-1910 national economic downturn and corresponding upsurge in industrial agitation. Between 1910 and 1914 trade-union membership grew from 2.6 to 4.1 million.[23] More and more of Rowntree's workers wished for representation, and the Quaker directors felt morally unable to reject those demands, though Seebohm Rowntree was among those who maintained resistance, despite his approval of unions in principle. These tentative moves, common across the confectionery industry, were not translated into general industrial practice in York until during and after the First World War.[24]

The consequences of Seebohm Rowntree's *Poverty* went beyond the world of social investigation to affect the chocolate company itself. Though in the Quaker tradition it had been alert from the first to its employment and wages policy, the pioneering system which evolved in the York factory henceforth needed to be assessed not merely against the yardstick of Quaker ethics or business efficiency, but in the light of general community well-being. Rowntree needed to be seen to be paying a living wage, and in characteristic Quaker fashion, those who proved inadequate were edged out. That way, at least, Rowntree was guaranteed a clean bill of health on this question.

Yet it is easy to be retrospectively cynical. The Rowntree family proved themselves to be well ahead in the theory and practice of employment, and ever conscious of their ethical obligations to their workers and the local community. The fact that Rowntree recognised many of the principles of an increasingly assertive socialist movement is not to say that Quakers were socialists at heart. Seebohm Rowntree, in particular, believed that wages should be higher and that employers who felt unable to oblige should abandon their role. Starvation wages had no place in a modern civilised economy.[25]

Seebohm Rowntree proved indefatigable. As well as leading a full career at the Cocoa Works, his publication record would grace the most industrious of academic careers.[26] Both aspects reveal that he had moved beyond a man of conscience wrestling with local problems, faced with the fact that most employers remained wedded to an intransigent authoritarianism, and the untramelled self-interest associated with it, that had once made commercial sense. This had provided the rough theoretical framework around which early Victorian progress had moulded itself. When that self-interest was allied to the traditional Quaker sense of social good, it was able to produce a working environment both congenial and profitable. But such experiments were mere oases: pockets of enlightenment in a wasteland of conflict between management and labour. The industrial history of Britain in the years immediately preceding the First World War was characterised not by the practices pioneered by successful Friends, but by the alienation of millions of workers which drove them towards the unions and the Labour party, to the exasperation of political leaders. Seebohm Rowntree echoed the belief that state compulsion was required 'to over-ride the immediate interests of the employer by imposing on him obligations which are to the advantage of the nation rather than his own'.[27]

It was a major shift in industrial thinking which remained anathema to the dominant traditionalists in industry and politics. More importantly, it was a marked break with a fundamental Quaker principle that harboured a suspicion about the state and had sought to keep a distance between it and the Society of Friends. This drift towards promoting state interference in areas of life generally regarded as private or corporate was one natural consequence of Rowntree's social enquiries, and the use of the social survey as a means of laying bare prevailing patterns and habits established the centrality and power of sociological expertise. Previous debates about what the poor required were henceforth rendered redundant. Rowntree's work allowed 'whole populations to speak for themselves systematically and incontrovertibly about what deprivation means'.[28] What was needed thereafter were those with the determination and might to do something about such findings. Whatever their failings, the reforms promoted by Lloyd George and Churchill constituted *the* most important attempt to grapple with Britain's manifold social problems before the utterly changed environment of 1945.

Early Quakers had been sorely treated by the state, and their early history had been characterised by efforts to secure their own rights in the teeth of official persecution. British life was unrecognisably different by the early years of the twentieth century, but so too were the Friends themselves. One insight into the changed nature of the Quaker way was the simple fact that the work of successful Friends had helped to show how to organise economic and political life differently. Clearly not everyone would be able to arrange their commercial affairs like the confectionery manufacturers, not everyone would be able to rejig their industries so that managerial self-interest worked in harmony with the social good, and not everyone would come to accept that the state, and the state alone, should provide a sure and steady defence of the most vulnerable and needy.

Quakers formed but one element in a motley coalition of interests keen to tackle the pressing issues of early twentieth-century Britain. They remained a Society characterised by success, and they continued to attract the attention of non-Quakers. They were persuasive and influential, heeded and respected by people in authority within a wide range of interests, even though their ranks were by now thin and underpopulated. By 1914, not for the first or last time, the Quakers had come to exercise an influence and power out of all proportion to their numbers.

Conclusion

At any point during the years 1700 to 1914 we are able to find contemporaries willing to praise or decry the story of Quaker commercial success. Of course this is also true of other religious groups, most notably the Jews, but which others acquired such a remarkable reputation at a time of comparable numerical decline? In 1914 their ranks had been reduced to perhaps one-quarter of the numbers of their early days. Today, however, it would be difficult to make a similar connection between Quaker life and business attainment. The most famous present-day companies are Quaker only by popular historical association, or where it suits the conglomerate ownership to maintain or promote the tradition. The revolution in economic affairs in the twentieth century, particularly since the Second World War, has so fundamentally recast the structure of global commercial and financial life that old ties between religion and business have been severed or utterly transformed.[1]

It was quickly assumed that Quakers were good at business. Certainly, in the late eighteenth as in the late nineteenth century, the Society of Friends was the spiritual home to an outstanding commercial élite. The Society itself and a host of local meetings were greatly influenced by the activities of its more prominent members: successful Friends can be recalled both for their economic contribution and for the dominant role they played in Quaker life. More difficult to answer, however, is the question of the relationship between the two: what importance did Quakerism play in the commercial lives of these Friends?

From the mid-seventeenth century there was a strong Quaker affinity with industry, frugality and self-help. From the days of George Fox, they were encouraged to be hard-working, financially prudent and honest in all their business dealings. Through the meeting house, in the home and in the workplace, Quakers sought to train themselves, their children and each other in those personal and social qualities which were at once a reflection of their living faith and a code of everyday conduct. The process would be continued by Quaker schools. But the ideals of Quaker life were not a simple mantra to be memorised and recited at particular moments. They were enforced by a structure of management which was more intrusive and manipulative than many have recognised, and was carried on throughout the nineteenth and into the twentieth century. To be a Friend necessarily involved subjecting oneself to possible scrutiny of one's personal and professional life; those whose behaviour left something to be desired were visited, questioned, helped – or excluded. This was a highly unusual arrangement. How many Anglicans were removed from their church because their commercial dealings were less than proper? Yet time and again Quakers across the country found themselves called to account before senior members for the conduct of their business affairs.

Although this internal regulation seems draconian, it proved to be extremely helpful. It was a form of specialist supervision, allowing commercially experienced Quakers to advise Friends in need. But it also meant the unsuccessful – those who transgressed the Society's conventions on dealing with the consuming public – were disowned. The purpose was to ensure that no shame would come the way of the Society because of the personal failings of individual members, thereby safeguarding its collective honest reputation.

Thus Quakers were nurtured in the ways of upright business and monitored to that same end.

Quakers also trusted each other. This enabled them to circumvent any commercial or financial risk by relying on each other for help. The Quaker network and the movement of senior Friends between London and the localities created a ready-made system of contacts. This made possible the flow of information and sympathetic assistance, in personal terms as well as in the efficient conduct of the Society as a whole. It also yielded family links through marriage, and the consequent creation of Quaker dynasties that straddled entire industries and a wide range of commercial interests. As their successes multiplied, so too did their ability to help each other. This was especially striking in financial matters, where the proliferation of Quaker banks offered access to funds, often on favourable terms, for further ventures. Quakers could be depended on to care for other people's money; Quaker borrowers could be relied on to use that money sensibly.

The rise of Quaker prosperity was not without its tensions. Material success in 1700 and 1900 threatened the plainness which had been their hallmark since the founding fathers. This and the unbending application of the marrying-out rule was responsible for the departure of many children of successful Friends, but along with deep-seated social changes in general, growing prosperity shifted the Society from its traditional introspective (not to say self-absorbed) quietism into a more committed engagement with the world at large. By the late eighteenth century, more and more Friends found it impossible to resist the social and political challenges of the time, and were using their unique standing to humanitarian ends. They sought to promote social reform sometimes through philanthropy, often as employers, but increasingly through the local council chamber and Parliament. The more affluent had the wherewithal to operate on an extraordinary scale. Some sought to create their own ideal communities in the shadow of their factories which, from the first, were purged of the social and urban problems which so blighted British life throughout the nineteenth and into the twentieth century. Quaker wealth was used during this time to pursue the decency which lay at the heart of Quaker social thought.

The formative Quaker experience of protecting each other against a hostile world had helped to foster a mistrust of the outside world and a suspicion that only fellow Friends were utterly reliable. Though times changed, the persecutions faded away and Quakers gradually came to play a full role in British life, the mutual trust which had succoured them in the lean years survived and remained a powerful force in years of plenty. And it was this reliance upon the probity and plain-dealing of fellow Friends that proved so vital for successful generations.

Moreover, outsiders also came to trust Quakers: their produce was sound, their prices fair, their services honest, their word good and their agreements honourable. In a world where such guarantees were less than universal, and suspicion reigned among consumers and customers, Quakers were exceptional. And therein lay the making of their success.

Notes

INTRODUCTION

1. *The Snake in the Grass; or Satan Transformed into an Angel of Light*, London, 1697, xvi
2. *Firms with Quaker Connections: A Tentative, Preliminary and Incomplete List*, London, 1996

I: GEORGE FOX AND FRIENDS

1. *The Journal of George Fox*, revised edition, John L. Nikalls, London, 1986, Chapter 1
2. There is, however, a debate about whether Fox can be claimed as the founder of the movement. Fox became leader by dint of his organisational and theological victory over other prominent Quaker pioneers. See William C. Braithwaite, *The Second Period of Quakerism* (1919), York, 1979, Chapter 16
3. Christopher Hill, 'Quakers and the English Revolution', in Michael Mullett, ed., *New Light on George Fox, 1624–1691*, York, 1991, 23
4. Entry for George Fox (1624–91), *Dictionary of National Biography*, VII, 558
5. Fox, *Journal*, 40
6. Ibid., 58
7. B. Reay, 'Quakerism and Society', in J. F. McGregor and B. Reay, eds, *Radical Religion in the English Revolution*, Oxford, 1984, 141

8. Nicholas Morgan, *Lancashire Quakers and the Establishment, 1660–1730*, Halifax, 1993, 13. For biographical sketches of this band of Quaker preachers, see Donald A. Rooksby, *The Man in Leather Breeches*, Colwyn Bay, 1994, 22–31
9. Fox, *Journal*, 114
10. Morgan, *Lancashire Quakers*, 14
11. Ibid., 142–5. For the role of women preachers, see Nesta Evans, 'The Descent of Dissenters in the Chiltern Hundreds', in Margaret Spufford, ed., *The World of Rural Dissenters, 1520–1725*, Cambridge, 1995, 300–302
12. Reay, in McGregor and Reay, eds, *Radical Religion*, 146
13. Christopher Hill, *The World Turned Upside Down*, London, 1975, 214. Also quoted in Reay, ibid., 146
14. Reay, ibid., 147
15. Ibid., 148–9
16. Fox, *Journal*, 158
17. Ibid., 99
18. For the history of the tithe, see Eric Evans, *The Contentious Tithe*, London, 1976
19. Quoted in Reay, in McGregor and Reay, eds, *Radical Religion*, 149
20. Quoted in Hill, in Mullett, ed., *New Light on George Fox*, 28
21. Quoted in ibid., 151
22. Reay, in McGregor and Reay, eds, *Radical Religion*, 155
23. Quoted in ibid., 158
24. Ibid., 161
25. Braithwaite, *Second Period*, 9–12
26. David Scott, *Quakerism in York, 1650–1720*, Borthwick Paper 80, York, 1991, 5–10
27. Bill Stevenson, 'The Social Integration of Post-Restoration Dissenters, 1660–1725', in Spufford, ed., *World of Rural Dissenters*, 365
28. Ibid., 366–7
29. Hill, in Mullett, ed., *New Light on George Fox*, 31
30. Ibid., 32
31. Reay, in McGregor and Reay, eds, *Radical Religion*, 158
32. Braithwaite, *Second Period*, 32–3
33. Quoted in ibid., 36
34. Ibid., 37
35. William Lamont, *Puritanism and Historical Controversy*, London, 1996, 24
36. Stevenson, in Spufford, ed., *World of Rural Dissenters*, 372–6
37. Ibid., 384–5
38. Braithwaite, *Second Period*, 109

39. Ibid., 114–15
40. Quoted in ibid., 54
41. Ibid., 154
42. Ibid., 435
43. Ibid., 457–60
44. Quoted in Rooksby, *Man in Leather Breeches*, 35
45. Morgan, *Lancashire Quakers*, 15
46. For the contemporary Quaker explanation of this process, see *Quaker Faith and Practice*, London 1995, section 1.04
47. Quoted in Rooksby, *Man in Leather Breeches*, 34
48. Morgan, *Lancashire Quakers*, 16
49. Harold Fassnidge, *The Quakers of Melksham, 1668–1950*, Bradford on Avon, 1992, 12–13
50. See Kenneth H. Southall, *Our Quaker Heritage: Early Meeting Houses*, York, 1984. See also Hubert Lidbetter, *The Friends Meeting House*, York, 1979

2: THE SHAPING OF QUAKER CULTURE

1. *Snake in the Grass*, xvi
2. H. Larry Ingle, 'Unravelling George Fox', in Mullett, ed., *New Light on George Fox*, 37
3. For these various views, see Morgan, *Lancashire Quakers*, 18–19
4. Scott, *Quakerism in York*, 7–10
5. Ibid., 11–13
6. *Quaker Faith and Practice*, 19.41
7. Ibid., 20.28
8. Ibid., 20.29
9. Ibid., 19.42
10. Lidbetter, *Friends Meeting House*, 4
11. Braithwaite, *Second Period*, 509
12. *The Journal of George Fox*, I, Leeds, 1896, 227
13. *Extracts from the Minutes and Advices of the Yearly Meeting of Friends held in London*, London, 1802, 195
14. Ibid., 195
15. Nicholas Morgan, 'The Social and Political Relations of the Lancaster Quaker Community, 1688–1740', in Michael Mullett, ed., *Early Lancaster Friends*, Lancaster, 1978, 23
16. Ibid., 24–5
17. John Brewer and Roy Porter, eds, *Consumption and the World of Goods*, London, 1994; James Walvin, *Fruits of Empire: Tropical Staples and Western Taste*, London, 1997

18. Morgan, in Mullett, ed., *Early Lancaster Friends*, 24
19. Scott, *Quakerism in York*, 13–14
20. Braithwaite, *Second Period*, 515
21. *Extracts*, 199
22. Braithwaite, *Second Period*, 499–500
23. Morgan, *Lancashire Quakers*, 24
24. Braithwaite, *Second Period*, 500
25. Ibid., 512
26. See archives, Ackworth School, *Career File*, sheets 13/5–8
27. Braithwaite, *Second Period*, 514–15 and 564–5
28. 'Epistle, 1739', *Epistles from the Yearly Meeting of Friends*, I, London, 1858, 227
29. 'Epistle, 1738', ibid., 221
30. See the essays in Neil McKendrick, John Brewer and J. J. Plumb, *The Birth of the Consumer Society*, London, 1983
31. 'Epistle, 1772', *Epistles*, II, 11–12
32. John Punshon, *Portrait in Grey: A Short History of the Quakers*, London, 1986, 130–32
33. Fox, *Journal*, 520
34. E. Jean Whittaker, *Thomas Lawson, 1630–1691*, York, 1986, Chapter 5
35. Punshon, *Portrait in Grey*, 87
36. 'Epistle, 1690', *Epistles*, I, 48
37. Ralph Randles, 'Faithful Friends and Well Qualified', in Mullett, ed., *Early Lancaster Friends*, 33–8
38. Stephen Allott, *Friends in York*, York, 1978, 63–4
39. Braithwaite, *Second Period*, 525–8
40. Keith Thomas, quoted in Christine Trevett, *Women and Quakerism in the Seventeenth Century*, York, 1991, 16. See also 14–15
41. Lidbetter, *Friends Meeting House*, 26
42. Braithwaite, *Second Period*, 270
43. Reay, in McGregor and Reay, eds, *Radical Religion*, 144–5
44. Trevett, *Women and Quakerism*, 123–6
45. Ibid., 128
46. Whittaker, *Thomas Lawson*, 71
47. Reprinted in George F. Clarke, ed., *John Bellers: His Life, Times and Writings*, London, 1987, 47–73

3: PLAINNESS AND PLENTY

1. For the use of this material for family reconstruction, see Richard T. Vann and David Eversley, *Friends in Life and Death: The British and Irish Quakers in the Demographic Transition, 1650–1900*, Cambridge, 1992

2. Arnold Lloyd, *Quaker Social History, 1669–1738*, London, 1950, Chapter 11
3. Clarke, ed., *John Bellers*, 170–71; Arthur Raistrick, *Quakers in Science and Industry*, New York, 1968, 49–50
4. R. Hingston Fox, *Dr John Fothergill and His Friends*, London, 1919, 10–17
5. *The Autobiography of William Tout of Lancaster, 1665–1752*, XIV, J. D. Marshall, ed., Manchester, 1967, 86
6. Ibid., 89–99
7. Hingston Fox, *Dr John Fothergill*, 11
8. Roy Porter, *English Society in the Eighteenth Century*, London, 1982, 102
9. Paul Langford, *A Polite and Commercial People: England, 1727–1783*, Oxford, 1989, 180
10. Quoted in ibid., 118
11. Thomas Clarkson, *A Portraiture of Quakerism*, III, London, 1806, 253–7
12. Lloyd, *Quaker Social History*, 9 and 69
13. *A Brief Account of the Life . . . of Christopher Story*, London, 1829, 12
14. *Extracts*, 54
15. Ibid., 28–9
16. 'Epistle, 1739', *Epistles*, I, 227
17. 'Epistle, 1688', ibid., 37
18. 'Epistle, 1691', ibid., 55
19. 'Epistle, 1692', ibid., 64
20. 'Epistle, 1706', ibid., 115
21. Neil McKendrick, 'The Consumer Revolution of the Eighteenth Century', in McKendrick et al., eds, *Birth of a Consumer Society*, 19
22. Quoted in A. S. Turberville, *Johnson's England*, I, Oxford, 1933, 175
23. McKendrick, in McKendrick et al., eds, *Birth of a Consumer Society*, 78–9
24. H. D. Willcock, ed., *Browns and Chester: Portrait of a Shop, 1780–1946*, London, 1947, 14
25. Walvin, *Fruits of Empire*, Chapter 10
26. For a discussion of Quaker artefacts, see Lidbetter, *Friends Meeting House*
27. McKendrick, in McKendrick et al., eds, *Birth of a Consumer Society*, 26
28. Porter, *English Society*, 237
29. 'Epistle, 1703' and '1754', *Epistles*, I, 106 and 290
30. 'Epistle, 1755', ibid., 294
31. 'Epistle, 1754', ibid., 290–91

32. 'Epistle, 1735', ibid., 210
33. 'Epistle, 1708', ibid., 120
34. 'Epistle, 1759', ibid., 312–13
35. 'Epistle, 1692', ibid., 64
36. Michael Mullett, 'The Social and Political Relations of the Lancaster Quaker Community, 1688–1740', in Mullett, ed., *Early Lancaster Friends*, 24
37. 'Epistle, 1735', *Epistles*, I, 210
38. Braithwaite, *Second Period*, 499
39. Ibid., 437
40. Ibid., 327
41. Ibid., 503
42. '1696, Liberality to the Poor', *Extracts*, 56
43. 'Epistle, 1768', *Epistles*, I, 351–2
44. Sheila Wright, *Friends in York: The Dynamics of the Quaker Revival, 1780–1860*, Keele, 1995, Appendix VI
45. For a good discussion of these general issues and a specific local case study, see Scott, *Quakerism in York*

4: MONEY MATTERS

1. *Autobiography of William Tout*, 89
2. F. Braudel, *The Wheels of Commerce*, London, 1982, 390–95
3. Henry Roseveare, *The Financial Revolution, 1660–1760*, London, 1991, 9–13
4. Ibid., 19
5. Mathias, *The First Industrial Nation*, London, 1983, 148–9
6. Sir John Clapham, *The Bank of England*, I and II, Cambridge, 1944
7. Roseveare, *Financial Revolution*, 43–4
8. P. J. Cottrell, 'Banking and Finance', in John Langton and R. J. Morris, eds, *Atlas of Industrialising Britain*, London, 1986, 144
9. Mathias, *First Industrial Nation*, 150
10. For the history of the country banks, see L. S. Pressnell, *Country Banking in the Industrial Revolution*, Oxford, 1956
11. Mathias, *First Industrial Nation*, 152
12. M. W. Kirby, *Men of Business and Politics: The Rise and Fall of the Quaker Pease Dynasty of North-East England, 1700–1943*, London, 1984, Chapter 1
13. Pressnell, *Country Banking*, 55
14. Quoted in Kirby, *Men of Business*, 7
15. Ibid., 18–19

16. Pressnell, *Country Banking*, 20, 55, 114 and 242
17. Raistrick, *Quakers in Science and Industry*, 326–9
18. Mrs Thomas Geldart, *Memorials of Samuel Gurney*, London, 1857, 10
19. See, for example, *Memoirs of Joseph John Gurney*, Joseph Bevan Braithwaite, ed., Philadelphia, 1857, 310
20. Audrey M. Taylor, *Gilletts: Bankers at Banbury and Oxford*, Oxford, 1964
21. Pressnell, *Country Banking*, 510
22. Hingston Fox, *Dr John Fothergill*, 281
23. For an analysis of the bewildering complexity of Quaker family links in this and related industries, see Jacob M. Price, 'Eighteenth-Century London Quaker Business Families', in Richard S. Dunn and Mary Maples Dunn, eds, *The World of William Penn*, Philadelphia, 1986
24. Ibid., 121
25. Ibid., 119–21 and 325; Mathias, *First Industrial Nation*, 323
26. Raistrick, *Quakers in Science and Industry*, 81–3 and 330–31
27. Pressnell, *Country Banking*, 27–8 and 128
28. George Harrison, *Memoirs of the Origin, Nature and Purpose of a Loan Fund Instituted at a General Meeting of Subscribers held at Devonshire House*, London, 1821
29. Quoted in Pressnell, *Country Banking*, 243
30. Quoted in Frederick B. Tolles, *Meeting House and Counting House: The Quaker Merchants of Colonial Philadelphia, 1692–1763*, Chapel Hill, 1949, 53
31. Ibid., 54–5
32. Quoted in ibid., 56
33. Ibid., 57–8
34. Ibid., 59–60
35. Pressnell, *Country Banking*, 27
36. Allott, *Friends in York*, 56–7
37. Langford, *A Polite and Commercial People*, 76
38. Allott, *Friends in York*, 58
39. John Brewer, *Sinews of Empire*, London, 1989
40. Allott, *Friends in York*, 59–60
41. 'Epistle, 1703', *Epistles*, I, 105
42. 'Epistle, 1709', ibid., 123
43. 'Epistle, 1716', ibid., 141
44. *Extracts*, 17
45. E. N. Chauhuri, *The Trading World of Asia and the East India Company*, Cambridge, 1978, 393–4
46. Walvin, *Fruits of Empire*, Chapter 2

47. 'Epistle, 1733', *Epistles*, I, 200. The satisfaction with Quaker tax payment was repeated later, in 'Epistle, 1757', ibid., 303
48. 'Epistle, 1769', ibid., 355
49. Allott, *Friends in York*, 57–8

5: NETWORKS

1. Letter, 26 July 1808, in *Letters of the Late John Thorp of Manchester*, Manchester, 1820
2. Kenneth Morgan, ed., *An American Quaker in the British Isles: The Travel Journal of Jabez Maud Fisher, 1775–1779*, London, 1992
3. For the London Quaker families, see Price, in Dunn and Dunn, eds, *World of William Penn*
4. *Autobiography of William Tout*, 98–9
5. Ibid., 12–13
6. For a discussion about the nature of Quaker organisation on both sides of the Atlantic, see Edwin R. Bronner, 'Quaker Discipline and Order, 1680–1720', in Dunn and Dunn, eds, *World of William Penn*, Chapter 18
7. Margaret Stiles, 'The Quakers in Pharmacy', in F. N. L. Poynter, *The Evolution of Pharmacy in Britain*, London, 113–30
8. Richard Palmer, 'Thomas Corbyn, Quaker Merchant', *Medical History*, XXXIII, 1989, 371–6; Roy Porter and Dorothy Porter, 'The Rise of the English Drugs Industry: the role of Thomas Corbyn', ibid., 277–95
9. Palmer, ibid., 372
10. Letter, Thomas Corbyn to Cadwaller Evans, 18th 2nd month, 1750 [Strict Quakers refused to name the month because of its pagan links], in *Letterbook, Corbyn and Company Papers*, Western Manuscripts 5442, Wellcome Institute Library, London, 132. See also letter on 182
11. Morgan, ed., *An American Quaker*
12. Letters, 18th 2nd month, 1750, and 5th 7th month, 1752, Western Manuscripts 5442, 132 and 182
13. Letters, 30th 7th month, 1740, to Dr Gamble, ibid., 10 and 145
14. I have benefited by being able to read the paper generously sent to me by Nuala Zahedieh, 'Credit, risk and reputation in late seventeenth-century trade'
15. Letter, Thomas Corbyn to Cadwaller Evans, 25th 2nd month, 1749, Western Manuscripts 5442, 96
16. Letter, 28th 2nd month, 1748, ibid.
17. Letter, no date, ibid., 128
18. Quoted in Price, in Dunn and Dunn, eds, *World of William Penn*, 367

19. Geoffrey Tweedale, *At the Sign of the Plough: 275 Years of Allen and Hanbury and the British Pharmaceutical Industry, 1715–1900*, London, 1990, 14–17
20. Stiles, in Poynter, *Evolution of Pharmacy*, 116–17
21. Price, in Dunn and Dunn, eds, *World of William Penn*, 371–2
22. Ibid., 373
23. Ibid., 375
24. Jacob M. Price, 'English Quaker Merchants and War at Sea, 1689–1783', in Roderick A. McDonald, ed., *West India Accounts*, Kingston, 1996, 64–86
25. Price, in Dunn and Dunn, eds, *World of William Penn*, 379–81
26. Ibid., 389
27. For a case study of these ethical business problems, see Price, in McDonald, ed., *West India Accounts*
28. Barbara M. D. Smith, 'The Galtons of Birmingham: Quaker Gun Merchants and Bankers, 1707–1831', *Business History*, IX, 1967, 132–50

6: EDUCATION

1. 'Epistle, 1767' and '1768', *Epistles*, I, 348 and 352–3
2. John Stephenson Rowntree, *Quakerism, Past and Present: Being an Inquiry into the Causes of its Decline in Great Britain and Ireland*, London, 1859, 71–4. For the most recent demographic analysis, see Vann and Eversley, *Friends in Life and Death*, 22–3
3. Quoted in Hingston Fox, *Dr John Fothergill*, 184
4. *The Cupola* (Ackworth School magazine), 1935, 'Fothergill Supplement', 4
5. Elfrick Vipont, *Ackworth School*, London, 1959, 16–17
6. John Fothergill, *A Letter from John Fothergill to a Friend in the Country*, London, 1778, 6
7. Hingston Fox, *Dr John Fothergill*, 280–81
8. For Fothergill's account of this transaction, see archives, Ackworth School, *Letters*, 1775, file 24
9. Allott, *Friends in York*, 63–4
10. Hingston Fox, *Dr John Fothergill*, 282
11. Fothergill, *Letter to a Friend*, 61
12. Ibid., 17
13. Vipont, *Ackworth School*, 26–9
14. Thomas Pumphrey, *The History of Ackworth School*, York, 1853, 34–5
15. Ibid., 36–7
16. Vipont, *Ackworth School*, 28 and 33–4

17. Pumphrey, *History of Ackworth School*, 23
18. Porter, *English Society*, 146 and 314
19. Hingston Fox, *Dr John Fothergill*, 284
20. Ibid., 288
21. *So Numerous a Family: 200 Years of Quaker Education at Ackworth, 1779–1979*, Ackworth, 1979, 12
22. Ibid., 22
23. David Tregoning and Hugh Cockerell, *Friends for Life: Friends' Provident Life Office 1832–1982*, London, 1982
24. Quoted in Anne Digby, *Madness, Morality and Medicine: A Study of the York Retreat, 1796–1914*, Cambridge, 1985, 60
25. Punshon, *Portrait in Grey*, 131
26. H. Winifred Sturge and Theodora Clark, *The Mount School, York*, London, 1931, 5
27. 'Prospectus', in ibid., 5
28. Wright, *Friends in York*, 17–18
29. Quoted in ibid., 8
30. Clare Midgley, *Women Against Slavery*, London, 1992
31. Sturge and Clark, *The Mount School*, 12
32. Lindley Murray, *English Grammar*, York, 1795. I am grateful to David Reibel for his expert comments on Murray. See also 'Lindley Murray', in D. A. Reibel, ed., *A Bibliographical Guide to the History and Structure of English*, London, 1997, 21ff
33. Ibid., 30–31
34. Allott, *Friends in York*, 68–9
35. Silvanus Thompson, ed., *Memorial of John Ford*, York, 1877, 2, 22 and 43

7: INDUSTRIALISTS, SCIENTISTS AND SHOPKEEPERS

1. Raistrick, *Quakers in Science and Industry*, Chapter 4 and 95–107
2. Charles K. Hyde, *Technological Change and the British Iron Industry, 1700–1870*, Princeton, 1977, 16
3. Pat Hudson, *The Industrial Revolution*, London, 1992, 132
4. Quoted in Raistrick, *Quakers in Science and Industry*, 134 and 139
5. Ibid., Chapter 5
6. Sidney Pollard, *The Genesis of Modern Management: A Study of the Industrial Revolution in Great Britain*, London, 1965, 72–3 and 193
7. See the classic essay, E. P. Thompson, 'Time, Work, Discipline and Industrial Capitalism', *Past and Present*, December 1967
8. These details are taken from the standard work, Arthur Raistrick, *Dynasty of Iron Founders*, London, 1989

9. Ibid., Chapter 2
10. David Richardson, ed., *Bristol, Africa and the Eighteenth-Century Slave Trade to America,* I: *The Years of Expansion 1698–1729*, Bristol, 1986, xx
11. A. P. Woolrich, *Ferrner's Journal 1759/1760: An Industrial Spy in Bath and Bristol*, Eindhoven, no date, 35. A copy of this booklet can be found in the library of the Friends Meeting House, Euston Road, London
12. For the moral problems facing Quaker international traders in times of warfare, see Price, in McDonald, ed., *West India Accounts*
13. Ibid., 65–7. See also James Walvin, *Black Ivory: A History of British Slavery*, London, 1992, 30
14. See Smith, 'The Galtons of Birmingham'
15. Both quoted in Raistrick, *Dynasty of Iron Founders*, 71–2
16. Morgan, ed., *An American Quaker*, 264–7
17. Raistrick, *Dynasty of Iron Founders*, Chapter 5
18. Ibid., Chapter 6
19. Raistrick, *Quakers in Science and Industry*, 202–10
20. A. E. Musson, *Enterprise in Soap and Chemicals: Joseph Crosfield and Sons Ltd, 1815–1965*, Manchester, 1965, Chapters 1–2
21. Ibid., Chapter 5
22. Ibid., 54
23. Ibid., Chapter 10
24. See Lorna Weatherill, 'The Meaning of Consumer Behaviour', in Brewer and Porter, eds, *Consumption and the World of Goods*, Chapter 10
25. Raistrick, *Quakers in Science and Industry*, 200–202
26. See archives, Ackworth School, *Career File*, sheets 13/5–8
27. Tweedale, *At the Sign of the Plough*, 15
28. See Raistrick, *Quakers in Science and Industry*, Chapter 7
29. G. N. von Tunzelmann, 'Technological Progress During the Industrial Revolution', in R. C. Floud and D. McCloskey, eds, *The Economic History of Britain since 1700*, I, Cambridge, 1981. For an older but still important view, see A. E. Musson and E. Robinson, *Science and Technology in the Industrial Revolution*, Manchester, 1969
30. Keith Thomas, *Man and the Natural World*, London, 1983, 227
31. Ibid., 237

8: THE QUAKER CONSCIENCE

1. William C. Braithwaite, *The Beginnings of Quakerism*, Cambridge, 1961, 315–16
2. Joseph John Gurney, *Observations on the Religious Peculiarities of the Society of Friends*, Philadelphia, 1832, 273

3. George Harrison, *Second Address to the Right Rev. Prelates of England and Wales*, London, 1795, 6
4. Braithwaite, *Beginnings of Quakerism*, 47–50
5. Braithwaite, *Second Period*, 558–9
6. Ibid., 560–64
7. Ibid., 565–71
8. Ibid., 584
9. Ibid., 594
10. Morgan Godwyn, *The Negro and Indians Advocate*, London, 1680, 9
11. *George Fox's Journal*, London, 1765, 437
12. Hingston Fox, *Dr John Fothergill*, 99–101
13. *Extracts*, 176
14. Ibid., 176–7
15. J. R. Oldfield, *Popular Politics and British Anti-Slavery*, Manchester, 1995, 41–2
16. Ibid., 51–3
17. Ibid., Chapter 4
18. Mark Jones, *The Nature of the Liverpool Movement for the Abolition of the Transatlantic Slave Trade, 1787–1807*, dissertation, University of York, 1995
19. Quoted in Tweedale, *At the Sign of the Plough*, 35
20. Ibid., 39
21. Stephen Allott, *Quaker Pioneers*, London, 1963, 74
22. Punshon, *Portrait in Grey*, 190–92; Anne Vernon, *A Quaker Business Man: The Life of Joseph Rowntree*, York, 1987
23. Gillian Wagner, *The Chocolate Conscience*, London, 1987, 45
24. Rowntree, *Quakerism, Past and Present*, Chapter 8
25. Ibid., 154

9: THE MODERNISERS

1. Rowntree, *Quakerism, Past and Present*
2. Elizabeth Isichei, *Victorian Quakers*, Oxford, 1970, 112–13
3. There is a useful discussion in Edward Royle, *Modern Britain: A Social History, 1750–1985*, London, 1987, 313–19
4. Rowntree, *Quakerism, Past and Present*, 156
5. Rowntree, 86 n. 13 and 88 n. 14. On Quaker emigration, see also the details in archives, Ackworth School, *Career File*
6. Isichei, *Victorian Quakers*, 115
7. Wright, *Friends in York*, 18
8. Isichei, *Victorian Quakers*, 2 and 16–25
9. Wright, *Friends in York*, Chapter 6

10. Ibid., 100–104. See also Midgley, *Women Against Slavery*
11. For details, see Wright, *Friends in York*, Chapter 7
12. Ibid., 124
13. Ibid., 133
14. Ibid., Chapter 7
15. Alex Tyrrell, *Joseph Sturge and the Moral Radical Party in Early Victorian Britain*, London, 1987, 233
16. Isichei, *Victorian Quakers*, 160–65
17. Ibid., 192
18. Ibid., 195–7
19. Ibid., 202–208
20. Ibid., 215
21. James Walvin, *Questioning Slavery*, London, 1996
22. For details, see David Turley, *The Culture of Anti-Slavery*, London, 1991
23. For the full story of this campaign and its context, see Brian Harrison, *Drink and the Victorians*, London, 1971
24. For details, see Isichei, *Victorian Quakers*, Chapter 9

10: CHOCOLATE

1. Sidney Mintz, *Sweetness and Power*, London, 1985
2. Walvin, *Fruits of Empire*, Chapter 6
3. 'Historicus', *Cocoa: All About it*, London, 1896, 46
4. 24 November 1664, *The Shorter Pepys*, R. Lathem, ed., London, 1985, 445
5. Quoted in A. W. Knapp, *Cocoa and Chocolate: Their History from Plantation to Consumer*, London, 1920, 8
6. Quoted in A. L. Butler, '"The Indian Nectar": The Introduction of Chocolate to Seventeenth-Century Europe', paper at Social History Conference, London, 1993, 12
7. Letter from John Royton, 5 April 1723, in W. E. Minchinton, ed., *The Trade of Bristol in the Eighteenth Century*, Bristol, 1957, 89
8. T. Fry, *A Brief Memoir of Francis Fry, FSA*, privately published, 1887, 10. See also Stefanie Diaper, 'J. S. Fry & Sons: Growth and Decline in the Chocolate Industry, 1753–1918', in Charles E. Harvey and Jon Press, eds, *Studies in the Business History of Bristol*, Bristol, 1988, 33–54
9. Wagner, *The Chocolate Conscience*, 13; John Latimer, *The Annals of Bristol in the Eighteenth Century* (1893), Bath, 1970, 177
10. J. Othick, 'The Cocoa and Chocolate Industry in the Nineteenth Century', in Derek Oddy and Derek Miller, eds, *The Making of the Modern British Diet*, London, 1976, 79

11. Diaper, in Harvey and Press, eds, *Studies*, 35–6
12. Raistrick, *Quakers in Science and Industry*, 215–16
13. Diaper, in Harvey and Press, eds, *Studies*, 38–9
14. For details of food adulteration, see John Burnett, *Plenty and Want: A Social History of Diet in England from 1815*, London, 1979, Chapter 5
15. Diaper, in Harvey and Press, eds, *Studies*, 39
16. Ibid., 40–41
17. Ibid., 42–3
18. Robert O. Mennell, *Tea: An Historical Sketch*, London, 1926, 28–9
19. Circular, 1 July 1862, Rowntree Paper HIR/4A/9, Borthwick Institute, University of York
20. Letter from H. I. Rowntree, ibid.
21. Ledger HIR/1/2, Borthwick Institute, contains newspaper advertisements, letters of reply, notes kept by Rowntree on the interviews, and descriptions and drawings based on information received from interviewees and correspondents
22. Ibid., 4–12
23. Report by Thomas Neal, ibid., 22
24. Ibid., 48 and 55–6
25. Ibid., 60–66 and 93–110
26. Ibid., 183
27. Interview with W. Winfield, ibid., 135
28. Ibid., 151 and 153
29. Ibid., 159 and 209–11
30. Robert Fitzgerald, *Rowntree and the Marketing Revolution, 1862–1969*, Cambridge, 1995, 47–51
31. Iolo A. Williams, *The Firm of Cadbury*, London, 1931, 2–6
32. Ibid., 10
33. Ibid., 14
34. Ibid., 22–8
35. Ibid., 39
36. Fitzgerald, *Rowntree and the Marketing Revolution*, 51
37. Ibid., 51–2
38. Ibid., 53–4
39. Ibid., 55
40. Diaper, in Harvey and Press, eds, *Studies*, 43
41. See Chapter 11 below
42. Diaper, in Harvey and Press, eds, *Studies*, 44–5
43. Ibid., 45–6
44. Fitzgerald, *Rowntree and the Marketing Revolution*, 57–8
45. Ibid., 64–5
46. Vernon, *A Quaker Business Man*, 121

47. Ian Campbell Bradley, *Evangelical Entrepreneurs,* London, 1987, Chapter 4
48. Diaper, in Harvey and Press, eds, *Studies*
49. Ibid., 45
50. Ibid., 49
51. Vernon, *A Quaker Business Man*, 122
52. Fitzgerald, *Rowntree and the Marketing Revolution*, 69–73
53. *Cocoa Works Magazine: A Journal in the Interests of the Employees of Rowntree and Company Ltd,* no.152, October 1915, 1775, and no.153, December 1915, 1894. The 24 bound volumes covering the years 1902–67 are held in the Factory Archives Department, York. I was granted access to them by the then librarian/archivist, Christine Theaker
54. See the case studies in Bradley, *Evangelical Entrepreneurs*

11: QUAKERS AS EMPLOYERS

1. Punshon, *Portrait in Grey*, 170–71
2. See essays in David J. Jeremy, ed., *Business and Religion in Britain*, Aldershot, 1988
3. T. A. B. Corley, 'How Quakers Coped with Business Success: Quaker Industrialists 1860–1914', in ibid.
4. Fitzgerald, *Rowntree and the Marketing Revolution*, 64
5. T. A. B. Corley, *Quaker Enterprise in Biscuits: Huntley and Palmers of Reading, 1822–1972*, London, 1972, 96
6. For the details of the Clark company, see George Barry Sutton, *C. and J. Clark, 1833–1903*, York, 1979
7. Helen Cadbury Alexander, *Richard Cadbury of Birmingham*, London, 1906, 191–2
8. This theme is best dealt with in Fitzgerald, *Rowntree and the Marketing Revolution,* Chapter 8
9. Corley, *Quaker Enterprise*, 98–9
10. Corley, in Jeremy, ed., *Business and Religion in Britain*, 174–5
11. Corley, *Quaker Enterprise*, 100–101
12. Ibid., Chapter 10
13. For details, see Fitzgerald, *Rowntree and the Marketing Revolution*, 224–43
14. Ibid., 224–6
15. *Cocoa Works Magazine*, no. 1, March 1902
16. Ibid., 2
17. Ibid., 4–11
18. Ibid., no. 4, 28 June 1902, 40; no. 42, August 1905, 74; no. 46,

December 1905
19. Ibid., no. 57, November 1906, 252
20. Fitzgerald, *Rowntree and the Marketing Revolution*, 226
21. Ibid., 230
22. Ibid., 230–31
23. B. Seebohm Rowntree, *Poverty: A Study of Town Life*, London, 1901. For a discussion of that and subsequent York surveys, see Stephen Jenkins and Alan Maynard, 'The Rowntree Surveys: Poverty in York since 1899', in Charles Feinstein, ed., *York, 1831–1981*, York, 1981. See Chapter 12 below
24. *Cocoa Works Magazine*, no. 70, December 1907
25. Gerald Burke, *Towns in the Making*, London, 1971, 137–47
26. W. Alexander Harvey, *The Model Village and its Cottages: Bournville*, London, 1904, 9–11
27. Quoted in L. E. Waddilove, *One Man's Vision: The Story of the Joseph Rowntree Village Trust*, London, 1954, 6
28. Vernon, *A Quaker Business Man*, 147
29. Ibid., 150
30. Fitzgerald, *Rowntree and the Marketing Revolution*, 227
31. Ibid., 235–6
32. Ibid., 233
33. Ibid., 239
34. Corley, in Jeremy, ed., *Business and Religion in Britain*, 173–5
35. Ibid., 178
36. Ibid., 178–9
37. Price, in Dunn and Dunn, eds, *World of William Penn*, 387
38. Corley, in Jeremy, ed., *Business and Religion in Britain*, 180–84

12: POVERTY AND SOCIAL CHANGE

1. David Englander and Rosemary O'Day, eds, *Retrieved Treasures: Social Investigation in Britain, 1840–1914*, Aldershot, 1995, 5
2. For details, see Introduction, ibid., 1–40
3. Philip Waller, 'Charles Booth, 1840–1916', in Paul Barker, ed., *Founders of the Welfare State*, London, 1984, 42
4. Derek Fraser, *The Evolution of the British Welfare State*, London, 1980, 127
5. Quoted in Asa Briggs, *Social Thought and Social Action: A Study of the Work of Seebohm Rowntree, 1871–1954*, London, 1961, 17
6. Ibid., 14
7. Ibid., 22–4
8. Rowntree, *Poverty*, x

9. Ibid., 120–21
10. Ibid., 133
11. Briggs, *Social Thought*, 31
12. Randolph S. Churchill, *Winston S. Churchill*, II: *The Young Statesman, 1901–1914*, London, 1967, 30
13. Ibid., 31–2
14. Rowntree, *Poverty*, 305
15. Briggs, *Social Thought*, 50
16. Ibid., 56–7
17. Ibid., 59–60
18. Quoted in ibid., 66
19. Ibid., 71–3
20. Ibid., 93
21. Ibid., 104
22. Fitzgerald, *Rowntree and the Marketing Revolution*, 218
23. Ibid., 240
24. Ibid., 240–43
25. Briggs, *Social Thought*, 108–109
26. For a bibliography of Seebohm Rowntree's writings, see ibid., 344–8
27. Ibid., 110
28. J. H. Veit-Wilson, 'Paradigms of Poverty: A Rehabilitation of B. S. Rowntree', in Englander and O'Day, eds, *Retrieved Treasures*, 230

CONCLUSION

1. See especially David J. Jeremy, *Capitalists and Christians: Business Leaders and the Churches in Britain, 1900–1960*, Oxford, 1990

Bibliography

Readers will be able to trace the more specialised sources and collections used in the book in the notes to each chapter. Though many of the books mentioned here should be readily available in good city libraries, British readers will be able to consult publications by and about Quakers in the library of the Religious Society of Friends, Euston Road, London.

The fine detail of early Quaker history can be traced in two (revised) volumes by William C. Braithwaite: *The Beginnings of Quakerism* (1912), Cambridge, 1961, and *The Second Period of Quakerism* (1919), York, 1979. There is a general account in John Punshon, *Portrait in Grey: A Short History of the Quakers*, London, 1991. An invaluable compendium of Quaker culture can be found in *Quaker Faith and Practice: The Book of Christian Discipline of the Yearly Meeting of the Religious Society of Friends (Quakers) in Britain*, London, 1995. We are told, with characteristic Quaker rectitude, that this book 'is made with pulp from sustainable, responsibly managed forests in Finland'.

The most recent book on George Fox (with an excellent bibliography) is H. Larry Ingle, *First Among Equals: George Fox and the Creation of Quakerism*, New York, 1994. There are useful essays in Michael Mullett, ed., *New Light on George Fox*, York 1991. The early days of the Quakers can be approached via two local studies: Nicholas Morgan, *Lancashire Quakers and the Establishment, 1660–1730*, Halifax, 1993, and David Scott, *Quakerism in York, 1650–1720*, York, 1991. For the broader religious context of the early Quakers, see William Lamont, *Puritanism and Historical Controversy*, London, 1996, and Margaret Spufford, ed., *The*

World of Rural Dissenters, 1520–1725, Cambridge, 1995. There are many versions of Fox's *Journal.* The most accessible edition is *The Journal of George Fox*, John L. Nickalls, ed., London, Religious Society of Friends, 1986. For the role of Quaker women, begin with Christine Trevett, *Women and Quakerism in the Seventeenth Century*, York, 1991. There is a concise account of Quaker buildings in Kenneth H. Southall, *Our Quaker Heritage: Early Meeting Houses*, York, 1984.

The best analysis of Quaker demography, though not an easy read, is Richard T. Vann and David Eversley, *Friends in Life and Death: The British and Irish Quakers in the Demographic Transition, 1650–1990*, Cambridge, 1992. For a general account of eighteenth-century British life, the best place to begin is Paul Langford, *A Polite and Commercial People, England 1727–1783*, Oxford, 1989. The rise of consumer consumption in the seventeenth and eighteenth centuries is traced in John Brewer and Roy Porter, eds, *Consumption and the World of Goods*, London, 1993. But see also James Walvin, *Fruits of Empire: Exotic Produce and British Taste, 1660–1800*, London, 1997.

On the background to Quaker financial history, begin with Henry Roseveare, *The Financial Revolution, 1660–1760*, London, 1991. The history of banking is best approached through the (dated) book by L. S. Pressnell, *Country Banking in the Industrial Revolution*, Oxford, 1956. A regional study is available in M. W. Kirby, *Men of Business and Politics: The Rise and Fall of the Quaker Pease Dynasty of North-East England, 1700–1943*, London, 1984.

Quaker networks are best illustrated in the remarkable filigree scholarship of Jacob M. Price. A starting point would be his essay 'Eighteenth-Century London Quaker Business Families', in Richard S. Dunn and Mary Maples Dunn, eds, *The World of William Penn*, Philadelphia, 1986. That volume contains a number of crucial essays on Quaker culture, but see also Jacob M. Price, 'English Quaker Merchants and War at Sea, 1689–1783', in Roderick A. McDonald, ed., *West India Accounts*, Kingston, Jamaica, 1996. There is an excellent analysis of Quaker networks at work in Kenneth Morgan, ed., *An American Quaker in the British Isles: The Travel Journal of Jabez Maud Fisher, 1775–1779*, London, 1992.

There are many useful clues about Quaker business practices in the older volume, Frederick B. Tolles, *Meeting House and Counting House: The Quaker Merchants of Colonial Philadelphia, 1692–1763*, Chapel Hill, 1949. A helpful case study of Quaker business can be found in Geoffrey Tweedale, *At the Sign of the Plough: 275 Years of Allen and Hanbury and the British Pharmaceutical Industry, 1715–1900*, London, 1990. See also Humphrey Lloyd, *The Quaker Lloyds in the Industrial Revolution*, London, 1975.

Bibliography

The standard studies of Quaker industry and science remain the two books by Arthur Raistrick, *Dynasty of Iron Founders*, London, 1989, and *Quakers in Science and Industry*, New York, 1968. A recent general account of industrial change can be found in Pat Hudson, *The Industrial Revolution*, London, 1992. But look, too, at the essays in Patrick O'Brien and Roland Quinault, eds, *The Industrial Revolution and British Society*, Cambridge, 1993. For a detailed case study of a Quaker industry, see A. E. Musson, *Enterprise in Soap and Chemicals: Joseph Crosfield and Sons Ltd., 1815–1965*, Manchester, 1965.

On the chocolate magnates, begin with Gillian Wagner, *The Chocolate Conscience*, London, 1987. For the Fry family, see the essay by Stephanie Diaper, 'J. S. Fry and Sons', in Charles Harvey and Jon Press, eds, *Studies in the Business History of Bristol*, Bristol, 1988. The history of Rowntree has recently been covered in detail in Robert Fitzgerald, *Rowntree and the Marketing Revolution: 1862–1969*, Cambridge 1995. It contains much of interest on the other chocolate companies. See also Ian Campbell Bradley, *Evangelical Entrepreneurs*, London, 1987.

Recent Quaker business practice can be studied in David J. Jeremy, ed., *Business and Religion in Britain*, Aldershot, 1988. Individual Quaker companies are discussed in T. A. B. Corley, *Quaker Enterprise in Biscuits: Huntley and Palmers of Reading, 1822–1972*, London, 1972; George Barry Sutton, *C. and J. Clark, 1833–1903: A History of Shoemaking in Street, Somerset*, York, 1979.

The contribution of Quakers to social reform is discussed in David Englander and Rosemary O'Day, *Retrieved Treasures: Social Investigation in Britain, 1840–1914*, Aldershot, 1995. Still important is Asa Briggs, *Social Thought and Social Action: A Study of the Work of Seebohm Rowntree, 1871–1954*, London, 1961.

Index

Index